DEEP WATER

*Murder, Scandal, and Intrigue
in a New England Town*

KENNETH M. SHELDON

Down East Books
CAMDEN, MAINE

Down East Books

An imprint of Globe Pequot, the trade division of
The Rowman & Littlefield Publishing Group, Inc.
4501 Forbes Blvd., Ste. 200
Lanham, MD 20706
www.rowman.com

Distributed by NATIONAL BOOK NETWORK

British Library Cataloguing in Publication Information available

Library of Congress Cataloging-in-Publication Data
Names: Sheldon, Ken, author.
Title: Deep water : murder, scandal, and intrigue in a New England town
    / Kenneth M. Sheldon.
Description: Camden, Maine : Down East Books, [2022] | Includes
    bibliographical references.
Identifiers: LCCN 2022001832 (print) | LCCN 2022001833 (ebook) | ISBN
    9781684750276 (paperback ; alk. paper) | ISBN 9781684750283 (ebook)
Subjects: LCSH: Dean, William K., -1918. | Murder—New
    Hampshire—Jaffrey—Case studies. | Jaffrey (N.H.)—History—20th
    century.
Classification: LCC HV6534.J337 S54 2022 (print) | LCC HV6534.J337
    (ebook) | DDC 364.152309742/9—dc23/eng/20220204
LC record available at https://lccn.loc.gov/2022001832
LC ebook record available at https://lccn.loc.gov/2022001833

♾™ The paper used in this publication meets the minimum requirements of American National
Standard for Information Sciences—Permanence of Paper for Printed Library Materials, ANSI/
NISO Z39.48-1992.

CONTENTS

III. JUSTICE

DRAMATIS PERSONAE

William Kendrick Dean, the victim
Mary Dean, his wife

SUSPECTS AND ASSOCIATES
Lawrence MacLay Colfelt, Jr., Dean's tenant
Margaret Mary "Daisy" Colfelt, wife of Lawrence Colfelt
Natalye Colfelt, stepdaughter of Lawrence Colfelt
Frank Romano, Colfelt's hired hand
Charles L. Rich, banker, friend of William Dean
Lana Rich, wife of Charles Rich
Georgiana Hodgkins, sister of Lana Rich
Susan Henchman, bank cashier and friend of the Riches
Russel Henchman, brother of Susan and friend of Charles Rich
Edward Parsons Baldwin, worked for Charles Rich

INVESTIGATORS AND OFFICIALS
Edward Boynton, selectman
Peter Hogan, selectman
William Coolidge, selectman
Roy Pickard, Cheshire County solicitor
Oscar L. Young, New Hampshire state attorney general
Harry L. Scott, Pinkerton Detective Agency agent
William de Kerlor, aka "Kent," journalist, lecturer, detective
Edward H. Lord, sheriff of Cheshire County
Walter E. Emerson, deputy sheriff
George Nute, Jaffrey chief of police

Perley Enos, acting chief of police
George Parker Wellington, fish and game warden

FRIENDS AND NEIGHBORS
Charles Bean, aka "Crazy" Bean, nurse, photographer
Charles Deschenes, storeowner, neighbor
Martin Garfield, farmer, neighbor
Frank Humiston, horseman
Arria Morison, summer resident
Margaret Robinson, summer resident
Leon Turner, farmer, neighbor
Mary Lee Ware, summer resident

BUSINESSMEN
Delcie D. Bean, box manufacturer
Guy H. Cutter, banker
George H. Duncan, postmaster and pharmacist
Wilbur Webster, tack manufacturer
Homer White, mill owner
Dr. Frederick C. Sweeney, Charles Rich's friend and physician
Merrill Symonds, box manufacturer
John G. Townsend, banker and town clerk

CLERGYMEN
Reverend Myron L. Cutler, Universalist minister
Reverend F.R. Enslin, Baptist minister
Winifred Enslin, wife to Rev. Enslin
Father Herbert Hennon, Catholic priest

I

MURDER

1

THE FARMER

THE ROAD LEADING TO WILLIAM K. DEAN'S HOME WAS A WINDING country lane that rose gradually, twisting and turning, passing fewer than half a dozen houses until it reached a point overlooking the town of Jaffrey, New Hampshire. In 1918, Jaffrey consisted of two villages: Jaffrey Center, which lay to the west with the larger and grander homes of the more affluent residents, and East Jaffrey, a typical New England mill village with a river running through it, the factories, railroad depot, and homes of millworkers nearby. Jaffrey's residents were a mix of hard-rock Yankees whose parents and grandparents had tilled the soil, raised sheep, and cleared the hillsides, living alongside recent immigrants who worked in the mills and factories.

On the evening of August 13, 1918, William Dean rode down to East Jaffrey in his buggy, reluctantly leaving his wife Mary at home. The Deans had been happily married for 38 years, but in recent years Mary had begun to suffer from a mild form of senility that was attributed to "softening of the brain." While not a complete invalid, she was nevertheless prone to memory lapses and occasionally mixed up her words.

Neighbors who saw Dean driving to town that evening thought he seemed somber and distracted, as if something was weighing on his mind. It was a Tuesday evening, the night that stores in East Jaffrey stayed open until 9 p.m. to accommodate those who could not conduct business during the day.

Dean first stopped at Goodnow's, the flagship store of a dry goods chain that would eventually spread across New England. He made a few purchases, then walked up the street to the post office and Duncan's drugstore, which shared a building. He chatted with a friend named Georgiana Hodgkins, then crossed the street to drop off some laundry at Meyers dry goods store. He crossed back over the street, bought some currant buns at Vanni's market, then walked back to his buggy parked behind Goodnow's.

According to Georgiana Hodgkins, Dean gave her a ride to the nearby home of her brother-in-law, Charles Rich, who was perhaps Dean's best friend. Just before Dean and Hodgkins arrived, Rich had sustained a kick in the face from his horse and was bathing his wounds with the help of his wife, Lana. Dean visited with the Riches for a time and then headed home.

It was twilight of a sweltering summer day, and as Dean drove his buggy out of town, children were playing in the road—not unusual at a time when few horses or vehicles would come along to interrupt them. Dean rode past the home of Mrs. Emma Chouinard, who beckoned to her children to let him pass. According to Mrs. Chouinard, he tipped his hat "in his polite way," and continued on his way. A number of other villagers, relaxing in hammocks or rockers on their porches in hopes of catching a cool breeze, also saw Mr. Dean as he drove by. They waved, bid him good evening, or simply nodded pleasantly.

They did not know it was the last time they would ever see him.

2

THE TOWN

By the fall of 1918, the United States had been at war with Germany for over a year. The war brought victory gardens, Liberty Bonds, and reports of German U-boats prowling the waters off the East Coast. Despite the war, day-to-day life in East Jaffrey proceeded as it had for decades, much as Thornton Wilder described it in *Our Town*, the quintessential New England play set in the southwest corner of New Hampshire. "You come up here on a fine afternoon and you can see range on range of hills—awful blue they are," says the Stage Manager, who narrates *Our Town*. "And, of course, our favorite mountain, Mount Monadnock's right here—and all around it lie these towns—Jaffrey 'n North Jaffrey, 'n Peterborough, 'n Dublin ..."

The Stage Manager, from his vantage point in Peterborough where Wilder wrote the play, could well have seen William Dean's hilltop home some six miles away to the southwest. At the time, most of the region had been cleared of trees to provide pasture for sheep and wood for fuel, and incidentally providing unencumbered views of mile upon mile of rolling hills.

The Deans lived in a small bungalow perched on a windswept knoll a hundred yards off the Old Peterborough Road. Past the bungalow another hundred yards was a large summer house that the Deans had built and which they had been forced to begin renting out when finances became tight. Between the two houses and down a slope was a barn where Dean kept his few animals: one or two cows, his horse, a flock of white turkeys for which he was locally known, and an assortment of stray and cast-off animals that the Deans had taken in. Standing in their yard, one could see Mount Monadnock rising majestically to the west, Massachusetts to the south, and on a clear day, the Atlantic Ocean eighty miles to the east. It was an isolated but starkly beautiful location, with only the sounds of wind, birds, and the occasional night-calling owl to disturb the peace.

William Dean's father had been a Baptist missionary in China and then Siam, where William grew up playing with the crown prince of Siam. In later youth, he lived with his uncle Henry, a physician in Rochester, New York, who inspired William to go to medical school. Dean studied and trained to be a doctor, but never actually practiced medicine. His wife, Mary—who was also his first cousin—knew the stress that a medical career had caused her father and married William only when he agreed not to practice. They moved to Jaffrey in 1887, in part because Dean was suffering from a throat ailment that threatened tuberculosis; it was thought that the clean country air of their hilltop retreat would aid in his recovery.

In Jaffrey, the Deans were much loved for their kindness and hospitality. They appreciated literature, music, and art and hobnobbed with wealthy summer residents who descended on the region during the warm months to attend the theatre, concerts, and art exhibitions. The summer people often brought visiting guests to the Deans' hilltop farm to see the magnificent views of the mountains and the surrounding towns and villages. Mary recorded the visitors' names in a guest book, and in one season she noted as many as 600 visitors. It was an idyllic way of life that came to a sudden, tragic end on the night of Tuesday, August 13, 1918.

According to Mary Dean, her husband arrived home at about 9:30 that evening, his usual time when returning from the village. He brought in his purchases, ate one of the currant buns he had purchased in town, and smoked a cigarette. At about 11 o'clock, he went to milk the cow; Dean was viewed as somewhat eccentric by his neighbors in that, contrary to accepted practice, he milked his cows at noon and midnight, so that he could sleep late in the morning. The Deans were accustomed to staying up into the early hours of the morning, reading by a light that locals reported could be seen a great distance away. Before he headed to the barn, William told Mary he would return at midnight and asked her to have a hot supper ready for him when he returned. He took a lantern and pail and left to do his chores.

Mary heated some soup and waited for William's return, but he didn't come. An hour passed, then two. She began to grow anxious; the Deans were creatures of habit, and it was unlike him to deviate from his usual routine. She felt certain some mishap had befallen him. Why else would he leave her alone for so long?

She waited through the night, occasionally dozing, then startled awake by the rustling of wind in the trees or the shrill bark of a fox in the woods. Her husband never returned.

3

THE SEARCH

AT THE BREAK OF DAY MARY WENT TO THE BARN, WHERE SHE HAD NOT been for months and had not dared to go at night. She entered through the small side porch and found the lantern tipped over, its light extinguished. The lantern still had oil in it, which meant it had not run out on its own.

She searched the barn but found no sign of Billie, as she called him. Panicking, she returned to the house and began telephoning friends and neighbors. She called Martin Garfield, perhaps the nearest neighbor, who arrived a short time later with his young son. They found Mrs. Dean talking anxiously with Arthur Smith and a neighbor boy who had arrived that morning to hay the Deans' fields.

Garfield and Smith searched the barn, the summer house, and the surrounding fields, while the two boys climbed up to the hayloft, but there was no sign of Mr. Dean. Garfield, knowing of Mrs. Dean's sometimes confused mental state, asked her if he could look around their house—perhaps Mr. Dean was simply sleeping late as was his habit and she had gotten confused about his whereabouts. But Dean was not in his bed, nor anywhere else in the house.

Not far from the Deans' porch was an uncovered well protected only by a low stone wall. It occurred to Garfield that Dean might have tripped and pitched into it in the dark. He asked Mrs. Dean if her husband might have stumbled into the well without her hearing it, a suggestion that would have unfortunate consequences for her later. "She looked queer and didn't answer," Garfield said. But by now, she seemed convinced that her husband was dead, certain that he would have returned unless something had happened to him.

Pondering the situation, Garfield walked to the barn and sat down to rest on the steps of the side porch. Looking down, he saw a drop of blood on the ground. Arthur Smith's young helper, standing nearby, also saw the blood and asked what it was.

"I guess Mr. Dean killed a chicken or something," Garfield said, not wanting to alarm the boy. But by now he suspected that something had happened to Mr. Dean and that this was not chicken blood.

He looked around casually and saw more blood on the porch steps, as well as on the door to the barn. He said nothing to the boys, but returned to the Dean house and telephoned William Coolidge, the town's head selectman, telling him simply that Mr. Dean was missing.

Coolidge responded quickly, heading to the Dean farm and stopping along the way to pick up fellow selectman Peter Hogan and acting police chief Perley Enos. As they drove to the Dean place, Coolidge told the others that they would start by looking the house over. "The old lady is out of her mind, and you see if you can find anything there," he said. "Just as likely as not, she might have killed him."

The men arrived at the Dean farm and searched the houses, the barn, and the surrounding woods and fields, but Mr. Dean was nowhere to be found. Coolidge proposed calling for more help to scour the area, but Garfield argued that Dean couldn't have gone far. "I know Mr. Dean couldn't walk a great ways because his legs troubled him," he said. Then, remembering his talk with Mrs. Dean about the well by the bungalow, Garfield suggested they search the rainwater cistern next to the summer house. The cistern had an old wooden cover that was level with the ground except for a single layer of loose bricks surrounding it. It would not have been noticeable from any distance, and only a person who was familiar with the place would have known about it.

Coolidge, Hogan, and Garfield walked up to the cistern and lifted the cover. "Mr. Garfield got a pole and began to poke around in the cistern," according to Coolidge, "and apparently he hit something, and we asked him what it was and he said it felt like a bag. I took the pole and knocked what felt like a body, and I said, 'He is there all right.'"

4

THE BODY

By now, it was noon. The men found an ice hook in the barn and used it to pull the body out just enough to confirm that it was William Dean. He had been bound, his hands tied behind his back, a rope around the knees, and a rough burlap sack over his head.

They released the body back into the water and telephoned the county authorities, waiting for them to arrive before removing the body from the cistern. While they waited, William Coolidge became concerned about Mrs. Dean and decided she should have someone with her. He called the Monadnock National Bank to speak with Dean's friend Charles Rich, who was manager of the bank, hoping that Rich's wife could come to look after Mrs. Dean.

Coolidge heard the phone ring, but before it was answered, a car pulled into the Deans' yard. In it were Charles and Lana Rich, Georgiana Hodgkins, and William Leighton, the town undertaker. Their arrival struck Coolidge as odd. How could they have heard the news so quickly, given that Dean's body had just been found?

When the Riches arrived, Mrs. Dean was in the barn tending to the turkeys and other animals, which seemed odd to Charles Rich. "She was down there doing that instead of being overcome with grief," he testified later. "I was a little surprised at that, knowing she was an invalid. And from that day to this she hasn't, to my knowledge, inquired what became of Mr. Dean or mentioned it."

Mrs. Dean emerged from the barn, and Lana Rich and Miss Hodgkins took her aside to keep her from seeing what was going on at the cistern. Mr. Rich joined the other men by the cistern, at which point Martin Garfield noticed that Rich had a severe black eye and cuts on his face and ear. Rich also made what seemed to Garfield like a foolish comment. "Mr. Rich came to the well and looked in and said he thought Mr. Dean was nervous and intimated that he probably put himself out of the way," Garfield said. "I told him I didn't think Mr. Dean could commit suicide the way he was fixed up."

"Mr. Dean was a pretty smart man," Rich said.

"He must have been a mighty smart man to tie his legs together, his hands behind his back, pull a bag down over his head, put a stone around his body, jump into the cistern and pull the cover over it," Garfield replied. He offered to have Dean's body pulled up for Rich to see, if he had any doubts about the matter.

Rich turned white. "I don't care to see him."

At that, Rich left and rejoined the women. Mrs. Dean saw him approach and said, "Oh, Mr. Rich, Mr. Dean is dead in the deep water."

"Yes, Mrs. Dean, he was in deep water," Rich replied.

Georgiana Hodgkins found Mary Dean's reaction to the news disturbing. "She didn't seem to be impressed by the fact that her own idea had been confirmed, and just went on talking," Hodgkins said.

The Riches and Miss Hodgkins were the only people present to hear Mrs. Dean's comment about deep water, words that would cause her no end of trouble in the days to come.

It was not until 2 p.m. that the person responsible for investigating the murder, Cheshire County Solicitor Roy Pickard, arrived on the scene. Pickard, a graduate of Middlebury College, had been a schoolteacher before becoming a lawyer. From there, he was elected county solicitor, equivalent to district attorney. Although he had been in office for only four months at the time of the Dean murder, Pickard had already earned a reputation for prosecuting cases aggressively. He arrived at the Dean farm accompanied by the county medical examiner, Dr. Frank Dinsmore, and two county sheriffs.

The officials stood by as Dean's body was pulled from the cistern and laid on the grass. The ropes binding Dean's knees and arms had been tied with square knots, and rather than untie them, the men cut the ropes to preserve the knots as evidence. They removed the burlap sack from Dean's head, revealing a blood-stained horse blanket that had been wrapped around it, along with a stone estimated to weigh about twenty-five pounds, apparently added to keep the body from floating to the top of the cistern.

The searchers unwrapped the blanket, revealing deep cuts on the left side of Dean's forehead and bruises to his left eye. A horse halter had been looped around Dean's throat and pulled so tightly that it left an indentation in his neck. If there had been any doubt before, there certainly was none now; William Dean had been brutally murdered.

The body was placed in a basket and carried to the kitchen of the summer house, where Dr. Dinsmore conducted a preliminary examination. He determined that the lacerations on Dean's head had been caused by one or more blows, which were perhaps strong enough to render him unconscious, but probably not to kill him. He also concluded that Dean had not been drowned. "There was no water in the lungs," he testified, an indication that the victim had not been breathing when he was dumped in the cistern. However, the lungs did provide evidence for the actual cause of death. According to undertaker Leighton, who was present at the examination, "The lungs showed a dark color, proof of suffocation." The conclusion seemed clear: William Dean had been stunned by a blow to his head, choked to death, and then bound and thrown into the cistern.

The examiners checked Dean's clothes and found, in his right hip pocket, a silver box containing tobacco and cigarette papers. The farm-hand Arthur Smith, who was present, had seen the case many times while working about the farm. "It was a little square box and just like an engraving on top," he said.

The engraving consisted of the initials H.W.D., those of Dean's uncle and father-in-law, Henry Walter Dean, who had given the case to William. It was a cherished heirloom, one that he carried everywhere; Dean was an inveterate smoker, and townspeople had often seen him roll his own cigarettes with the papers he carried in the box.

While the examination of the body proceeded, County Solicitor Pick-ard, the sheriffs, and volunteers searched the farm for clues. They found bloodstains on the barn door, the doorknob, the porch steps, and the floor of the barn. They concluded that Dean had been murdered in the barn and his body carried 150 feet to the cistern; the grass from the barn to the cistern did not appear flattened or compressed, indicating that the body had been carried rather than dragged.

The searchers were unable to find anything that might have been used as a murder weapon. Nor could they find the milk pail that Mr. Dean had used on the night of his death, which perplexed them. Accord-ing to Mrs. Dean, that night he had used a tin pail with a strainer on the side. She had found another pail, a blue and white pail, "but I couldn't find the strainer pail anywhere," she said.

In any event, it appeared that Mr. Dean had finished milking the cow before his murder. Fish and game warden George Wellington arrived, milked the cow, and found that it gave no more than the ordinary amount, establishing that it had been milked the night before. But the milk pail had disappeared. It was suggested that perhaps the murderers had washed their bloody hands in the pail and disposed of it, wanting to hide the evidence. If so, where was the pail, and what had they done with the milk?

Then, as if there weren't already enough complications, New England's weather—well-known for being fractious and changeable—dealt the search a sudden and disastrous blow.

That summer had been exceptionally hot and dry, with temperatures soaring to over 110 degrees and less rainfall than in the previous 35 years. Social events were cut short due to the intense heat, and gardens withered for lack of rain. But if people wanted rain, they got it in spades on the day William Dean's body was found. At about 3 p.m., a violent thunderstorm struck, the worst in anyone's memory. The storm took down electrical systems, knocked out street lights, and hurled lighting that burned a barn with 30 tons of hay to the ground.

At the Dean farm, the storm brought all activity to a halt. Curiosity seekers scattered to their homes, and most of the officials, deciding that not much more could be done in the way of searching, left as well. When the thunderstorm abated, undertaker William Leighton took Dean's body from the summer house to his mortician's parlor in the village.

The question then arose as to what to do about Mary Dean. Neighbors and friends felt she was incapable of caring for herself, and as far as county officials were concerned, she was the only possible suspect in the case.

Lana Rich took charge of the situation. She contacted the district nurse Marie Hiller with a request and a warning. According to Hiller, "Mrs. Rich told me to watch Mrs. Dean and said that it would not be safe to stay alone with Mrs. Dean as she had me to believe that Mrs. Dean might be the murderess, and that I should get some other woman to stay with me."

The problem was finding someone willing to help Hiller watch over Mrs. Dean, a woman who was suspected of murder and possibly insane. A solution presented itself in the aftermath of the thunderstorm, which had wreaked havoc throughout the region. At the tack factory, the storm caused electrical problems that brought work to a standstill, its workers temporarily furloughed. Nurse Hiller asked one of the workers, Elizabeth Bryant, if she would stay with her at the Dean farm to watch over Mrs. Dean. Hiller admitted to being spooked by the nature of the murder, but Mrs. Bryant was, in her own words, "one of the kind that don't let anything trouble me."

Nevertheless, a gruesome murder had been committed at the farm, and the murderer, as far as anyone knew, was still at large. That night, three men stood guard over the Dean premises, while the women stayed with Mrs. Dean in the bungalow. The night passed without incident, although the watchers were tense, and Mrs. Dean's erratic behavior—wandering from room to room, forgetting who these people were and why they were in her house—only exacerbated their jitters. They found it hard to believe that Mrs. Dean could commit such a horrific crime, but there was still the very real possibility that they were spending the night with a madwoman.

5

THE INVESTIGATORS

THE NEXT DAY, AUGUST 15, THE FIRST NOTICE OF DEAN'S MURDER appeared in the *Peterborough Transcript*.

Brutal Murder in East Jaffrey

The community was stirred Wednesday by the discovery of the brutal murder of William K. Dean, a retired farmer, 70 years old, living about two miles from this village, who was killed sometime between midnight and morning.

The article appeared at the bottom of the second page, in the community news section for East Jaffrey, a placement that seems odd. In a region where homicides were not everyday occurrences, the murder of a well-known resident would certainly seem like front page news, but perhaps the placement resulted simply from a rush to get the news into the paper. The brief story sketched the outlines of Dean's disappearance, the finding of his body in the cistern, and the fact that authorities were at a loss to know the motive for the murder. "They are making a close investigation of the premises," the article concluded.

To assist with the investigation, County Solicitor Pickard contacted the Pinkerton Detective Agency, an organization famous for protecting Abraham Lincoln during the Civil War and somewhat infamous for their part in strike-breaking activities at the turn of the 20th century.

The agency assigned detective Harry L. Scott to the Dean murder case, reporting directly to Roy Pickard.

At the same time, agents of the Department of Justice's Bureau of Investigation (predecessor to the FBI) also began looking into the murder. The agents had already been in the area, investigating reports of possible German espionage made by citizens who had been told to be alert for any signs of enemy activity on the home front. The people of the Monadnock region had taken the charge seriously. They reported high-powered automobiles—still enough of a novelty to be remarked upon—traveling on little-used country roads and sometimes driven by foreigners. International visitors had always frequented the area's resort hotels, but now seemed more suspect as they hiked in the woods, made long-distance telephone calls, and socialized with locals reputed to have pro-German sympathies.

But the largest number of reports concerned lights coming from Mount Monadnock or the surrounding hills. Sometimes flashing, sometimes steady, occasionally colored or moving horizontally or vertically, the lights were reported throughout the summer and fall of 1917. Typical was a brief notice in the *Peterborough Transcript* for September 20, 1917, noting that, "For the past few evenings about 7 o'clock, a light has been seen near the south end of Monadnock mountain, which appears to be a signal, but what for we have no idea. It may need investigating."

Locals, the year-round residents of the region, were sometimes hesitant to report such sightings to the authorities for fear of looking foolish. Or it might simply have been the Yankee tendency to reticence. But the wealthy summer people—with a greater sense of entitlement, as well as homes and connections to government officials in Boston and New York—felt no such compunctions. They made their concerns known, concerns that came to the attention of the Bureau of Investigation, which sent agents to look into the matter.

In the spring and summer of 1918, federal agents had interviewed a number of witnesses about signal lights and other suspicious sightings in the Monadnock region, but they had found no solid evidence of enemy activity. Their initial response to the reports of signal lights was muted, if not dismissive, noting that the lights generally appeared near a farm or highway, or were simply the result of "physiological causes."

In other words, people were seeing things. Despite their best efforts over many months, agents of the Bureau of Investigation had failed to uncover any real evidence that the lights had anything to do with enemy espionage or the actions of pro-German sympathizers. Agent J.C. Leighton summed up his findings in a report of August 10, 1918. "A great many of these reports on the lights have come from women who are intimately acquainted with one another and it appears to have become a hobby with them to report these occurrences. During interviews which agent has had with them, they constantly refer to one another relative to what has been seen. Apparently, no one living in the immediate vicinity from which these lights are alleged to have been displayed has seen them."

Then, three days after Agent Leighton filed his report, William Dean's body was found in the very neighborhood where the Bureau had been investigating the lights. Suddenly, the focus of investigation shifted. Now the agents weren't simply looking into flashing lights. Now it was murder.

On the morning of August 15, Jaffrey selectman Edward Boynton contacted the Concord office of the Bureau of Investigation and asked them to help the county solicitor investigate the murder of Mr. Dean. Agent Guy Reeve traveled to Jaffrey, inspected the scene of the crime, and spoke with the selectmen and the county solicitor.

As the investigators conferred, the Dean farm was already in the process of being broken up. Mrs. Dean had called Russel Henchman, a near neighbor, to take away the cow and bull, telling him she could not care for them by herself. That afternoon, Henchman loaded the bull onto a truck and then proceeded to sweep the barn floor. Henchman, who was the superintendent of the town water works, next went to the summer house, where he turned off the water and drained the pipes.

Meanwhile, Roy Pickard, the sheriffs, and Harry Scott continued their search for the murder weapon and the missing milk pail. They combed the houses, the barn, and surrounding fields without success. Finally, it occurred to them that the murderer might have tossed the murder weapon or the milk pail into one of the farm's wells or the cistern where Dean's body had been found. Deputy Sheriff Walter Emerson brought in a gasoline-powered engine to pump the water from the cistern, but he found no weapon or milk pail there. Instead, a more significant clue turned up: a silver cigarette case, shining at the bottom of the cistern.

One of the men who assisted with the pumping pulled the case from the water and handed it to Emerson, who laid it on the grass to dry in the sun. A number of witnesses saw the cigarette case, including Selectman Boynton. "I saw taken from the cistern after the water had been pumped out, a flat white metal cigarette case which was noticed at the bottom of the cistern, this was thrown on the grass," Boynton said. "Walter Emerson took same to hold for evidence."

By that time, newspapers in Concord, Manchester, and Boston had begun to report on the brutal murder, not always accurately. "Farmer Bound and Drowned in Cistern," the *Boston Globe* reported, mistakenly stating that Dean "met his death by drowning."

"Mystery Shrouds Murder," the *Boston American* reported, and included the first mention of Dean's tenant, Lawrence Colfelt. Colfelt, a wealthy and somewhat aloof character, had lived with his wife and stepdaughter in the big house on the Dean property until a couple of months before Dean's death.

On August 17, in an article headlined "No Clue to Motive for Murder at East Jaffrey" the *Boston Post* noted, "The authorities are practically convinced that whoever did the work of killing was familiar with every detail of the Dean premises and habits."

6

THE FUNERAL

WILLIAM DEAN WAS BURIED ON FRIDAY, AUGUST 16, DESPITE AN ODD and somewhat gruesome incident that threatened to delay the event. On the morning of the funeral, medical examiner Dinsmore came to undertaker William Leighton at the Baptist church and said he had overlooked something in the examination of Dean's body. He wanted Leighton to take the body back to the undertaking parlor and remove the stomach for further examination. Leighton argued against this as a great inconvenience to him and the many folks planning to attend the funeral. Rather than delay the funeral, he suggested they go ahead with the service, then hold a committal ceremony at the town vault, after which he would remove the stomach and proceed with the burial. Dinsmore agreed and the service proceeded.

A large number of townspeople attended the funeral, but sadly, Mary Dean did not. In fact, she was never told about the funeral, as those watching over her apparently deemed it best that she not be there.

Another person notably absent was Dean's friend, Charles Rich. By now, a number of people had seen Rich with a greatly bruised and scratched face, which he attributed to the kick from his horse that he had received on the night of the murder. The cuts and bruises on Rich's face caused no end of gossip in town, gossip that only intensified when Rich did not appear at Mr. Dean's funeral, especially since he was supposed to be a pallbearer.

In fact, Rich had been preparing to leave for the funeral when County Solicitor Pickard, Selectman Coolidge, and Agent Reeve arrived at the bank, seeking to examine the contents of William Dean's safety deposit box. Rich explained that he was just on his way to the funeral, but the officials told him they would be done in time for him to attend.

A problem immediately arose in that Rich did not have a key to Dean's deposit box. Oddly enough, Rich's wife, Lana, did have a key, having found it at the Dean bungalow and been told by Selectman Edward Boynton to hold on to it for safekeeping. Rich sent home for the key, and the box was opened. Inside were the Deans' wills, a box with some jewels and pearls, some family memorabilia, Liberty Bonds valued at $1,800, and other bonds of lesser value—nothing that seemed to give a clue as to the motive for Mr. Dean's murder. By the time the investigators had examined the contents of the box to their satisfaction, the funeral was over. Charles Rich had missed it.

As far as we know, the only family member to attend William Dean's funeral was his brother, Frederick, who had arrived from his home in New York City the night before. It was the first time he had been to Jaffrey in years, as he and William had been estranged for some time.

As the closest relative, Frederick assumed responsibility for Mrs. Dean. He arranged for Dr. Charles E. Thompson, superintendent of the Gardner, Massachusetts, State Colony for the insane, to examine her and assess her mental condition. On Saturday, the day after the funeral, Dr. Thompson followed Mary around the farm for two hours accompanied by Frederick Dean, New Hampshire Attorney General Oscar Young, and detective Harry L. Scott. They retraced William Dean's final movements from the house to the barn, then to the cistern where his body had been dumped, all the while watching Mrs. Dean closely for her reaction. In his report, Dr. Thompson stated, "I am of the opinion that Mrs. Dean is suffering from a progressive deteriorating mental disease which has already lasted for several years and which will undoubtedly continue."

Almost immediately, Frederick Dean applied to Probate Judge Robert A. Ray, who declared Mary Dean to be insane and—based on Frederick's recommendation—assigned Lewis W. Davis, vice president of the Monadnock Savings Bank, to be her guardian and administrator of her estate.[1] Davis quickly made the decision to send Mrs. Dean to a sanitarium for observation. This was not a formal commitment, although as Judge Ray stated, "She was regarded at that time as dangerous."

Apparently, Agent Reeve agreed. In a brief report filed on August 19, he wrote, "From the facts as presented by the County Solicitor and by the selectman, this office has concluded that Dean's wife was the one who committed the murder, especially in view of the fact that she had been reported as gradually losing her mind for the last few years."

On the morning of Tuesday, August 20, Marie Hiller and Elizabeth Bryant arrived at the Dean bungalow to accompany Mrs. Dean to the sanitarium. Mary, who had become used to them coming in the evening, remarked, "But you have come here early today, haven't you? Why, you are all dressed up."

"We're going for an automobile ride, wouldn't you like to come with us?" Bryant asked.

Mrs. Dean was resistant to the idea until Oscar Dillon, a driver who had once taken her for an enjoyable ride to Boston, asked her. "You'll go with me, won't you?"

Mary finally agreed, but changed her mind when it was time to go. At that point, Marie Hiller gave her a sedative injection, and the elderly woman was bundled into the car. The women were accompanied by Frederick Dean and Dr. Alfred Childs of Dublin, New Hampshire.

Mary seemed to enjoy the ride at first, until it became a longer trip than she had expected and the countryside was no longer familiar, at which point she asked to be taken home. The women began singing to calm her and they eventually arrived at the Herbert Hall Hospital in Worcester, Massachusetts, which billed itself as "A Hospital for the Care and Treatment of those afflicted with various forms of Nervous and Mental Diseases." Mary Dean did not know why she was there and expected to be returned to her home at any moment.

She never saw her home again. Within a few weeks, all of her personal property had been removed from the estate and put into storage, awaiting an auction that would disperse her belongings to the homes of friends, neighbors, bargain hunters, and morbid curiosity seekers.

7

THE DETECTIVE

On the Saturday that Mary Dean's mental stability was being assessed, the Ladies' Aid Society of Peterborough held a rummage sale in support of a new hospital that had been proposed for the town of Peterborough. The sale raised $400 for the cause, and among the items sold were several donated by William Dean on the eve of his murder.

That same day, the first notice of Dean's murder appeared Jaffrey's weekly paper, the *Monadnock Breeze*. The *Breeze*, as its editor and publisher often referred to it, appeared every Saturday with farm news, recipes, and items of local interest: who was visiting whom, who was recovering from illness, whose son was serving in France. The news from East Jaffrey and Jaffrey Center appeared in separate columns as if the villages were two distinct towns, reflecting what those who lived in them generally felt.

The tone of the *Monadnock Breeze* was chatty, Republican-leaning, and editorially sanguine. From the beginning, it encouraged patience and trust in the officials investigating the Dean murder, even as time dragged on with no apparent progress being made in the case. "People are naturally anxious and some are getting nervous and timid knowing that such a horrible deed could happen," the *Breeze* reported, "but cooler heads are willing to wait patiently while those in authority continue their work upon the case."

Meanwhile, locals lived in fear that the murderer remained on the loose. The milk pail was still missing, no murder weapon had turned up, and there was still no clue as to a motive for the killing. The once-quiet town of Jaffrey became a hotbed of rumors and hearsay. The rumors—of which there were plenty—pointed to three possible suspects: Dean's wife, Mary; his friend, Charles Rich; and his former tenant, Lawrence Colfelt.

Frederick Dean, perhaps discouraged by the lack of progress in the case, returned to his home in New York on Thursday, August 22. There, his wife encouraged him to contact William Wendt de Kerlor, a self-styled criminal psychologist, lecturer, and psychic with whom she had become acquainted. De Kerlor had a long and somewhat checkered history, including a stint on vaudeville. He also had a conviction for fortune telling, which was illegal at the time and resulted in him being deported from England. Like modern-day celebrities, de Kerlor had learned the tricks of self-promotion, including providing sensational copy to newspapers as a way of heightening his acclaim. He was assisted in his many enterprises by his wife, Elsa Schiaparelli, who would later achieve fame as a fashion designer.

Frederick Dean spoke to de Kerlor about his brother's murder and asked for his psychological view of the case. De Kerlor, in addition to his other enterprises, was a correspondent for the *New York World* newspaper and always looking for a good story. He agreed to help.

The next day, Dean and de Kerlor traveled by train to East Jaffrey. Before arriving, de Kerlor suggested that he go by the pseudonym "Kent" among the locals, explaining that he was very well known and his reputation might elicit scorn from "people more or less skeptical of psychological methods"—a fear that was justified, as it turned out.

Dean and de Kerlor arrived on Friday evening and checked into a boarding house in town. On Saturday morning they went to the Monadnock National Bank, where Dean introduced de Kerlor to banker Charles Rich, without revealing that he was a criminal psychologist and a private investigator. Upon meeting Rich, de Kerlor took note of the bruises on the banker's face, about which Dean had warned him ahead of time. De Kerlor was skeptical that the injuries could have been caused by a kick from a horse, but said nothing.

The three men spoke cordially for a time, then Dean and de Kerlor went to the Dean farm where the estate administrator, Lewis Davis, was busy sorting books, letters, and papers. De Kerlor inspected the barn and noted the blood stains on the steps, along with three scratch marks that looked as if they had been caused by some implement. He examined the cistern and found similar scratches on one of the stones that ran around it. He took photographs of everything, including some that would later cause doubts about his methods, if not his sanity.

The next day, an incident took place that did nothing to bolster de Kerlor's credibility. He and Frederick Dean returned to the Dean farm in the company of Sheriff Emerson and George Wellington. De Kerlor wanted to view the surrounding range of hills, perhaps to study the possibility that someone had been signaling from the Dean place. To that end, he had asked Wellington to bring his field glasses.

The four men stood on the verandah of the summer house, from which vantage point de Kerlor surveyed the surrounding area through the binoculars. After a minute, he pointed in the direction of Turner's farm, a neighbor east of the Dean farm. "You will observe an iron trestle," he said.

Wellington took the glasses, but didn't know where de Kerlor was looking.

"Directly back of the building," de Kerlor said. "It's a wireless."

"Is that what you call them out in New York?" Wellington asked.

"Yes."

"Well, here in New Hampshire we call them windmills."

The following Monday, Dean and de Kerlor went to Greenville, New Hampshire, where the Colfelts had moved after leaving the Dean farm. At the Greenville train station, they spoke with a brakeman who said Colfelt's daughter had given him some letters to mail from the station in Ayer, Massachusetts, and had come back later to confirm that he had done so, which struck de Kerlor as suspicious. From Greenville, they proceeded to the Cheshire County seat in Keene, New Hampshire, where de Kerlor presented his suspicions about Colfelt to County Solicitor Pickard. Pickard told Dean and de Kerlor that he appreciated their efforts but saw nothing to implicate Lawrence Colfelt in the murder. And he warned that "if Colfelt were to hear his name mentioned as a pro-German or as a

German spy in connection with those lights he, Colfelt, wouldn't hesitate to bring a libel action against anyone," as de Kerlor recalled.

The warning undoubtedly rattled Frederick Dean, who had a history of financial problems; the last thing he needed was to defend himself against a lawsuit from an adversary with deep pockets. According to de Kerlor, Dean hadn't even had enough money to pay for the train tickets from New York and had to borrow it.

Roy Pickard had another reason for exculpating Lawrence Colfelt. He told Dean and de Kerlor that, in his opinion, Mrs. Dean was probably the guilty party and had murdered her husband in a fit of insanity.

Before they left, Pickard took Frederick Dean aside and spoke to him privately. De Kerlor did not know what the conversation was about, but it seemed to him that after that conversation, Frederick Dean's attitude about the case changed completely.

8

THE ARGUMENT

THAT EVENING, DEAN AND DE KERLOR RETURNED TO THEIR BOARDING house, where they argued. Dean said to de Kerlor, "Those people in Keene seem to resent your activities, or your intelligence, or something."

"It's unfortunate," de Kerlor agreed.

"Can't you see they don't want you? What will you do?"

"There's but one thing to do," de Kerlor said. "That is to go back."

Dean agreed, and the two made plans to return to New York the next day. In the morning they stopped at the bank to return a book that de Kerlor had borrowed from Charles Rich. After handing Rich the book, de Kerlor asked for his opinion about the murder. Rich called Dean and de Kerlor into a private office and spoke confidentially, perhaps because he knew they were leaving town and would be unlikely to repeat what he said.

"I've told Mr. Dean once or twice that I thought Mrs. Dean did it," Rich said.

"What leads you to believe that Mrs. Dean could do this murder?" de Kerlor asked.

"Well, those old ladies when they grow to a certain age they become senile, but although they're senile, they are not physically weak," Rich said. "Sometimes they are physically very strong."

De Kerlor found that doubtful, but said nothing. He then asked how much money William Dean had left. They talked for a few minutes about Dean's finances, then Frederick and de Kerlor departed.

As they went to purchase tickets for the train, de Kerlor confronted Dean about the issue of his brother's finances and Rich's involvement. "Don't you see there is something wrong and crooked about those bonds being there and he having the key, having access to the safe box of your brother?"

"No, no, no," Dean said. "Nothing of the kind. I don't believe it."

They argued further. "Mr. Dean, I don't think you are playing a square game to the memory of your brother."

"Well, I'm going back and you are coming with me," Dean insisted.

"Mr. Dean, if you talk like this, remember that I am not going to talk to you anymore," de Kerlor said. "Goodbye."

With that, the two parted ways. Frederick Dean returned to New York and de Kerlor stayed on in Jaffrey. He immediately met with the town's selectmen—who appear to have approved of de Kerlor's methods— and offered his services.

"He wanted to take up the case and investigate it, and we let him go ahead," said selectman William Coolidge. The agreement was that the selectmen would pay Kent's expenses only; De Kerlor perhaps expected to be compensated by the sale of a sensational news story he planned to write.

De Kerlor threw himself into the investigation with a vengeance, traveling the countryside, interviewing anyone and everyone who knew anything about the murder, at all hours of the day and night. In contrast to the county investigators, who had seemed slow-moving and over-cautious in their investigation, de Kerlor tackled the case with a zeal that impressed—and sometimes annoyed—the townspeople.

Case in point: de Kerlor knocked on the door of Alfred J. Hutchinson, next-door neighbor to Charles Rich, at 11:15 p.m., an unheard-of hour for country folks, if not for a New Yorker like de Kerlor.

"What do you want?" Hutchinson yelled through the door.

"This is Mr. Kent and I would like to have you tell me what you know about the Dean murder."

"I know nothing about the Dean murder."

"Well, please excuse me if I have disturbed you. I have no intention of disturbing you, but I will try to come and see you tomorrow."

"You needn't come," Hutchinson snapped. "I have nothing to tell you."

Hutchinson was serious about not wanting to talk to de Kerlor. When the detective returned the next day to apologize for intruding, Hutchinson yelled, "Get out of here. If you don't get out of here, I will chuck you out."

Later, when asked why he had taken such a dislike to de Kerlor, Hutchinson explained that "he was a perfect stranger to me, a foreigner at that, and it made me mad to have him follow me." It made him mad enough that Hutchinson went to his boss, Wilbur Webster—owner of the tack factory—who gave him a gun. According to de Kerlor, Hutchinson told others "that he had this gun to shoot me with, that it was no use my going to his house at any time of the day because he would shoot me dead."

Merrill Symonds, cofounder of the Bean & Symonds match factory in town, was not impressed by de Kerlor either. "I believe that Kent has some of these men here hypnotized," he said. "You may think that he is a good man, but I don't think so, and it is a wonder to me that we haven't come to blows yet."

Still, many of the townspeople were captivated by the energetic de Kerlor, pleased that someone was making a real effort to find Mr. Dean's murderer, someone who was not afraid to ruffle feathers to get the job done.

Perhaps de Kerlor's most audacious act took place two days after Frederick Dean left town. Just before leaving, Dean had obtained a permit to have his brother's body exhumed, probably at the urging of de Kerlor. The fact that permission had been granted to Frederick Dean and not to de Kerlor does not appear to have fazed him. On August 29, de Kerlor had Dean's grave opened, the casket brought to the surface, and the body re-examined.

A number of local men were present, including the undertaker, the medical examiner, selectmen, police chief, and Charles Rich, who had apparently overcome his squeamishness about seeing Dean's body.

De Kerlor's main reason for exhuming the body was to study the cuts on Dean's skull to see if they matched up with the scratches he had seen on the barn floor and the stone by the cistern. When the casket was opened, de Kerlor placed a piece of paper on Dean's head and traced the path of the three irregular wounds. A local photographer took photographs of Dean's body, the grave was closed up again, and William Dean was allowed to rest in peace, at least for the time being.

From the cemetery, de Kerlor and the other men proceeded to the Dean farm, where de Kerlor compared his drawing of Dean's wounds to the scratches on the porch and the stone by the cistern. De Kerlor, at least, was satisfied that they matched.

Then de Kerlor did something unexpected and astonishing. He held the drawing up to Charles Rich's head to compare the cuts on his face to those on Mr. Dean's skull. "You see, gentlemen," de Kerlor told the group, "these marks are corresponding to those on Mr. Rich's face and Mr. Rich will have to explain how he got them. His explanation so far is not satisfactory."

Rich was dumbfounded, as were the other men. "You could have knocked those fellows down with a feather," said William Leighton, who was frankly surprised that Rich didn't take a punch at de Kerlor. "Instead he gave a grunt and a sneer, as he is capable of doing."

Edward Boynton was even more shocked and noted, "it was a surprise to me because knowing Mr. Rich as well as I did, I expected murder to be committed right there."

De Kerlor pressed the issue with Rich. "We have been told hitherto by yourself that a horse kicked the pipe in your mouth. We have no desire to presume that you have committed this murder, but the coincidence is really extraordinary."

Rich was livid. "When the time comes, I will explain," he said through gritted teeth.

9

THE COUNTY SOLICITOR

WILLIAM AND MARY DEAN HAD NO CHILDREN—A CONSCIOUS DECISION they had made because they were first cousins—but they were especially close to Dean's nephew and namesake, William Dean Goddard, who lived in Rhode Island. Shortly after the murder, Goddard telegrammed County Solicitor Roy Pickard, "Please report any clue regarding my uncle, William K. Dean."

Nearly two weeks passed with no reply. Now Goddard wrote to Pickard, repeating his request for information. "I am anxious to hear what motives, if any, have been suggested as prompting the crime; and whether you have any one under suspicion."

Pickard responded a few days later, outlining the details of the murder and admitting that it was a baffling case. He noted that Dean had no enemies and no money to steal. No one in the area had reported any tramps who might be suspected in the crime. "My present opinion is that Mrs. Dean is the solution to the mystery," Pickard wrote, and went on to dismiss an alternate theory regarding Dean's death. "There has been a rumor which has developed nothing, that a former resident in Mr. Dean's house was a German and that Mr. Dean in some way came to know some of his acts and practices and that Mr. Dean was put out of the way because of fear that he might reveal something. This matter has been investigated by me, by secret service men in the employ of the United States Government and by one of the best detectives I could secure. We have found absolutely no basis for this theory and we are as much in the dark at this time about the crime as we were the day Mr. Dean's body was taken from the cistern. I say this with a little reservation, however, because I did not know at that time of Mrs. Dean's peculiar statements and actions." Then Pickard dropped what must have seemed like a bombshell to Goddard. "I am frank to tell you this, that if Mrs. Dean were sane and she had said the things and done the things which she has said and done I should indict her for murder at the October term of our Superior Court. There is no need, however, to do that at this time because she is insane and is where I can find her at any time."

Goddard responded to Pickard's letter, in part agreeing with him. "The act itself appears so insane and motiveless that the theory of an insane perpetrator seems temptingly natural." But he wanted more details. "I should want to know, however, precisely what peculiar things Mrs. Dean had said and done before adopting the theory that it was her act."

Pickard provided those details in a letter dated September 11, 1918. "We are still seeking for some ray of light which will cause us to look elsewhere than to her but at the present time there is nothing which would arouse any suspicions at all in any other direction."

Pickard went on to cite jealousy as a possible motive. "It is a fact that Mrs. Dean was very jealous of her husband and has been ever since he married her thirty eight years ago." He explained that on the night Dean was murdered, he had brought home a bunch of sweet pea flowers from Georgiana Hodgkins, sister to Mrs. Rich. Pickard speculated "whether this was the spark which brought the explosion we do not yet know."

Furthermore, there was Mrs. Dean's remark—made before her husband's body had been found—that he was "dead and in deep water, that he was down deep where people could not see him and that he had fallen in because of a pain in his head." To Pickard, this was particularly incriminating. "How she should be able to give information which later proved to be so extremely accurate is beyond my comprehension."

Pickard also mentioned a stick of wood found shortly after the murder and which Mrs. Dean insisted be sawn in two and burned up. The women caring for Mary had obliged her and the stick had been burned, a grave mistake in Pickard's book. "This stick of wood might or might not have been the weapon with which Mr. Dean's head was struck," he told Goddard.

Finally, Pickard noted that Mrs. Dean had the exclusive opportunity to commit the crime, and he wondered why, if her husband had been missing since the night before, she did not call anyone until 8 o'clock the next morning.

Pickard did not mention to Goddard two particularly damning pieces of evidence that investigators had uncovered at the Dean farm. The first was a woman's tortoiseshell hairpin, found near the cistern where William Dean's body had been dumped. The other was a calendar from the Deans' kitchen with a note written on it: August 13, the day Dean was murdered, had been circled in pencil and marked with the words "Billee die."

10

THE FIRST SUSPECT

THE INITIAL REACTION OF TOWNSPEOPLE TO THE IDEA THAT MRS. Dean had killed her husband was one of disbelief. To begin with, they wondered whether she was physically capable of committing such a crime given her enfeebled condition.

"Some have asked whether she had the physical strength to have done it," Charles Rich said. But he noted that Mrs. Dean often loaded large chunks of wood on the fireplace for her husband, who had heart trouble.

Alfred Sawyer, president of the Monadnock Savings Bank and an associate of Rich's, agreed. "Mr. Dean wasn't known as a man of any great actions, but Mrs. Dean was always known as a very strong and robust woman, up to the past two years, while Mr. Dean was known as a sickly man."

Wilbur E. Webster, owner of the W.W. Cross tack factory and another friend of Rich's, said, "I am pretty sure that when they come to see, Mrs. Dean could have done it at a time she was out of her head."

Even Georgiana Hodgkins, who considered herself a friend of the Deans, allowed the possibility that Mrs. Dean had committed the crime. "I have known of a case of a woman who had suddenly seized a knife and killed her little girl—a woman who was not considered at all dangerous," she said. "And she never knew it, but did it in a sudden frenzy, and her husband came back and found the little girl with his wife and took the knife away and she never knew it, and I thought as I watched Mrs. Dean whether she could be like that."

One objection this theory was that William Dean had weighed 135 to 140 pounds. Could his frail wife have carried his body from the barn to the cistern? "Not in her regular physical condition," Hodgkins admitted. "But it seems to me a frenzy might have seized her and she might have done it."

Judge Ray, who had declared Mrs. Dean to be insane, agreed. "To me it seems, that notwithstanding the weakness of that woman, it must be taken in consideration how much an insane person can do. They are simply fiendish. Why, I have known some insane people that were ten to [a] hundred times stronger than you would suspect they possibly could be and they were shrewd and astute and all sort of things. I think it is the general belief of people here that Mrs. Dean is the guilty one."

If Mrs. Dean was the prime suspect, what was her motive? On September 22, the *Boston Herald* ran a full-page article summarizing the details of Dean's murder and including details of his home life. "His retirement is said in East Jaffrey to have been occasioned by the jealousy of his wife," the article noted. "Nor is much known about the home life of the Deans during their 25 years of semi-seclusion, although it is recalled that the woman repeatedly said her husband would take to himself another wife after her death. But this is certain—in East Jaffrey the former doctor was safe forever form the smiles of women patients, and here his wife could rest secure from the peril, be it real or fancied, that troubled her."

Did William Dean's attitude toward other women provide any basis for jealousy on his wife's part? Charles Rich, who knew Dean as well as anyone else in town, described him as "a great entertainer to ladies," and Dean's former tenant Lawrence Colfelt said that Dean "liked very much the company of ladies." According to Colfelt, Dean kept an album with photographs of women. "Very refined, nothing vulgar, but always refer-ring to pictures of good-looking women."

Georgiana Hodgkins recalled Mrs. Dean saying that Billy "liked all young girls." She explained that Mrs. Dean "was a little older than Mr. Dean and she continued to be conscious of it." Was Mrs. Dean kidding when she said her husband liked all young girls? "I think she spoke of it intentionally, as a joke," Hodgkins said, "but I think there was something behind it a little."

Others who had known the Deans for years—including many from the fashionable summer set—declared the rumors of Mrs. Dean's jealousy to be vile lies. According to Mary Lee Ware, a wealthy resident of Boston and Rindge, New Hampshire, "The relations between Mr. and Mrs. Dean were delightful. I never have seen a greater intimacy, or really a closer companionship between husband and wife than they had." When asked whether Mrs. Dean was the jealous sort, Ware said, "I don't think Mrs. Dean had the slightest jealousy. I think people who had seen her only the last few years—since her mind has begun to go—have heard her say things really quite silly with regard to Mr. Dean and that might be taken for jealousy." Ware admitted that Mrs. Dean had remarked, "When I am gone Billy will marry again. He likes the young girls." But, she explained, "Mr. Dean was very jolly and cheerful with everybody, old and young, but I never saw a touch of jealousy in Mrs. Dean."

According to nephew William Dean Goddard, jealousy was not an issue in the Deans' relationship. "That is something I never heard or thought of in connection with this couple during all the 36 years since I first knew them," he said. According to Goddard, there was only one relative who supported the jealousy theory, and the authorities "have entertained suspicions regarding that one relative's motives"—undoubtedly referring to Frederick Dean.

Margaret Robinson—another wealthy Bostonian and a friend of the Deans who maintained a second home in Jaffrey Center—was so upset by the rumors of Mrs. Dean's jealousy that she countered them in a lengthy letter sent to newspapers. "Instead of Mrs. Dean having torn her husband away from his city practice because of jealousy of women patients, the fact is that she, a handsome, charming woman, in the prime of life, left her friends and the comforts and pleasures of city life to bring her husband, who had contracted a serious throat trouble which threatened tuberculosis, to a New Hampshire hilltop to nurse him back to health. Although he had studied medicine, he had never practiced it," she wrote, "so he never had any patients, either men or women."

The letter concluded, "Mrs. Dean's care for her husband during the years he was in ill health was repaid with interest during their last years when her failing powers, due to hemorrhage of the brain, made it impossible for her long to do her household tasks."

Notwithstanding these testimonies to the Deans' relationship, there was still Mrs. Dean's disturbing and weirdly prophetic comment about her husband being dead in deep water. But according to neighbor Martin Garfield, there was a simple explanation for that: his suggestion to Mrs. Dean that perhaps her husband and tripped and fallen into the open well near their home. She had not responded but immediately started for the telephone. "Up to that time she hadn't mentioned anything about him being dead," Garfield said.

Arthur Smith, the first person to see Mrs. Dean that morning, corroborated Garfield's account. "Mrs. Dean didn't mention anything about deep water or any water until after the body was found, when she pointed toward Peterborough and said, 'Mr. Dean has gone to the deep waters,'" Smith testified.

In fact, Mrs. Dean remarked to several people that Mr. Dean was in deep water—but each time, she pointed toward a swampy area and a muddy brook that ran through it, not toward the cistern where his body was found. Her fears related to the swamp may have echoed those of her husband. According to local shopkeeper Frank Baldwin, the area was a wet bog in winter and spring, and Mr. Dean had an aversion to it and to ponds or open water in general. He had once gotten stuck in the mire of the swamp, and after that Mrs. Dean had always worried about him wandering into it and being lost.

It is also possible that when Mrs. Dean said "deep water" she actually meant "shallow water." The doctors at the sanitarium where she was staying determined that she was afflicted with "word blindness," an outmoded term for a kind of verbal dyslexia, in which a person may say the opposite of what she means. One instance of this was Mrs. Dean's description of the stick of wood that had been burned and which had concerned County Solicitor Pickard so much. According to Elizabeth Bryant, who was present at the time, the stick was simply too long to fit in the woodstove. Mrs. Dean told Bryant, "This naughty stick is too short for the stove," and continued to harp on it.

Acting police chief Perley Enos confirmed Bryant's account of Mrs. Dean's confusion. "She got it mixed up, and she kept that up," he said.

Finally, Elizabeth Bryant had had enough. She told Enos, "Saw it in two and she will get her mind at rest." Enos sawed the stick in two and the pieces were burned.

Could the stick of wood have been the murder weapon as County Solicitor Pickard wondered? Bryant dismissed that idea as nonsense. "Do you think if she used that wood to kill him, she would have it around so long a time?"

Elizabeth Bryant also had a simple explanation for the disturbing calendar entry "Billee die." Like many farm people, the Deans used their calendar as an informal diary, recording major and minor events, weather, and daily temperatures. On the evening after her husband's death, Mary asked Bryant what day it was.

"It's Wednesday," Bryant replied.

"Well, what's the number?"

"Fourteenth."

"Yes," Mary said. "Billy died the 13th. Now, I must set that down."

The next morning, Bryant saw that Mary had drawn a circle around the date of the 13th and written the ominous words, "Billee die."

"That was all there was to that," said Bryant, who was fully convinced of Mary Dean's innocence in her husband's death. "I could stake my life on it that that woman never done it, and I doubt if any sane man could have done it alone. The distance that corpse had to be carried, it took someone stronger than Mrs. Dean to do it."

The mental health professionals agreed. Dr. Charles E. Thompson, who had examined Mary Dean after the murder, said, "While it is conceivably possible for one in the stage of the disease in which I find her to commit a crime, I am of the opinion that in this case Mrs. Dean showed no sign whatever to lead me to think she had any part in, or knowledge of, the crime." In the report he submitted to County Solicitor Pickard, Dr. Thompson stated, "Several tests were made to determine her physical strength and it was clearly shown that her strength was that of a feeble

woman and not such as to allow me to assume even for the sake of argument, that she could have exerted the force necessary to do it."

To neighbors and friends who had known Mary Dean, the idea that
she had murdered her husband was not just ridiculous, it was contempt-
ible. "I knew Mrs. Dean couldn't have had anything to do with it and it
made me indignant to have her accused," Martin Garfield said. "A man
who knew the circumstances the way Mr. Dean was fixed, a man who
says that she has done it is either a knave or a fool."

11

THE TENANT

To most people in East Jaffrey, the idea that Mrs. Dean killed her husband was ridiculous. But if not her, then who? The most obvious suspect was Dean's former tenant, Lawrence Colfelt.

According to Colfelt, he and his wife had first come to Jaffrey in the summer of 1916 seeking a healthier climate for their daughter, Natalye, who was actually Colfelt's stepdaughter, child of his wife's first marriage. "I'd always heard about New Hampshire being so wonderful, and I made up my mind I would come up here," he said. "My daughter is very delicate. Tuberculosis is in the family and she seemed to benefit in the mountains."

During their first stay in Jaffrey, the Colfelts rented a hilltop home not far from that of William Dean and became acquainted with the Deans. The Colfelts stayed in Jaffrey until October and then returned to their home in New York.

The following summer, the Colfelts returned and rented the big summer house at the Dean property. According to Colfelt, Natalye was attending Radcliffe College in Boston, and he and his wife, Margaret, wanted to be near her. Their choice of the Dean place was also partly altruistic, according to Mrs. D.M. White, a Peterborough realtor who helped the Colfelts find the rental. "Mrs. Colfelt, a very kind woman who is supporting several French and Italian orphans, knew that Mrs. Dean was not well and that the Deans needed the money and the Colfelts wished to help them all they could." White added, "Mrs. Colfelt comes from a very old American family, one of whose ancestors signed

43

the Declaration of Independence and Mr. Colfelt comes from ancient English stock."

To be precise, Lawrence Colfelt generally claimed to be of Irish extraction. His father, a Presbyterian minister, had separated from Lawrence's mother when the boy was 12 years old. Colfelt's mother did not appear to suffer financially as a result, thanks to a large bequest from her father, millionaire industrialist James McManes, as Colfelt explained when questioned by County Solicitor Pickard.

> PICKARD: Do you mind speaking something about what you have done? About what your life work has been?
> COLFELT: Well, 1906 and 1907 I was with the firm of Marshall, Spader & Co. They were in the brokerage business. You see, I inherited from my grandfather an income and I have always had, since that time, from ten to twenty thousand dollars a year.
> PICKARD: Without any effort whatever on your part?
> COLFELT: Without any effort on my part at all.
> PICKARD: And you have used that by living and going about and having a good time?
> COLFELT: Yes, and I have always lived right up to it. You know, it doesn't go very far nowadays, with all the comforts of life, horses, and help, it all takes up money.

Indeed, it must have. In today's terms, Colfelt's annual allowance would amount to half a million dollars or more. Given that, it is perhaps not surprising that Lawrence Colfelt carried himself like a wealthy man, proud and erect. The residents of Jaffrey, unused to his aloof, patrician manner, were not quite sure what to make of him.

"Colfelt acted as if he thought that he was above the people living around here," said Anna Bagley, a Peterborough telephone operator. "He looked to me like a military man."

Jaffrey farmer Harry Mack said, "I always thought that Colfelt was a damned crank. I never had any use for him. You know loads of these town fellows come from the city and they are some damned cranks, and we'll let it go at that."

Others found the Colfelts to be pleasant enough. Lana Rich said of Margaret Colfelt, "I like her very well. She seems rather pleasant."

The manager of the Shattuck Inn, a resort hotel at the foot of Mt. Monadnock, described Lawrence Colfelt as "rather a large man, with a little black mustache, large head, pleasant and agreeable to talk to. He looks more like a foreigner."

Therein lay the problem. By "foreigner," most people meant "German." Prior to World War I, being "pro-German" was no worse than being "pro-English" or "pro-Polish"—an ethnic and political leaning based on culture and heritage.

Then the United States declared war on Germany. Suddenly, anyone with pro-German sympathies learned to keep their thoughts to themselves, or had overnight conversions to a more patriotic mindset. An intensive government campaign warned citizens to be on the lookout for subversive activities. Even Hollywood did its part. *The Spy Menace*, a popular movie serial of 1918, was so viciously anti-German that some theaters in larger cities refused to book the film, either for fear of incurring the wrath of the German populace or of inciting violence against them.

In Jaffrey, the *Monadnock Breeze* advised, "If you have reason to suspect anyone of being disloyal to Uncle Sam keep your eye on that person. Give his or her name to the proper officials. The free air of New Hampshire is too good for the man or woman who is in sympathy with the Kaiser."

A notice in the *Peterborough Transcript* proposed a ban on the teaching of German in schools. In Dublin, a book written by a summer resident that defended Germany was removed from the town library and burned in public. "That's how hot the people were getting," said Charles Thomas, the town's postmaster.

"There was so much anti-German feeling that even little German Dachshund dogs would be kicked," said Delcie Bean, Jr., who was eight years old at the time.

Against that background of anti-German sentiment, it is perhaps not surprising that Jaffrey residents came to believe the unconventional Lawrence Colfelt to be a German and a spy. According to federal agents, Colfelt said locals were suspicious of him because "he had nothing in common with the villagers and did not mix with them; that they therefore, did not understand him and became antagonistic and proceeded to gossip irresponsibly about him."

When asked, Colfelt strenuously denied having any German connection.

> PICKARD: What is the fact? Were you ever in any way connected with the German military government?
>
> COLFELT: Absolutely no. I never even put my foot in Germany. My daughter has a few school friends that were German descent. That's all I know about Germany.
>
> PICKARD: You never were in the employ, or never acted in any capacity or in any way for Germany, or any of her agents?
>
> COLFELT: No, no way.
>
> PICKARD: What were your sympathies in connection with the war?
>
> COLFELT: Well, of course, I wanted the United States to win, the Allies to win. There was nothing about that.
>
> PICKARD: Were you pro-English, or how was that?
>
> COLFELT: No, I wasn't pro anything. I was pro-American.

Colfelt went on to state he had been purchasing Liberty Bonds "to help the thing along," meaning the war effort. Colfelt's wife, Margaret, was similarly adamant in declaring her patriotism. When asked by Pickard where her sympathies had been, she replied, "Well, where they only could be, in America. Heavens! Where do you think they would be?"

During World War I, every citizen was expected to contribute to the effort in some way. The War Department's "work or fight" rule directed that every able-bodied male should either enlist or be engaged in some occupation that supported the war effort. New Hampshire Attorney General Oscar Young summed up the attitude saying, "Along about that time there was a considerable sentiment in this part of the country, New England particularly, that a man ought to be something more than a consumer while we were engaged in this World War and everybody was doing all they could to make it a success. It was felt that an able-bodied man ought not be sitting around using what other people produced but not contributing to it some way."

William Dean, for one, was highly patriotic. It pained him that he wasn't able to contribute to the war effort; at one point, he wrote to a friend "bemoaning the fact that he could not carry a gun," the friend said. Two weeks before his death, Dean told another, "I am so sorry I haven't got a son of my own to be in France."

In part, Dean had rented his property to Lawrence Colfelt in hopes that the younger man would make use of the farm to produce something useful for the war. Instead, according to folks in Jaffrey, Colfelt spent his time riding his horse and driving his large, gray Marmon car all over the countryside. "I met Colfelt in the winter of 1917 to 1918 on snowshoes most every place I went," neighbor Leon Turner said. "He knew the lay of the land for 50 miles."

Nevertheless, by the summer of 1918 Colfelt apparently became worried enough about the work or fight rule to apply for employment at local companies. No company would hire him, perhaps because of the rumors of him acting suspiciously and being a foreigner. Finally, Colfelt applied for and was given a position with the Atlantic Shipbuilding Company in Portsmouth, New Hampshire. Leaving his wife in Greenville, he went to Portsmouth on Sunday, August 11 and began work at the shipyard on Monday, August 12, the day before William Dean's murder.

It was fortuitous timing for Colfelt, of which he was well aware. According to a Bureau of Investigation report, "When asked his opinion as to the author of the murder he replied by stating that he himself was covered with luck on that occasion that he happened to be in Portsmouth at the time and in view of the accusations since made he considered it providential as he might have been at Jaffrey or in some place where he could seriously be suspected of being implicated."

Colfelt reiterated his good fortune when interviewed by Attorney General Oscar Young just a few days after the murder. "We never were mixed up in anything like this before, and I'm very anxious to tell everything that I can and want everybody to know that I have a perfect alibi," he said.

County Solicitor Pickard, at least, believed there was nothing to the suggestion that Colfelt was a German spy, or that he had killed William Dean to keep him quiet. When William de Kerlor presented Pickard with information that he felt implicated the Colfelts, Pickard responded, "We have investigated them and their alibis, which to us were perfectly reasonable, and we were bound to let them go."

12

THE BANKER

SUSPICION ALSO FELL ON CHARLES RICH, GENERALLY CONSIDERED TO BE among Dean's closest friends. Born and raised in Vermont, Rich had attended MIT, graduating third in his civil engineering class. After graduation he had taught school in Vermont and then in Peterborough. In 1883, he accepted a position at the Monadnock National Bank and rose to the position of head cashier.

While working at the bank, Rich founded an insurance agency that is still in business today. In time, he served as town moderator, treasurer of the school district, state legislator, and judge of the police court. To many locals, he was best known as "Judge Rich."

Rich served with the National Guard, as choir director at the Universalist Church, and as Worshipful Master at the local Masonic lodge, the highest position in a lodge.

Judge Rich's peers and business associates considered him to be a pillar of the community. "He is a man with a fine brain and very able," Dr. E. Channing Stowell commented, adding that, "I rather think you will find he had been the motive power and perhaps the planning power behind the prosperity of East Jaffrey."

"There isn't a man in this town that has done so much as he had," said businessman Merrill Symonds.

Apparently though, Judge Rich's personality may have left something to be desired. Police Chief George Nute noted that, "Rich is not always fair nor of an even temper in trying the cases that come before him."

Jaffrey businessman Delcie Bean, more commonly known as D.D. Bean, was a close associate of Rich and sometimes found his personality to be problematic. "I will just tell you one incident that happened to me with Rich which rather surprised me and will throw light on his character," Bean said. "I had gone to the bank many, many times and was rather friendly with Rich. One day I happened to come in and he was at the counter and I wanted to check my deposit slips, and therefore asked him to lend me his lead pencil. He positively refused in a very ugly tone. Of course, later on he would be sorry. But I could never forget it. He had very queer spasms. He will turn you down for absolutely nothing."

On another occasion, Bean went to the bank on business and greeted Rich with, "Fine weather, Mr. Rich."

"I don't know anything about the weather," Rich snapped.

If Rich was discourteous to leading citizens like Bean, he could be even more offensive to average, workaday people. "Mr. Rich had always been hateful and surly to people in the bank," Jaffrey resident Alice Humiston said.

Perhaps Rich's harsh manner contributed to rumors that his background was German or that he had pro-German sympathies. Local gossip held that he had taught German language lessons at his home before the war, and his friend Herbert Sawtelle admitted, "C.L. Rich is a German scholar and speaks German fluently." Rich also sported an imperious handlebar moustache, perhaps too reminiscent of the one worn by Kaiser Wilhelm.

Given all that, it's not surprising that the cuts and bruises on Rich's face—which Attorney General Oscar Young described as "a beautiful black eye"—caused such talk on the day after William Dean's murder. "I should always think it rather funny that Rich should have a black eye the next morning," said liveryman Ralph Davis.

Still, Rich's explanation seemed straightforward enough. According to Rich, "That night Mr. Dean went missing, just before I went into the house to go to bed, Mrs. Rich said, 'You better give this basket of pea pods to the horse.'" Rich went to the barn. "I slapped the horse as I stepped through the door, and the lights weren't on and she was frightened and kicked, striking me in the side and knocking me over, but something knocked that basket up, broke my pipe. It didn't cut the flesh any, but some vein under the flesh, so that for a day or two my eye was considerably black."

Rich's friends found his explanation perfectly reasonable. "Well, it is a very queer thing that C.L. Rich had a black eye the next morning, after the murder," Merrill Symonds admitted, but he blamed any suspicion about the matter on William de Kerlor. "I would just as well believe that if a real detective came here, a man that was a real man, the man Rich would never have been suspected. They would have found that he was a great friend of Dean, and Colfelt, but as for linking his name with the murder, they would have never thought of it. It is a very unfortunate thing that Rich had the black eye the next morning. I admit that."

Rich's presence at the exhumation of Dean's body, and the incident following when de Kerlor put the ghastly piece of paper to his face, only added fuel to the fire. Rich had been speechless, but according to Symonds that didn't mean he was guilty of anything. "I don't think that he had anything to cover up. I think he was kind of provoked for a minute and rather resented Kent's attack. But, damn it, I would have made the same answer, under similar conditions," Symonds argued.

Furthermore, given that Rich and Dean were good friends, what possible motive could Rich have had to be involved with Dean's murder? "I have always believed Mr. Rich to be a great friend of Mr. Dean's, and his personal financial adviser," banker Alfred Sawyer said. "I can think of nothing that would be a motive for Mr. Rich to murder Mr. Dean."

Others argued that Rich's character ruled out any involvement. "I would as well think my father or anybody else being connected with the murder than Mr. Rich," said Henry Allison, postmaster in Dublin. "I cannot conceive of any man of Rich's standing or character having anything to do with an affair of that sort."

County officials likewise appear to have dismissed Charles Rich as a suspect early on. According to Merrill Symonds, when County Solicitor Pickard met with local businessmen to discuss the case, "He told us from his own mouth that he had not one percent of evidence against Rich." Whatever the rumors on the street held, as far as the leading citizens of Jaffrey were concerned, Charles Rich was in the clear.

13

THE SOCIALITE

In the fall of 1918, New England weather, changeable by its very nature, seemed especially cantankerous. After the intense heat of the summer, an early frost in mid-September demolished gardens, dealing a blow to those who hoped to save money by canning vegetables.

The fourth Liberty Loan had begun, and local papers urged readers to purchase bonds and practice other, somewhat more unusual habits to support the war effort. A notice in the local papers urged residents, "Save your Peach Stones. 200 stones make a gas mask, and a mask saves a soldier. It may be your boy."

By now, over a month had passed since William Dean's murder and county officials had made no real progress in their investigation. They had submitted the bloody doorknob from the barn for fingerprint analysis, but it was too smeared to be of any use. Neither the murder weapon nor the milk pail had been found, and no motive had come to light. Agents from the Concord office of the Bureau of Investigation had wrapped up their investigation into the mysterious signal lights from the mountains. Pinkerton agent Harry Scott had submitted his report to the county and moved on. The selectmen had offered a $300 reward for information leading to the discovery of the murderer, but nothing new had turned up. The county had declined to offer any similar reward. "I do not feel that a reward will be of any value at this time," said County Solicitor Pickard. "If anyone has any information he should and will come forward without being paid for his information."

Dean's nephew William Dean Goddard was still anxious for news of any progress in the case. Pickard wrote to Goddard, "I am still working on the case and attempting to find any clues that may lead to the discovery of the murderer. The German spy theory is the puzzling theory in East Jaffrey but at present I have no evidence of any sort to substantiate it. Rumors are numerous but every rumor that has been chased has resolved itself into nothing."

The *Boston Sunday Herald* summed up the situation: "More than a month has elapsed since the unknown hand struck down the New England farmer on the night of that 13th of August, and the mystery of his end grows deeper rather than clearer."

If locals were unhappy at the lack of progress in the case, most felt there was nothing they could do about it. The investigation was up to the selectmen and county officials, and average citizens hesitated to question the authorities, even if they didn't think the job was being done right. However, at least one resident felt no qualms about making her dissatisfaction known, and she was no average citizen.

Mary Lee Ware of Rindge, New Hampshire, was the daughter of a wealthy Boston family and a graduate of Radcliff College. Her father was a physician and professor at Harvard Medical School. Today, Ware is best known for funding a collection of highly detailed glass flowers for the Harvard Museum of Natural History. She was, by all reports, a force to be reckoned with.

Impatient with the lack of progress in the Dean case, Ware contacted Norman L. Gifford of the Boston office of the Bureau of Investigation and asked what he was going to do about it. Gifford wasted no time in assigning Robert Valkenburgh, one of his top agents, to the case.

Valkenburgh began his investigation by studying the records on the case at the Bureau's Concord office, which do not appear to have been much. From there, he traveled to Keene and met with County Solicitor Pickard. According to Valkenburgh, Pickard told him that "Mrs. Dean was the author of the crime, and only her irresponsibility, which was due to her suffering from senile dementia, prevented him from indicting her before a grand jury."

Valkenburgh knew that the medical experts had ruled out the possibility of Mrs. Dean committing the crime. He also knew that the federal government had no jurisdiction to investigate a local murder. But the possibility that the murder was somehow connected to German espionage gave him sufficient cover to continue working on the case. "If you investigate the lights in East Jaffrey, you will fall over the murder," Valkenburgh said. "If you make an investigation of the murder, you will fall over the lights. You can't separate them."

County Solicitor Pickard seemed amenable to Valkenburgh's investigation and even provided the agent with his files on the case. It was a level of cooperation that would come to be greatly tested in days to come.

On September 19, 1918, Valkenburgh, Gifford, and other federal agents arrived in Jaffrey. They were met by a detachment of soldiers from nearby Camp Devens in Ayer, Massachusetts, who had been sent to help the agents search for signal lights.

The agents began by inspecting the Dean farm, where they made a curious discovery at the summer house: panes of glass in windows facing east toward Pack Monadnock had an odd appearance. According to Agent Feri Weiss, "These window panes present the appearance as if they had rusted, the glass is discolored in circles of red-blue, but this effect cannot be seen from the inside of the house, but only from the outside. Only when standing on the outside and looking at a certain angle, could we observe the peculiar discoloration of these two window panes."

The agents also noticed that the screen on the front door was extremely brittle, so much so that a mere touch would cause it to crumble to pieces. They removed one of the window panes and a section of the screen to be sent to the Massachusetts state chemist for analysis.

At the barn, agents found another clue that previous investigators seemed to have missed, one that was even more suspicious: a bloody heel mark on the floor which "by its size seems to come from a woman's heel," Weiss reported.

14

THE PRIEST

IN THE DAYS FOLLOWING THEIR ARRIVAL IN JAFFREY, FEDERAL AGENTS interviewed suspects, selectmen, neighbors, business leaders, and townspeople—anyone who might have any connection or information regarding the murder or possible German espionage. In all this, they had the assistance of an unlikely ally, Father Herbert A. Hennon, pastor of the local Catholic church.

Father Hennon was an outgoing, athletic Irishman, a football and baseball star in college. He had arrived in Jaffrey in 1912 to a parish that was growing rapidly thanks to an influx of workers at the town's mills and factories, people of French-Canadian and Italian descent. Realizing the need for a bigger church, the energetic and frugal Hennon hit upon a plan. He encouraged parishioners to collect fieldstones—of which New England has an embarrassment of riches in its fields and pastures—and bring them to church on Sunday in their wagons. Within a few years, Hennon and his flock had collected enough rough stones to build a new, 600-seat Saint Patrick's church complete with a tower topped by Celtic crosses, still in use today.

Father Hennon had attended William Dean's funeral, where Deputy Sheriff Emerson approached him and asked him to help with any information he might come upon. As it happens, two of the town's three selectmen were also members of Hennon's congregation, and they also asked for his help because "they were not getting the proper support in certain quarters," according to Hennon.

Father Hennon was perhaps uniquely positioned to pick up tidbits about the Dean murder, whether informally or perhaps even via the confessional booth. People who were concerned about what they may have seen or heard, those who were too afraid to speak up publicly, and those who were simply dissatisfied with the lack of progress in the Dean case, all made their concerns known to the priest.

And Father Hennon acted. The church's parish hall became the unofficial headquarters for those unhappy with the county's handling of the case. The selectmen held meetings there, as did agents of the Bureau of Investigation. William de Kerlor stayed with Hennon at the parish house. Hennon acted as the agents' guide to the region, introduced them to those with stories to tell, assisted them in searching for signal lights, and accompanied them to meetings with government officials. In a letter to her mother, Alice Humiston wrote, "Father Hannon [sic] has done wonders. Not only in creating the proper sort of public opinion among the people of his church, but also by giving money, by lodging officials, and by doing all sorts of things to help clear up the mystery."

Hennon also passed on information he had picked up, information that may have been more or less reliable. Federal agent Weiss reported, "Agents then heard from Father Hannon [sic] that Louis Cournoyer learned from Joe Levesque that he heard a Mr. Burpee, who is a dyer in the White Mills, state that Miss Hodgman [sic] told somebody in front of Davis' store the morning after the murder that they could not sleep all that night on account of a conversation they had to listen to between Dean and Rich." Sadly, a good deal of what we know about the Dean murder comes to us from this kind of report, which is practically a textbook definition of hearsay. In life, as in the game of telephone, the gossip that reaches the last person in line is sometimes unrecognizable from the original.

If residents had been on the alert for suspicious lights before Mr. Dean's death, they were even more vigilant in its aftermath. Now, reports of strange lights flew fast and furious. Shafts, brilliant flashes, streaming trails, colored lights, and searchlights were all reported, as were balloons, rockets, and even "aeroplanes." At times, so many people were out at night looking for signals that they were likely to mistake each other—and their lanterns and flashlights—for spy activity. Federal agents may even have contributed to the confusion. As Agent Weiss reported on one occasion, "We flashed one light from our auto all across the mountains, to find out whether anybody will report signals tomorrow morning, just as a test."

Many in Jaffrey were adamant that the signal lights were real. Others, including the county officials charged with the murder investigation, scoffed at the idea, dismissing the supposed signal lights as simply automobile headlights, campfires, planets, stars, or other natural occurrences. Perley Enos, the town's acting police chief, dismissed the reports as mere imagination. "You look at any star long enough and unless you get in line with something, if you stand perfectly still, you will see that move. That is, you imagine it."

Pinkerton agent Harry Scott agreed. "We chased around and tried to catch up with the lights. We didn't find any and we finally came to the conclusion we were men laboring under an optical illusion."

Even department of justice agents admitted that it was difficult if not impossible to separate real from imagined signal lights, given the increase in electric lighting in homes and the number of automobiles traveling at night.

County Solicitor Roy Pickard summed up the general attitude of county officials: "After all the prolonged investigations and searches and watching, not only by many patriotic private citizens but by state and federal authorities, without a single practical result of importance, the conclusion forces itself upon me that the probable solution is found simply in natural events, and that there was no signaling in the interest of alien enemies."

By the fall of 1918, the war was building to a conclusion. The Allied operation known as the Hundred Days Offensive had begun. Germany and its allies, accepting that victory was impossible for them, began to look for diplomatic solutions.

In Jaffrey, residents remained on edge over the failure to track down the murderer of Mr. Dean. Rumors continued to run rife, and even children were struck with a sense of foreboding. One young boy reported seeing a man with a mask looking through his window and soon rumors flew about a masked man stalking the town. The rumors amounted to nothing, and some suspected the boy dreamed the episode based on a movie he'd seen. "It may have something to do with the moving picture serial which is just now going on in the local theater," said Alfred Hutchinson.

Then, as if the war and the anxiety over the Dean murder were not enough, the flu struck.

15

THE FLU

THE FIRST CASES BEGAN APPEARING IN LATE SEPTEMBER. ROY ELLISON, a private at Camp Devens had been sent home to recuperate from pneumonia. Gladys Leighton, who had only recently begun working as an operator at the telephone exchange, was sick with influenza.

Two weeks later, the *Monadnock Breeze* reported that entire families were down with the flu. "Dr. Childs of Dublin is a busy physician caring for the sick in town, and the District Nurse has no idle moments." Schools were closed and mills shut down for lack of workers.

By October of 1918, the so-called "Spanish flu" was raging across the globe. Millions were sick and dying. Hospitals were overwhelmed, and rural areas were hit as hard as urban centers.

East Jaffrey was among the hardest hit towns in New Hampshire. Doctors and nurses came from surrounding states to help out. Local businesses and factories cut their hours or closed entirely for lack of workers. The annex of the old high school was converted into a hospital. The *Peterborough Transcript* reported, "The Board of Health has worked in heroic manner and has met the situation in a way which would do credit to a much larger town than this." The paper especially called attention to Charles Bean, "who is a first class nurse of wide experience and been placed in charge of the men's ward."

The flu epidemic exacerbated tensions that residents were already feeling. In an unpublished account of the Dean murder, Alice Humiston wrote of two people who had died of the flu. "I will just mention in passing that the district nurse who took care of them is a German,"

Humiston wrote, adding that one victim "was not seriously sick until this nurse began taking care of him"—a classic case of xenophobia if ever there was one.

The flu numbered among its victims several people connected with the Dean case, further complicating efforts to track down Dean's murderer. Nevertheless, federal agents continued investigating the murder and chasing down reports of signal lights. On October 20, Agent Valkenburgh and others drove to Greenville, New Hampshire, to examine the house that Lawrence Colfelt had rented after leaving Mr. Dean's farm. The house was empty, Colfelt having gone to work in Portsmouth and his wife, Margaret, having left on September 13 for her home in New York.

The agents found nothing of note at the house. But next to the property was another, deserted house that belonged to the same landlord. Valkenburgh reported, "Agent found that two lights of glass on second floor were partly discolored as if they had come in contact with a strong heat. This discolorment was not as great as the one in the big house on the Dean Farm."

By now, the agents had received the report of the Massachusetts state chemist regarding the window pane removed from the Deans' summer house. The chemist, Walter L. Wedger, reported that the glass had been treated with some kind of alkali solution. According to Norman Gifford, "When it was suggested to Mr. Wedger that it might be a solution such as is used on the outside of windshields to keep the raindrops from collecting, he immediately stated that in his opinion that is exactly what it is." The purpose of the treatment, Gifford presumed, was to keep the rain from diffusing lights shining from inside the house.

The chemist had also examined the crumbling window screening from the Deans' summer house. "After testing this wire, the chemist informed me that that came in contact with a very strong heat, thereby making it so brittle you would see it, as you touched it, it would be powder," Valkenburgh stated.

The findings made Valkenburgh suspicious enough that he decided to interview Lawrence Colfelt again. But before doing so, he acted on a hunch. He dropped hints in Jaffrey that he and other agents would be traveling to Portsmouth at some point "to give Colfelt the third degree."

When the agents arrived at the Rockingham Hotel in Portsmouth where Colfelt had been staying, they learned that he had left three days earlier. Apparently, Colfelt had gotten over his concern about the "work or fight" law. As far as Valkenburgh was concerned, someone in Jaffrey had tipped Colfelt off to the agents' impending visit.

Despite the efforts of the federal agents, there was still no progress in finding the murderer of William Dean. The *Boston Sunday Post* reported that "the 1,895 men, women, and children, who constitute the all-the-year-around population of Jaffrey, are disappointed. They have been see-ing private detectives and Secret Service men and hearing about them for eight long weeks and the mystery of the Dean farm is tonight quite as much of a mystery as it was on the 13th day of last August."

County Solicitor Pickard understood that some were dissatisfied with the lack of progress in the case, but noted that, "the thing that we lack up to the present time are any concrete facts which will direct us to a proper end."

The only real progress in the case, and a minor one at that, involved the milk pail that Dean had used on the night of his murder. Mrs. Dean had said he used a tin pail with a strainer on the side. But according to Arthur Smith, Mr. Dean had discarded that dilapidated pail in favor of the blue and white enamel pail that had been found in the barn the next morning. As Pinkerton agent Scott testified later, "I found from the investigation they were very certain Mr. Dean had milked in the blue and white enamel milk pail."

It seems clear now that Mrs. Dean, in her confusion, was simply wrong about which pail her husband had been using that night. County officials had spent weeks searching for the wrong pail; the actual pail had been in Sheriff Emerson's possession the entire time.

16

THE AUTOPSY

The Great War was grinding to a halt. In Europe, Germany attempted a last-ditch naval effort to salvage her honor if not a victory, but German sailors would have none of it. Naval units refused to participate in the operation, and the spirit of resistance spread across the country. Revolution erupted, resulting in the establishment of a German republic and the abdication of Kaiser Wilhelm on November 9, 1918. The armistice quickly followed on November 11, ending World War I.

In Jaffrey, the summer people were long gone, having returned to their year-round homes in Boston and New York. "There are over 40 houses in and around the Centre and only ten or a dozen of them will be occupied in the coming winter," the *Monadnock Breeze* noted.

With the end of the war and the exodus of the summer people, interest in the Dean murder seems to have waned as well. Perhaps this was simply exhaustion in the aftermath of the war and the flu pandemic. Fears about foreign espionage may have seemed moot at that point. But for whatever reason, newspapers—large and small—largely fell silent regarding the Dean case.

The state and county authorities had, to all intents and purposes, concluded their work on the case. But federal agents doggedly continued their investigations. On November 14, Bureau of Investigation agents met with U.S. Attorney Fred H. Brown in Concord and presented him with a summary of the Dean case, perhaps hoping his influence would light a fire under the state and county officials. To that end, Brown invited State Attorney General Young to the meeting and shared the agents' report with him.

Along with the report, the agents made two suggestions: first, that a formal autopsy on Mr. Dean's body be conducted by Dr. George Magrath, a well-known and respected medical examiner from Boston. The Harvard-trained Magrath had, in 20 years as medical examiner for Suffolk County in Massachusetts, undertaken over 10,000 investigations of suspicious deaths and performed 4,000 to 5,000 autopsies.

The agent's second suggestion was that a formal judicial inquiry be held, to include the calling of witnesses to testify under oath. According to Norman Gifford, Attorney General Young seemed agreeable to the idea of an autopsy, but said he would "confer with County Solicitor Pickard, who had previously been investigating the state's phase of this case."

Twelve days later, the agents again met with Young, this time with Roy Pickard present. Pickard rejected the idea of an autopsy on William Dean's body out of hand, arguing that Mr. Dean had already been bothered enough and that his body should be allowed to rest in peace. "Mr. Pickard waxed facetious at the thought of Dr. Magrath entering the case for the purpose of performing an autopsy," Norman Gifford said.

In the end, Attorney General Young yielded to his county solicitor's objection regarding the autopsy. Furthermore, according to Gifford, "Mr. Young stated that at this time he did not feel there was sufficient evidence to warrant any sort of Judicial inquiry and that he would not proceed at this time." Young and Pickard did say they appreciated the cooperation of the federal government and expressed a desire that federal and state authorities continue to work together on the case.

If Roy Pickard felt that an autopsy on Mr. Dean's body was uncalled for, the selectmen of East Jaffrey disagreed. With the aid of the federal agents, they contacted Dr. Magrath themselves and asked for his assistance with the case. Magrath agreed, and on a frigid January 6, 1919, he traveled to Jaffrey and conducted a complete autopsy on the body of William Dean in the vault of the East Jaffrey Cemetery.

The town's selectmen—Boynton, Coolidge, and Hogan—were present, as were agents Valkenburgh and Weiss. The stone walls of the cemetery vault only added to the chilly setting, and the selectmen brought a small oil stove to help keep the doctor's hands from freezing.

As to be expected after four months in the ground, Dean's body was "much decomposed," as Magrath stated in his report. The body had not been embalmed, and reading the autopsy suggests that Dr. Magrath must have been a man of cast-iron stomach: "The skin of the face dark greenish brown, soft and slimy . . . the skin of the arms and to a great extent the muscles, soft and putty-like . . . the hands dry, brown, leathery."

The lungs were clear, according to Magrath, confirming that Dean had already been dead when put into the cistern and did not drown. He had sustained a fracture of the skull, which was probably enough to render him unconscious but not to kill him. His neck was broken at the fourth cervical vertebra and the hyoid bone—a small horseshoe-shaped bone that lies under the tongue—had been fractured, findings that confirmed Dean had been strangled and suffocated to death.

There was more. According to Agent Weiss, "It is also evident that the former medical examination had been practically a joke." Although the stomach had been removed on the day of the funeral, the heart, liver, lungs, and kidneys had not been touched.

From his years of experience in suspicious deaths, Dr. Magrath concluded that the murder was not committed in a hurry to get the body out of the way. The aim had not been simply to hide the body, but to make absolutely certain it was dead. "In other words," Magrath said, "it impressed me, the description of the body, as showing an intent or desire on the part of the assailant or assailants to leave no doubt as to the matter of death, and the tying of the hands and feet being in that condition as to prevent the man's releasing himself if he could free any of the ties or ropings."

Dr. Magrath also noted that based on his findings, "Mrs. Dean could not have committed the murder. It required more strength than she possessed. She was too frail, mentally and physically. They have to look elsewhere."

After finishing the autopsy, Magrath went to the Dean farm to examine the cistern and the rest of the premises. He also stopped at the home of Reverend and Mrs. Enslin, where Mrs. Dean had been living since her release from the hospital in Worcester. He interviewed her briefly, then accompanied the agents to the parish hall of Saint Patrick's church, where a surprise awaited him.

When Dr. Magrath arrived at the parish hall, Father Hennon introduced him to Charles "Charlie" Bean, the nurse who had been so helpful during the Spanish flu epidemic. Bean had been told that Dr. Magrath was in town and he had taken the opportunity to bring Magrath something that might interest him.

Charlie Bean, in addition to being a nurse, was a photographer, handyman, and well-known gossip. He was also somewhat eccentric, to a degree that folks in town called him Crazy Bean. "He really is not crazy, but he is rather eccentric and is a regular town character," Alice Humiston wrote. "He knows everybody's business and is fond of peddling gossip about town. I am not always sure when he is telling the exact truth and when he is embellishing it somewhat." According to William de Kerlor, Bean had suffered a nervous breakdown following the death of his wife a few years earlier, and had become a sleepwalker as a result.

Bean told Dr. Magrath and the agents that in November of the previous year, he had been wandering about the now-vacant Dean farm looking for clues to the murder. His search took him along a path and a stone wall that ran by the barn. About 250 feet from the barn he noticed a stone propped up against a large boulder by the wall. He moved the stone and found beneath it a five-pronged hand cultivator, the type used to weed a garden. "It laid underneath the boulder as though a person had taken and placed it in like that," Bean said.

Bean recognized the weeder as one he had seen in Dean's barn, hanging near the ladder that led up to the hay loft. He took the weeder home, handling it carefully to avoid disturbing any fingerprints that might be on it. Rather than give the weeder to the local authorities—whom he believed had given up on the case—he decided to hold on to it until he could hand it over to the federal authorities. He had kept it for almost two months when he learned that Dr. Magrath was in town and decided that was the man to have it.

Bean handed the weeder to the agents, who saw what looked like blood stains on it and hair stuck to the prongs. The agents turned it over to Dr. Magrath, "who promised to examine it microscopically so as to decide the nature of the blood spots and hair," according to Agent Weiss.

17

THE DOCTOR AND THE PHOTOGRAPHS

THE REMAINDER OF JANUARY WAS UNSEASONABLY MILD, TO THE CON-
sternation of lifelong Yankees. "Not in the memory of the oldest inhab-
itant have we had a January like this," the *Monadnock Breeze* reported.
"Practically all through the month we have had March weather, minus
the winds."

There were a few chimney fires—not surprising in a region where so
many people burned wood for heat—and at least one fire in a surprising place. "It was a new burning experience when Dean George Adams
found his bed on fire," the *Breeze* reported. "A fireplace spark did it. The
Deacon hustled, so did everybody."

Regarding the Dean murder, there was nothing new to report;
the papers even failed to acknowledge the autopsy performed by Dr.
Magrath. Perhaps to make up for the lack of news on the case, the *Boston Sunday Post* published a lengthy article lionizing William de Kerlor,
whom it described as "one of the noted psychologists of the world and an
author of repute," comparing his work to that of Sherlock Holmes. (It is
quite likely that de Kerlor, acting as his own press agent, provided most
of the information for the laudatory article himself.)

By now, de Kerlor had relocated to Boston. In the interview about
the Dean murder, he claimed that he knew who the guilty party was, but
could not name him yet. Also, the culprit was not alone, according to de
Kerlor. "There were three of them at least, probably four; and one of them
was a woman."

De Kerlor went on to describe the scratches on the stoop of the barn porch that matched the scratches on Dean's skull, theorizing that both had been caused by the recently uncovered hand weeder. He also told of a bundle of bloodstained clothing that had been found not far from the murder scene. "Among the articles was a man's torn shirt and several other articles which led me to believe that the murder had been fully premeditated."

But de Kerlor's most astounding claim was related to a photograph he had taken of bloodspots on the barn porch. He had developed a negative that showed nothing, and was about to discard it when his eye was attracted to a small whitish spot on the plate. "I looked at it closely and was amazed to behold a human face," de Kerlor said. "There was no mistaking it. I had seen it before. As I studied the plate, three other faces appeared, one of them a woman's."

As De Kerlor explained the images on the plates, "the theory would be that as the blood of the murdered man spills at the time when his conscience is still with him, the particles of blood—which known scientific and psychological researches scientifically claim to be the vehicle of the electric body within man—would remain sufficiently conscious as to impress the more sensitive chemical ingredients of the photo filament within the retina of the eye."

The psychologist/detective understood that his findings were perhaps too revolutionary for the average person to accept. "Of course I do not intend, or hope, to convince everybody of the reality of the psychic pictures. But when the evidence has been presented—and the case settled—then the world will have them. And then the world will be one step nearer to a partial realization of the great cosmic forces of the consciousness and the superconsciousness."

The newspaper, at least, was convinced. "Well may the perpetrators of such crimes tremble if, as Dr. de Kerlor claims, such a consciousness remains behind, imprinted on the very substance of things, simply waiting to offer its mute but irresistible evidence."

In East Jaffrey, however, feelings about de Kerlor were still decidedly mixed. As an investigator, Merrill Symonds found him "untrustworthy and wholly unsatisfactory." Symonds's partner D.D. Bean called de Kerlor "a damn cheap cuss," and noted, "It seems to me that he is trying by public sentiment what he cannot get himself."

Attorney General Oscar Young told federal agents Valkenburgh and Weiss "that he cannot understand how two sensible men like we, meaning the two agents, could be tied up with a man like Kent, whom he, the Attorney General, regards as a lunatic."

18

THE MEETINGS

WINTER CONTINUED TO BE UNUSUALLY MILD, AS IF TO APOLOGIZE FOR the erratic behavior of autumn. Residents, now that they had gotten over the shock, reveled in the pleasant weather. The *Monadnock Breeze* declared, "Never have the skies been bluer, the sun brighter, the air sweeter and more nippingly delicious, the moon more radiant, the mountain more protective in his dignity, the hills and valleys more interesting, the trees more friendly and intimate all through this wonderful winter."

Along with crocuses and daffodils, the early spring seemed to bring a revival of interest in the Dean murder case. County Solicitor Pickard continued to assert that there was no new evidence to warrant any kind of judicial action. But the people of Jaffrey would not rest. George Duncan, owner of the town drugstore, began circulating a petition requesting state and federal officials to conduct "a searching and complete judicial investigation into the crime which resulted in the death of William K. Dean." Several hundred citizens signed the petition in short order.

Among those who did not sign were business partners D.D. Bean and Merrill Symonds. When criticized for failing to add their names to the petition, Symonds said that they were not opposed to further investigation, just to William de Kerlor being involved. Symonds even offered to put up his own money to hire a different investigator than de Kerlor, whom he considered to be "a damn poor stick." D.D. Bean went further: "I believe that this man Kent is crazy and ought to be locked up."

The argument about conducting a judicial investigation into the case continued on street corners, in places of business, and in meetings, both formal and informal. The Jaffrey Board of Trade, which had not met in two years because of the war, held a special meeting open to all citizens on February 17. "As you may well surmise, one of the prominent topics for discussion was the Dean case," said George Duncan, president of the Board. "During the discussion, considerable criticism was expressed by various speakers, of the apparent lack of interest and cooperation on the part of the county and state authorities, whose attitude no one present was in a position to explain."

Among the complaints speakers at the meeting leveled against county and state authorities were: that that they had accused Mrs. Dean but failed to take any action against her that would bring the case to a conclusion; that they had declined to have an autopsy performed; that they failed to protect the crime scene; and that they had resisted calling a grand jury to look into the crime.

After the meeting, Duncan wrote to County Solicitor Pickard explaining that a follow-up meeting would be held, "and we would be pleased to have you present, if you see fit, to explain your position and that of General Young." Pickard was initially reluctant to attend such a meeting for fear it would devolve into a personal attack, but he agreed to come as long as the only matters discussed "are those having to do with an honest endeavor to adjust differences and solve this case." It was a noble goal, or perhaps simply wishful thinking.

While local, county, and state officials argued about the lack of progress in the case, Bureau of Investigation agents continued to press for action on the federal level. On February 19, agents met once again with U.S. Attorney Fred H. Brown. Brown felt there was insufficient evidence of espionage to initiate judicial proceedings, but suggested that he and the agents meet with Attorney General Young and County Solicitor Pickard to go over the autopsy report and Dr. Magrath's conclusions. They met on February 25, having also invited Jaffrey's selectmen, Dr. Magrath, and Father Hennon "representing the interested residents of the town," according to Agent Weiss.

Dr. Magrath presented his autopsy report, the result of which was "to overthrow the original theory of County Solicitor Pickard that Mrs.

Dean—a feeble-minded woman—had committed the murder," according to Agent George Kelleher.

Furthermore, it was clear from the autopsy that more than one person had been involved in the murder of William Dean. "They couldn't strike a man in the face and at the same time squeeze his Adam's apple with the same blow," Agent Valkenburgh said. "So it must have been two distinct persons, if not three."

The selectmen then presented the townspeople's petition requesting that a grand jury be held. "All present, with the exception of the State officials, urged for a thorough Grand Jury investigation of the Dean matter," according to Kelleher. True to form, County Solicitor Pickard "appeared antagonistic to any Grand Jury investigation," Kelleher said. Attorney General Young, apparently still bowing to Pickard's judgment, said he would take the matter of a grand jury under advisement. The meeting ended with no action taken.

On March 12, 1919, Jaffrey held its annual town meeting, a New England tradition revered as grass-roots democracy but which often deteriorates into an argument about why it cost so much to paint the fence in front of the meetinghouse. That year, along with the usual discussions of road maintenance and plowing, an argument arose about the spending on the Dean case, which amounted to $2,000. The lion's share of that was for William de Kerlor's expenses, to which Charles Rich's supporters objected strongly.[2]

The meeting included the election of officers, in which selectmen Boynton, Coolidge, and Hogan were up for reelection. The vote was, in essence, a referendum on the handling of the Dean case; those who objected to the county solicitor and attorney general's conduct of the case favored reelecting the selectmen. Those who supported Charles Rich voted for a new slate of selectmen put up by the town's leading businessmen.

The result was a resounding victory for the selectmen.

19

THE TOWN DIVIDED

Two days after town meeting, the selectmen held a second public meeting on the Dean case, this time with County Solicitor Pickard in attendance. For two hours, Pickard defended the work county and state officials had done on the Dean case. He held that a secret grand jury would do nothing to quell public unrest about the case, perhaps revealing his primary concern: keeping a lid on things rather than finding the murderer.

"For the last thirty years there had not been a special grand jury called in the State of New Hampshire," Pickard told the attendees. "I have conferred on the subject, but can find no precedent and I frankly state, I don't know how to call a special grand jury"—an attitude that seems disingenuous on the face of it.

The detective/psychologist William de Kerlor was also present at the meeting. De Kerlor spoke after Pickard, and not surprisingly, his appearance sparked controversy. Alice Humiston recalled, "Somewhere in the midst of it all he told about the exhuming of the body and that fact that the mark on the face of a certain man was exactly like that on the face of the body."

At that point, the supporters of Charles Rich had had enough. "That's a damn lie," Wilbur Webster shouted, jumping to his feet. Rich's neighbor Alfred Hutchinson chimed in, rising to tell de Kerlor that he was going to shoot him if he ever came around his place again. Apparently, Hutchinson was serious, given the gun he'd been given by Wilbur Webster.

Rather than quell local discontent, the public meetings served only to stir the pot. "Rumors continue to fly and speculation is rife," the *Boston Sunday Post* reported. "High-powered motors, doctored window panes, visits made by strange men on dark nights to houses on the outskirts of town—and even the name of a woman—figure in the tale which Jaffrey people tell, a tale which makes them impatient with officials who show no results."

The town's business leaders were increasingly concerned, not just for their associate Charles Rich, but for the health and prosperity of Jaffrey. "That is a damn hard thing which you fellows want to understand, namely, that this town is getting one damn bad reputation out of this," D.D. Bean complained to federal agents.

Increasingly, the town of Jaffrey was divided into two angry camps. On one side were the supporters of Charles Rich, the businessmen who owned the mills and factories and came to be known as the Big Five: Bean, Symonds, White, Webster, and Meyers. They were, for the most part, Protestant, Republican, and members of the local Masonic lodge. On the other side were the people who worked in the mills and factories, people of French and Italian descent who were largely Catholic, Democrat, and not Masons; their Catholic faith forbade them to join secret societies. These people tended to be suspicious of Charles Rich, Lawrence Colfelt, and anyone who supported them.

The businessmen pushed back against rumors that they were downplaying the investigation of the Dean murder. "The fact of the case is that we welcome anything that will bring this murder out," said D.D. Bean. "We would be only too glad, only too pleased, tickled to death, to have this thing brought out regardless on whom it may fall."

While that was perhaps true, the businessmen's overriding desire was for Jaffrey to get back to business as usual, and they eventually decided there was only one way to do that. If the combined efforts of federal agents, the selectman, and a Catholic priest could not convince County Solicitor Pickard to call a grand jury in the Dean case, the Big Five expected to have more luck.

In late March, Jaffrey's most influential businessmen met Roy Pickard at a hotel in Winchendon, Massachusetts, a manufacturing town just over the state line. The goal of the meeting was to convince Pickard to conduct a grand jury investigation and thereby clear Charles Rich's name and put an end to the Dean affair.

The businessmen probably chose to meet in Winchendon so as to avoid the ever-present eyes and ears that supported the gossip network in the town of Jaffrey. And if distance alone were not enough to guarantee their privacy, conditions on the road to Winchendon would probably do the trick.

It was spring, and New England was experiencing its annual fifth season: mud. Then as now, the region's dirt roads freeze in winter and thaw in the spring, from the top down. Melting water, unable to percolate down through the frozen layers, mixes with the top layer of soil and turns roads into a viscous quagmire. In the Monadnock region, the spring of 1919 was worse than most. "The going at that time was wretched, and almost impossible to get through with an automobile anywhere," said Wilbur Webster.

"It wasn't really automobiling; it was mud time," Merrill Symonds noted. Rather than risk the treacherous roads, the businessmen took the afternoon train to Winchendon. Riding the train were D.D. Bean, Merrill Symonds, Wilbur Webster, and Homer White, each representing one of the major industries in Jaffrey. One person not present was George Duncan, a fellow Mason who had attended previous gatherings, but whose standing with the group would change dramatically in the days to come.

What the businessmen didn't know was that others also planned to be at the meeting, or at least within hearing range. Federal agents Valkenburgh and Weiss had received a tip about the secret meeting and wasted no time borrowing a car to drive to Winchendon. Despite the muddy roads—and in what must have been a Great Race scenario—they beat the train and arrived in town before the businessmen. The agents checked into the New Winchendon Hotel, taking the manager of the hotel into their confidence and securing a room next to the one the manager said he would give the businessmen.

The businessmen arrived and checked into their room, where they met Roy Pickard and Sheriff Edward Lord, whom Pickard had essentially dragged along with him. Little did they know that Agent Weiss was next door, his ear pressed to the adjoining door, while Agent Valkenburgh covered the outside of the hotel.

In the aftermath of the Winchendon meeting, rumors spread that the federal agents had recorded the businessmen's conversation with a dictograph, an early bugging device. But they had not; they simply eavesdropped. What they heard was this: the Big Five were able to achieve what others could not, convincing Pickard to conduct a grand jury investigation of the Dean murder.

On March 29, Pickard wrote to the selectmen of Jaffrey saying, "Upon going over the Dean matter very fully, the Attorney General and I have decided that we may bring the matter before the grand jury at the coming April term."

20

THE GRAND JURY

PICKARD'S SUDDEN TURNABOUT ON THE ISSUE OF A GRAND JURY HEAR-
ing caught local and federal officials off guard. "We worked all winter and
then he sprung it on us when we had only a few days' notice," said William Coolidge. The selectmen also complained that although they had
assisted the county solicitor and the attorney general in every way they
could, they were given no say whatsoever as to which witnesses would be
heard by the grand jury.

To assist them in preparing for the case, the selectmen hired Reginald H. Smith, a Boston attorney who had previously done work for
Mary Lee Ware. At Smith's suggestion, the selectmen—along with
federal agents and Father Hennon—met with Attorney General Young,
County Solicitor Pickard, and New Hampshire Chief Justice John Kivel
at the Keene courthouse on the day before the grand jury was to begin.

The meeting began with Selectman Boynton addressing the state
officials, making a request in the most diplomatic terms and suggesting
that federal and state officials might work together to conduct the grand
jury, increasing efficiency and improving the chances of success.

Judge Kivel dismissed the idea out of hand, saying that it was out
of the question and in any case would invalidate the proceedings. Agent
Norman Gifford stepped in, explaining that his department had spent
a great deal of time and effort on the case and that Attorney General
Young had already indicated approval of federal and state cooperation in
the case. "Judge Kivel replied that he should entertain no such request;

that it was a reflection upon the state authorities and that he had been prosecuting criminal cases before the Agent's birth," Gifford noted.

Agent Weiss spoke up but was similarly refused. Finally, Father Hennon spoke in support of the idea, "but was met by Judge Kivel with an even more abrupt and personal rebuff," according to Gifford.

The hearing began the next day. Before it did, Judge Kivel met with Agent Gifford once more. The judge was more conciliatory this time, but repeated that "he could not allow any procedure which would reflect against the state authorities," Gifford said. To Kivel, the offer of help from the federal government was tantamount to an insult about the state's ability to handle the case. The judge did, however, agree to have a stenographer take notes during the hearing and make those notes available to the federal authorities.

Gifford then tried to speak with County Solicitor Pickard about the case, but found him uncommunicative. As Gifford wrote in his daily report, "Agent is firmly of the opinion that Mr. Picard [sic] at least and very possibly higher State authorities, do not desire the presence of further cooperation on the part of the Federal authorities in this case."

Agent Feri Weiss was even more pointed. "Agent is convinced that the County Solicitor, as well as the Attorney General of New Hampshire, and more or less, Judge Kivel, are most unfavorably disposed toward the Federal authorities and to say the least, of prosecuting this case, in a most lukewarm, not to say, antagonistic manner."

Lawyer Reginald Smith had prepared an extensive, highly annotated brief of the case based on information provided to him by federal agents. His intention was to assist County Solicitor Pickard in conducting the case, though he admitted that the brief was incomplete because "Mr. Picard [sic], the prosecuting officer, did not inform us until ten days ago that he would present it to this April sitting."

In a letter to U.S. Assistant Attorney General John O'Brian regarding the case, Smith said, "The present stage is critical. We have to give our evidence to the Grand Jury through a man who knows very little about the case and who, I fear, is not endowed with brains. We are trying to supply both the brains and evidence, without his knowing it."[3] In any event, there is no indication that County Solicitor Pickard made any use of Smith's extensive report in his conduct of the grand jury hearing.

Because it was a closed hearing, the public knew nothing about what was happening inside the courtroom. Federal agents knew little more, other than what they could surmise from the witnesses they saw being summoned to the courtroom. Only one agent, Robert Valkenburgh, was called to testify. Another, Feri Weiss, spent his time cooling his heels in a small room next to the judge's chambers at the courthouse. When not otherwise occupied, the agents took the opportunity to interview witnesses in Keene who had not yet been questioned about the case. As they did, they could not have helped wondering what was happening at the grand jury hearing that they'd had little input into and no control over.

On April 22, 1919, after eight days of deliberation, the grand jury reached its conclusion, which chairman Stephen Bullock reported in a single terse paragraph: "The grand jurors announce that upon full consideration of all the evidence presented before them, they find that William K. Dean of East Jaffrey came to his death at midnight, August 13, 1918, at the hand of a person or persons unknown to them."

That may have satisfied Charles Rich's supporters, but not the majority of Jaffrey residents. "It cost more than $1,500 and took nearly three weeks to come to this conclusion that Dr. Dean was murdered," the *Boston American* reported. "Every man, woman, and child in East Jaffrey knew on the first day that it would have been physically impossible for Dr. Dean to have hit himself upon the head, choked himself with a halter, wrapped a horse blanket around his head, placed a 27½ pound rock on that, pull a bran sack down over his turbaned head, fasten the sack with twine to his belt loops, tie his hands, knees, and ankles, jump into a cistern and then pull the cover on after him."

By law, grand jury proceedings are secret, so nothing of what went on at the hearing was made public, generating even more frustration and gossip about the case. "There is something very funny about the whole business," said Jaffrey railroad station agent Robert F. O'Brien. "There is some whitewashing going on there, you can bet your life all right."

Reverend F.R. Enslin—at whose home Mrs. Dean was now staying—expressed his frustration over the grand jury in a letter to William Dean Goddard, saying, "Probably the guilty ones will go unpunished."

Federal agents were also unsatisfied with the results of the grand jury. "If there ever was any miscarriage of justice, it was before this Grand Jury," Agent Weiss said.

County Solicitor Pickard was unapologetic about the outcome of the grand jury. "Stories that the Grand Jury of Cheshire County was influenced are in line with other silly charges in this case," Pickard said. "The Grand Jury proceedings in the Dean case were judicially and carefully conducted along regular lines. The rights of every person were safeguarded and only facts which could be interpreted as legal evidence were considered. We naturally could not deal with rumors or country gossip. Everything connected with this case has been conscientiously weighed and acted upon. The county officials have no apologies to make."

Nevertheless, according to Pickard, the Dean case was still open, and the state welcomed any new evidence. But state and county officials took no further action to obtain any such evidence, despite numerous appeals from Dean's family members, townspeople, and even the federal government.

The record of the grand jury proceedings consisted of 20 notebooks of shorthand transcription. That transcript was, according to the *Keene Sentinel*, "now under seal, lock, and key and cannot be tampered with."

In fact, nothing so deliberate had been done with the records. At the end of the hearing, court reporter Lena Marsh simply wrapped the notebooks in brown paper and put them on a shelf in the Cheshire County Courthouse, where they would collect dust for the next several decades.

To all intents and purposes, the Dean murder case was over.

II
REVELATION

21

THE REPORTER

On April 23, 1919, the day after the close of the grand jury in the Dean murder case, the *Boston American* newspaper held a dinner at the posh Hotel Lenox in Boston. The *Boston American* was a Hearst newspaper, a designation that implied to readers at the time what Fox News does a century later. William Randolph Hearst, the Rupert Murdoch of his time, had built a publishing empire based on sensationalism and scandal, the cornerstones of "yellow journalism" and the predecessor to today's tabloid newspapers. The editorial stance of the *Boston American* was Democratic leaning, and its motto, printed at the top of every interior page, was "A Paper for People Who Think."

The dinner at the Hotel Lenox was held to honor Bert Ford, one of the paper's star reporters, who had just returned from France where he had served as a war correspondent—the equivalent of today's embedded reporters—with the 26th Division of the American Expeditionary Forces, known as the Yankee Division because it was made up entirely of troops from New England. Ford was the only reporter from New England to accompany the 26th Division in action along the Western front, action that culminated in the Meuse–Argonne offensive, the largest and one of the deadliest campaigns in U.S. military history, involving over a million American soldiers.

Although the war had officially ended in November, the Yankee Division did not return home until April 6, 1919; the abrupt ending of the war had left the army with the dilemma of demobilizing over 3 million troops, an operation that took many months to complete.

Bert Ford was the only war correspondent authorized by the war department to return from France with the Yankee Division and the publisher of the *Boston American* decided to mark his homecoming with a celebratory banquet. In attendance at the dinner in Ford's honor were 60 of his friends and associates, as well Col. Edward L. Logan, for whom the Boston airport was later named, and former governor and U. S. Senator David Walsh. Both men "told of the high esteem in which Mr. Ford is held by civilians and military members alike," according to an item that appeared in the paper the next day.

That same day, Ford returned to his job at the newspaper, where his boss had an assignment waiting for him. "See the chief," the city editor said. "He wants to talk to you about a murder pulled off in the Granite State while you were overseas."

The paper's managing editor, Robert McCabe, gave Ford the outlines of the Dean case. "I consider it a first-class mystery yarn," McCabe said. "I admit the trail is lean and cold with the passage of more than a year,[4] but take a turn up there and go to it."

Before heading to New Hampshire, Ford searched the paper's clippings file—the "morgue," in newspaper lingo—for articles about the Dean murder. He found them to be "disappointingly few and scant," containing little more than the circumstances of the murder and the victim's background. In search of more background on the case, Ford and a fellow reporter headed to Keene, New Hampshire, and met with the Cheshire County Solicitor Roy Pickard.

Pickard seemed surprised that anyone would still be interested in the case. "I supposed this case was closed," he said. "The grand jury investigated and failed to indict anyone. There is nothing more to be done." When Ford questioned this, Pickard explained that there was no new evidence and therefore no grounds for further action. "I have been on four murder cases, and when you've had that experience you will appreciate what I mean," Pickard said.

Ford chose not to tell Pickard that as a reporter, he had covered 10 times as many murder cases. Instead, he asked if he might see Pickard's records on the case. Pickard agreed, a decision he would have occasion to regret in the days to come. He had court duties that afternoon, so he allowed Ford to take the bulging file to his hotel room with the proviso that he "would be careful not to lose any of the records and return them next morning."

Ford and his colleague spent the night reading the contents of the file and making copious notes about what it contained. It was, in short, a treasure trove of documents about the Dean murder: Pinkerton agent Harry Scott's investigation report, witness affidavits, Bureau of Investigation reports, correspondence between Pickard and others involved in the case, and more. "What a gold mine that fat letter file proved," Ford recalled.

As Ford read through the file it became clear that Roy Pickard was a man caught in the middle of powerful forces. "Able, conscientious and with an excellent public record, he seemed to be trying to satisfy all factions in the murder squabble," Ford said, "but his official hands appeared to be tied."

Ford returned the file the next day and proceeded to East Jaffrey, where he met with the town's selectman, who told him of their dissatisfaction with the handling of the Dean case. "There was no doubting the sincerity and ire of the selectmen," Ford said. "They were as keen for action as if the murder had happened the day before our conference." The selectmen were also anxious to share information with him that was not contained in County Solicitor Pickard's files.

In the weeks and months to come Ford visited the murder scene, conducted his own interviews with townspeople and officials, and chased down leads. On September 15, as Ford was wrapping up his research, Mary Dean passed away, a little over a year after her husband's death. In her final days, Mrs. Dean's memory had continued to fail, rendering her unable to recall even the names of people or everyday objects; lemons were "those little yellow things," and the words for other foods escaped her as well.

Still, Mrs. Dean remained sweet and trusting to the end, never learning exactly what had happened to her husband. She took pleasure in playing the graphophone, especially records of old songs that she and Billie had enjoyed in the past. Friends visited her and found her as lovely and gentle as she had ever been despite her physical and mental infirmities.

The end came quietly, in stark contrast to her husband's passing. "She died very peacefully and suddenly," said Winifred Enslin, at whose home Mary lived during her final year. "She went into her room and said she would lie down and she passed away as if falling asleep."[5]

Mary Dean never saw the newspaper articles that would blow her husband's murder case wide open again.

22

THE ARTICLES

A LITTLE OVER A MONTH AFTER MARY DEAN'S PASSING, THE *BOSTON American* advertised an exposé series that would begin the next day: "Who Murdered DR. DEAN?" the ad demanded. "After months of investigation the *Boston American* publishes the FACTS that will startle all New England."

The first of Bert Ford's sensational articles appeared on the newspaper's front page the next day, October 22. The article opened with the revelation that William Dean, on the day before his death, had told a female friend he had important information for the federal authorities, information that was "too dangerous for a woman to know."

The series continued the next day, and ran every day for a month. For the first time, readers learned details from the grand jury that had not been made public before. They learned what eyewitnesses had said, what the Bureau of Investigation had done, and what state and county officials had and had not done.

The impact of the articles was explosive, reigniting the controversy over the Dean murder and breathing new life into the case. In a letter to the *Boston American*, the selectmen of Jaffrey wrote, "We wish to state that the *Boston American* has done a distinct public service in this matter. We are voicing the sentiments of hundreds of the best families in this region when we tell you this."

Even the federal government seemed encouraged by Ford's exposé, Dean's nephew William Dean Goddard visited the Boston office of the

Bureau of Investigation after the series ran and, as he wrote to a friend, "I could see there was a new atmosphere of hope because of Ford's articles."

The final article in the series concluded with a charge to New Hampshire authorities, including New Hampshire's governor, John H. Bartlett. "Treason is coupled with murder in the Dean case," Ford wrote. "What are you going to do about it, Mr. Governor?"

The answer was not long in coming. The next day, November 25, Bartlett invited Ford to share his findings at a meeting of the Governor's Council. Ford attended the meeting with two associates and met Attorney General Young, who revealed his attitude to Ford's work upon first meeting the reporters: "Haven't you fellows forgotten that case yet?" he asked. In the course of the meeting, Young also took the opportunity to complain that federal agents had spied on the Cheshire county solicitor and the Jaffrey businessmen when they met in Winchendon—a complaint that inadvertently revealed how the state and federal agents had been at loggerheads over the investigation.

For his part, Governor Bartlett seemed quick to jump on the Dean murder bandwagon. "You have made the 'lights' and the German spy activities seem very plausible to me," Bartlett told Ford, promising to take action. "No one will be spared. There is no desire to 'screen' anyone, of course. We mean to study this case and keep at it."

The *Boston American* lauded Bartlett's attitude, referring to him as "one of the ablest criminal lawyers in New Hampshire," and going on to say, "Such an announcement by Governor Bartlett is a tribute to his official sensibilities, his regard for the public welfare and his patriotism."

It was the kind of talk that politicians love. Unfortunately, Bartlett's attention was sidetracked for a time by personal and official matters. In the meantime, the *Boston American* continued to fan the flames of the controversy with articles critical of County Solicitor Pickard, Attorney General Young, and local officials like Sheriff Walter Emerson and Russel Henchman, a friend of Charles Rich who had been appointed postmaster of East Jaffrey a month after Dean's murder.

Even Jaffrey's local newspaper, the *Monadnock Breeze*—which had been largely silent on the matter of the Dean murder investigation—finally joined the fray. Acknowledging that many people believed justice had not been served, the *Breeze* excused itself as "a little country paper, going about its business week to week, not disposed to give circulation to every rumor that has been in the air." The editor, F.W. Crooker, undoubtedly found himself in a bind regarding coverage of the case, given that many of its advertisers were supporters of Charles Rich who wished for nothing more than to see the case go away.[6] But in the firestorm that followed the publication of Bert Ford's articles, even the restrained *Breeze* was forced to issue a statement, acknowledging that "a respected loyal American citizen was horribly murdered because he wanted to tell the truth," and declaring, "we would urge that the whole subject be brought before an impartial tribunal in order that this trying atmosphere of uncertainly, unrest and suspicion may be lifted from our community."

Roused to action by the *Boston American* articles, Jaffrey's residents began circulating a new petition, requesting a second, more comprehensive grand jury investigation. Once again, Rich's supporters refused to sign the petition. "I won't sign that petition and nobody can make me sign it," D.D. Bean declared, adding that, "Every person who puts his name on that is a Bolshevist." Postmaster Henchman went so far as to remove petition blanks from the post office. Meanwhile, William Dean Goddard began circulating a similar petition to members of William Dean's family.

A month after Governor Bartlett's meeting with Bert Ford, the governor announced he would be taking action on the Dean case. In fact, he would investigate it personally. The *Boston American* was pleased to report, "Governor John H. Bartlett has decided to do a little sleuthing on his own in the Dean murder case."

"There are many phases of this case which I wish to study myself," Bartlett said. "I want to go to Jaffrey and view the scene of the tragedy and to talk with witnesses. I want to ask questions and sort of sniff around. Being a criminal lawyer, I think I can get a scent if I take the trail myself."

Unfortunately, Governor Bartlett's attitude to the Dean case was to take a dramatic turn the very next day.

On January 13, 1920, the *Boston American* published an incendiary article about restaurants, dance halls, and movie theatres in Portsmouth, New Hampshire, which it alleged were centers of vice and immorality. At the time, social reformers across the country were engaged in efforts to close down such dance halls—sometimes called "dime a dance" halls—alleging that they were simply covers for prostitution. "In the lower dives, women of questionable character are employed as waitresses," the article noted. "At other places 'professional' waitresses used their positions as means of meeting their intended victims."

The article, which carried no byline, included mention of a "twilight dance hall" that was partly owned by Governor Bartlett, who lived in Portsmouth. Accompanying the article was a large cartoon with a carica- ture of Bartlett, relaxing and smoking a cigar in his dance hall while the ghost of William Dean hovered above, pointing to the governor accus- ingly. Apart from that, the article—which ran to several columns—made no mention of the Dean murder.

The article concluded, "In view of the fact that Governor Bartlett spends far more of his time in Portsmouth than in Concord, the State capital, which he visits one a week or a fortnight, it is obvious that con- ditions in his local playhouses could not have escaped his attention while he and his colleagues were counting the fat proceeds."

The timing could not have been worse. The governor had agreed to meet with Jaffrey's selectmen on January 15 to discuss the Dean case. They came to the meeting with the petition signed by over 500 residents of Jaffrey requesting a new grand jury.

They also brought an attitude. That morning, the *Boston American* reported that the selectmen would use the meeting to demand "a show- down" over the Dean case. "We have been buncoed so many times about this case," Selectman Boynton said. "We have been fighting this case for more than seventeen months and we have grown tired of big talk, empty promises and bluff."

During the meeting, one of the selectmen expressed a desire for an honest hearing in the Dean case. Governor Bartlett immediately took offense at the implication of "honest hearing" and said he would go no further until the selectmen filed formal charges against the attorney general and county solicitor. He would meet with them at a later date when those officials could be present and hear the charges made against them. "He also advised the Selectmen that they should come represented by counsel," according to Bert Ford, who covered the meeting.

That afternoon, the Governor met privately with Dean's nephew William Dean Goddard and Henry Dean, a lawyer and cousin of Dean. The relatives brought a more conciliatory attitude to the meeting with Bartlett, perhaps because they did not live in Jaffrey and had not been steeped in partisan bickering about the case.

Goddard and Dean presented the Dean family's petition, a carefully worded document that emphasized German culpability for the murder rather than the state's malfeasance. "We respectfully represent that new evidence has been discovered of sufficient importance to warrant a re-opening of the case," the petition stated. "We have been distressed and humiliated at the long delay of justice in the case, and we believe that prompt and decisive action is necessary to maintain American vigilance against the insidious machinations of a foreign foe."

Somewhat soothed by Goddard and Dean's diplomacy, Bartlett suggested that perhaps the state could appoint a special prosecutor to work with the county solicitor in a new investigation of the Dean case, someone acceptable to the selectmen, the Dean family, and federal authorities.

Dean's relatives were pleased with the results of the meeting, but they were not going to put all their eggs in one basket. They traveled to Washington, DC, with the Jaffrey selectmen and Bert Ford to discuss the case with Justice Department representatives and New Hampshire's congressional delegation. The party was accompanied by a Boston lawyer, Harry N. Guterman, who had vacationed at the Shattuck Inn in Jaffrey, become intrigued by the Dean murder, and offered his services to the selectmen. The selectmen, acting on Governor Bartlett's suggestion, had asked Guterman to act as a special prosecutor in the case and he agreed.

The assistant U.S. attorney general met with the group and assured them that he was deeply interested in the Dean murder and would prosecute the case regardless of the social, financial, or political connections of the persons involved.

The next day, the *Boston American* trumpeted the news in the type of front-page headline usually reserved for declarations of war and major disasters: "U.S. AGENTS TO RESUME PROBE OF DEAN MURDER."

23

THE BLOW-UP

TO THE PEOPLE OF JAFFREY, IT SEEMED THAT MOMENTUM WAS FINALLY building for a reopening of the Dean case. Roy Pickard and Oscar Young were on the defensive over their handling of the case, and the federal government was about to get involved.

In early February, Governor Bartlett agreed to meet with the selectmen again. An item in the *Boston American* published a few days before the meeting stated that the governor had ordered Attorney General Young and Cheshire County Solicitor Pickard to be there. "They will be given a chance to defend the position which they have taken in the Dean case and their methods of procedure," the paper reported.

The day before the meeting, the *Manchester Union*—a Republican and pro-business newspaper—struck a different tone, revealing what the state officials expected to happen at the meeting. "Governor Bartlett has stated that he will not listen to any charges which the selectmen may possibly wish to make regarding the official conduct of the attorney general or the county solicitor . . ."

The selectmen attended the meeting with attorney Guterman, William Dean Goddard, and Henry Dean—representing the Dean family—as well as Bert Ford and a fellow reporter. In retrospect, bringing the *Boston American* reporters to a meeting with Governor Bartlett—still smarting over the article about the dance hall—was a grave strategic error. Politicians, like elephants, never forget.

As expected, Attorney General Young and County Solicitor Pickard were present, along with three members of the governor's council and a stenographer. What the selectmen did not expect was that Charles Rich's business associates—Louis Meyers, Homer White, D.D. Bean, Merrill Symonds, and Guy Cutter, a New Hampshire state banking commissioner—were also there, along with some of their wives and a number of additional reporters; Attorney General Young had issued a public invitation to the other newspapers to attend the meeting, probably hoping for more sympathetic treatment than he expected to receive from the *Boston American*.

In all, between 25 and 30 people were present, far more than the governor claimed he expected at what he thought was to be "a little heart to heart talk with two of the selectmen." Bartlett scanned the crowd—the majority of which had not been invited by the selectmen—and claimed that he had been tricked into attending a judicial hearing rather than an informal meeting. "I am gathering from the number of people here that the matter has been interpreted to be something different than what was communicated to me," he complained.

Bartlett began the meeting by allowing Attorney General Young to make a statement. Young first denied that he had been ordered to attend and added, "We understand that charges are to be preferred here today against us by the Selectmen of Jaffrey and we wish to announce that we do not propose to be put on trial on a subject matter without knowing anything about what the charges are to be."

At this point, Bartlett called the selectmen to speak with him privately, away from the hearing of others in attendance. Harry Guterman objected to being left out of the conversation, stating that he represented the town of Jaffrey.

"I don't care to hear you now," the governor said, "I want to talk with these men here alone."

Bartlett continued to speak with the selectmen sub rosa, and Guterman again asked to be part of the conversation. "You sit down," Bartlett thundered, shaking his fist. Guterman insisted on his right to participate and Bartlett finally roared, "You sit down or you'll go to jail."

"I'm not afraid of arrest, if you insist on it," Guterman countered.

Bartlett again ordered him to sit down and reiterated that this was not a hearing, with the implication that no attorneys were required. Then he came to what was perhaps the heart of the matter, the memory of the *Boston American*'s recent attack clearly fresh in his mind. "There has been too much exploiting of the state of New Hampshire giving us a bad name and a bad reputation all over the world by newspapers, and I refer particularly to the *Boston American*, and I suppose you appear for them."

"I am not counsel for the *Boston American* or any other newspaper," Guterman replied. "I have been retained by the Selectmen and am special counsel for the town of Jaffrey in this matter."

"I don't believe it," said the governor.

"Do you mean to call me a liar?"

Bartlett dodged the question. "We don't want to hear from you anymore. If you want to stay here sit down and keep quiet, otherwise you'll be sent to jail."

"If that is your attitude, I shall not remain another minute," Guterman said.

"I don't think anybody will be sorry," Bartlett replied, playing to the pro-Rich crowd, which rewarded him with a round of applause.

Guterman took his leave just as a Concord policeman entered the room. Guterman did not, as the *Manchester Union* reported later, flee the chambers to avoid being arrested.

The selectmen—now lacking their counsel—presented Governor Bartlett with the brief they had prepared on the case, which contained a number of new witness statements they had acquired with the help of Bert Ford. But Bartlett paid no attention to the brief, choosing instead to lecture the selectmen and their few remaining supporters. Bartlett—a descendent of New Hampshire's fourth governor and signer of the Declaration of Independence Josiah Bartlett—waxed eloquent, wrapping himself in the New Hampshire flag and proclaiming that "the good name and reputation of New Hampshire will not be allowed to suffer if I can help it." Along the way, he also managed to insult the selectmen as being "ignorant of the law."

At that point, Bartlett essentially passed the buck on the Dean case to the federal government. "If the federal authorities can establish a motive for the lights seen on the hills of Jaffrey, they can probably also establish a motive for the Dean murder from the same source," Bartlett said. "If they take the matter into a federal court, they would thus establish a motive for the Dean murder, and the State would then be able to proceed with its murder charge." In other words, if the federal government figured out why Dean was murdered, the state would proceed to determine who did it—a curious attitude to take in a murder case, but the reasoning apparently satisfied him.

The meeting ended as quickly as it had begun. That evening, Governor Bartlett issued a statement that there would be no further hearings in the Dean case unless the selectmen submitted written charges of malfeasance in office or neglect of duty on the part of county and state officials.

There is no evidence that Governor Bartlett ever did anything with the brief that Bert Ford had helped the selectmen prepare. But Ford was not one to let good material go to waste. Over the next several months, the *Boston American* continued to run stories about the Dean murder, a steady drumbeat of criticism about the handling of the case alongside new revelations drawn from the eyewitness affidavits, published in the hope of encouraging federal officials to act where the state had not.

It is hard to overstate the importance of the Ford articles in unraveling the mystery of the Dean murder. In addition to the original witness statements Ford collected, his articles contain the only record of the investigation done by the Cheshire County Solicitor Roy Pickard; in the years since the Dean murder Pickard's original files have disappeared, whether by design or simple neglect. Given that a century has passed, it is entirely possible they were simply discarded in a routine housecleaning. It is also possible that someone decided they were too damning to preserve.

Ford's articles meant so much to William Dean Goddard that he arranged to have them compiled and printed as a book that was "Privately printed for the Relatives," according to the title page. The inscription was somewhat disingenuous, given that Goddard had a thousand copies of *The Dean Murder Mystery* printed, far more than Dean's relatives could use. As Bert Ford wrote to Goddard, "I think there will be a great demand for them in Jaffrey, Rindge, Peterboro and Dublin." (Then, as now, Peterborough was often spelled Peterboro.)

Goddard wrote an introduction to the book, in which he praised Ford for "inspiring confidence in those who had hitherto hesitated to give testimony lest it should be mishandled and they should only get into trouble themselves for their pains . . ."

The book sparked instant controversy in the town of Jaffrey. Few were willing to be seen reading it. Copies were burned and the library's copy disappeared. To this day, a copy of the book is kept at the Jaffrey Civic Center with strict instructions from the Center's founder that it be stored in the vault and its existence be kept discreet.

Bert Ford's articles and the ensuing book kept the controversy over the Dean case simmering through the spring and summer of 1920, which must have driven state and county officials to distraction. It certainly incurred the ire of Jaffrey's Big Five, who finally decided that they'd had enough.

24

THE LAWSUIT

By September of 1920, the relentless criticism and accusations from the *Boston American* must have seemed to Charles Rich's associates like the never-ending bark of a particularly exasperating dog. And just as a barking dog inspires every other dog in the neighborhood to join in, Bert Ford's articles provided new fodder for gossip in Jaffrey and encouraged the town's selectmen to keep fighting for justice in the Dean case.

Jaffrey's business leaders decided that only way to stop the gossip and rumor mongering was to file a slander suit against one of its prime instigators. The obvious choice was Edward Boynton, the most outspoken of the town's selectmen. The businessmen's antagonism toward Boynton went back as far as the Winchendon meeting with Roy Pickard, at which someone had allegedly remarked about Boynton, "he is the worst of the lot."

By this point, Wilbur Webster, Merrill Symonds, D.D. Bean, Homer White, and Dr. Frederick Sweeney (Charles Rich's physician) had come to be known to opponents as the "Soft Pedal Squad" for their tendency to downplay the controversy over Dean's murder. In late September, they met with Rich in Keene, at the law office of Orville E. Cain, who had previously served as the city's mayor and as the Cheshire county solicitor. He was also a banker, a Mason, and a former law partner of Roy Pickard.

The businessmen met with Cain to discuss the idea of suing Boynton, though they would later say the suit was entirely Rich's idea. Wilbur Webster claimed that he had just come along for the ride, while D.D.

Bean said he was simply a spectator at the meeting, interested only in obtaining justice for the town of Jaffrey. "I mean to say that this town has been practically demoralized, financially, socially and otherwise, by the methods that have been employed by our Selectmen," Bean said— unintentionally revealing that the suit was really against all the selectmen and that Boynton was merely their representative.

Regardless of the business leaders' denials, their influence in bringing the suit against Boynton seems obvious. Why else had they accompanied Rich to the lawyer's office? Wilbur Webster admitted later that he'd told Rich that if he didn't proceed to sue Boynton, "I could no longer support him."

The decision was made. On September 26, 1920, Rich sued Boynton for $10,000.[7] The suit alleged that Boynton did "falsely and maliciously speak and publish false, scandalous and defamatory words of and concerning the plaintiff . . ."

The next day, Boynton was arrested by Sheriff Edward Lord and taken to the county jail in Keene. Boynton's fellow selectmen offered to raise bail for him, but to their surprise, he declined the offer and chose to spend the night in jail. As the *Boston American* reported, "Friends rallied to Boynton's aid, but he refused bail and declared that he preferred to remain in a cell under the circumstances. This decision surprised his supporters, who are numerous in Cheshire county."

In fact, Boynton was cannier than Governor Bartlett had given him or the other selectmen credit for. Had Boynton paid the bail and avoided jail, the case could have dragged on for years and then been dropped by Rich whenever he pleased. But having been jailed, Boynton could charge Rich with false arrest if he were to drop the case. By spending the night in jail, Boynton guaranteed that the case would come to a public trial and that finally the truth might come out about the Dean murder. As the *Boston American* noted, "Judge Rich's action, in the opinion of the selectmen, their counsel and the townspeople, opens the way to present in a court of law, for the first time, sensational evidence relative to the murder of Dr. Dean by German agents."

Boynton posted bail the next morning, having achieved what he wanted, the promise of a public hearing about the Dean murder. His fellow selectmen, understanding that the suit was actually aimed at all of them, decided that the town would pay for Boynton's defense.

The slander case began heating up even before the actual trial, starting with the taking of depositions. Open to the public, the depositions were taken at the Union Hall on the second floor of the schoolhouse in Jaffrey, a location large enough to hold the crowds expected to show up.

And show up they did. "Today's proceedings brought out a throng to the Union Hall," the *Boston Post* reported. "Women were literally scattered about the benches, some sewing, some doing tatting, others with their husbands—all following with closest attention the testimony of the four witnesses called."

Lawyers for Judge Rich focused their questions on what Edward Boynton had said about Rich in public, while Boynton's lawyers—Robert and Alexander Murchie—concentrated on the events of the Dean murder and the events that followed it.

Because these were public hearings, newspaper reporters were also there in force, writing stories that exposed new revelations and caused sensation even before the trial began. "SECRETS OF DEAN CASE CAUSE STIR," the *Boston Post* blared on March 12. Most of the witnesses called on the first day were hostile to Charles Rich, causing his lawyer, Robert Upton, to issue a warning to the reporters present. "I want to say now that this is not a trial," he cautioned. "Whatever you print on this will be at your own risk for what will be heard here today will not be a fair presentation of the case."

Undaunted, the newspapers—led by the *Boston American*—published daily updates on the taking of depositions, right up to the day the trial began, on April 25, 1921.

25

THE TRIAL

CHARLES RICH'S LAWSUIT AGAINST EDWARD BOYNTON OPENED WITH the selection of jurors, 12 men who hailed from a number of the small towns in the Monadnock region and all of whom swore they did not know the principals in the case and had not formed an opinion about it. In today's media-saturated world this seems surprising, but it reflects the reality of small town life at the time; if it didn't happen in your town, it hadn't happened. It also means the jurors were unlikely to be influenced by Jaffrey's business leaders as those who lived in the town might have been.

Immediately after the jury selection, the jurors were taken to Jaffrey to view the scene of Dean's murder, an action that gave the case "every aspect of being a murder trial instead of a trial for slander," as the *Keene Sentinel* reported. From the Dean farm, the jurors were taken to a number of homes in town including those of Charles Rich, Edward Boynton, and a number of witnesses who had seen Mr. Dean drive home that evening.

To all intents and purposes, the actual trial began the second day, when Charles Rich took the stand. The pro-Rich *Keene Sentinel* downplayed the attendance at the trial, reporting, "The gallery was only sparsely filled and there were plenty of seats on the floor." On the other hand, the *Boston Globe* noted that "At the morning session the courtroom was comfortably filled and during the afternoon every seat was taken and many were standing in the gallery."

Charles Rich gave his testimony "between convulsive sobs," according to the *Boston Globe*. He told how school children shunned him on the street because of Boynton's slander. "I didn't mind the action of the adults of the town, but when the children ran away from me, it cut deep inside."

The *Boston Post* seemed to doubt the sincerity of Rich's tears, noting that "Judge Rich recovered himself rapidly, however, and appeared entirely composed, as he smiled and chuckled several times during the start of his cross examination shortly afterward."

Rich's lawyers called a number of witnesses to testify that Boynton had implicated Rich in the murder, but the only thing the witnesses appear to have agreed upon is that Boynton had said "Rich knows more about this than he has told," which Boynton himself admitted.

The defense opened the next day, and now the real fireworks began. Witnesses testified about when Dean left Rich's place, where Rich's horse was on the night of the murder, whether Rich had implicated Mrs. Dean, what he had told people about his bruised face, and whether Rich left his home after Dean departed that evening.

As the trial progressed, newspapers provided daily updates on revelations from the courtroom; if nothing else, the trial was good for circulation. "Never in the history of New Hampshire has so much interest been centered in a civil case," the *Boston Sunday Post* noted.

The week ended with a special Saturday edition of the *Boston American* that trumpeted "DEAN'S FEAR OF GERMAN PLOTS IS REVEALED." The revelation came, according to the paper, from Mrs. Arria Morison, a summer resident who was easily the star witness of the week.

Mrs. Morison's parents, Mr. and Mrs. John Whitcomb Cotton, were listed in the *Boston Blue Book*, a compendium of the elite upper class of Boston at the time. Her father was president of The American Tube Works, which produced seamless tubes for steam engines and indoor plumbing and heating.

As a young woman, Arria had been introduced to society in Paris in 1900. In 1905, she married Horace Morison, who was descended from the first permanent settler of Peterborough. During the war, Morison served in the office of the Surgeon General in Washington, DC, where the couple made numerous contacts within the government.

The Morisons maintained homes in Boston and Peterborough, where Mrs. Morison had made the acquaintance of the Deans. On the day before Mr. Dean's death, she spoke with him about the signal lights, which she had been observing for some time. In the course of the conversation, Dean asked her if she had any connections with the federal authorities, which she did, thanks to her husband's time in Washington, DC, and their social class. Dean told her he had important information for the authorities and "asked me if I would go to the office in Boston and ask them to send the best man they had to see him."

This news was a bombshell. For well over a year there had been rumors that Dean's murder had been connected to German espionage, but this was the first time anyone had offered concrete evidence to that end, proof that Dean had had information he wanted to give the government, but had been murdered before he was able to do so.

The second week of the trial was given over to cross examination of witnesses as the lawyers on both sides tried to counter testimony that might hurt their case. By the end, some 80 witnesses had been called to testify. Interestingly, Rich's friends—the members of the Soft Pedal Squad—were not among the witnesses, with one exception. "Merrill G. Symonds, Jaffrey manufacturer and state senator, was the only one of Rich's backers lauded by Attorney Murchie as having moral courage to appear and testify at the trial," the *Manchester Union* reported.

By the end of the week, the number of spectators at the Keene courthouse had swelled to 300. In his summation on Friday, May 6, Rich's attorney Orville Cain praised his client's unblemished reputation and pleaded with the jury for a verdict that would "close the mouth of this vicious defendant." Robert Murchie in turn argued that Boynton had only said what so many others in town had said about Rich, and that the real motive behind the suit was "to choke Boynton's investigations into the Dean murder."

The jury deliberated for three hours before dismissing the charges against Boynton. A jubilant Boynton said, "It seems to me that the result means that the people of Cheshire county are interested in a final solution of the Dean murder if possible."

The people of Jaffrey were equally pleased, as the *Boston Herald* reported: "Preparations were going on tonight in East Jaffrey for a torch light parade in honor of the victory of the selectman."

Charles Rich's lawyers tried to put the best face on the outcome. "While the verdict in the case is for the defendant," Robert Upton said, "the trial has resulted in a complete exoneration of C.L. Rich, so far as any complicity in the death of Dr. Dean is concerned." Needless to say, it had done nothing of the sort.

Upton immediately filed a motion to have the verdict set aside, arguing that "the jury misunderstood and misapplied the law." The judge took the weekend to think about it, and on Monday, May 9, denied the motion.

In the months to come, opposing factions in Jaffrey continued to argue about the lawsuit and its aftermath: the leading businessmen argued that the town's finances were in disarray because the selectman had paid for Boynton's lawyers, a sum totaling $6,000. As far as they were concerned the town was bankrupt, and they demanded that the state tax commission audit the town's books.

"Claim Jaffrey Is Bankrupt Town," a banner headline of the *Quincy Patriot Ledger* read, while the *Manchester Union* said, "Old Antagonism Stirred Up Anew in East Jaffrey." The *Boston Globe* summed up the situation in a short article on October 11, 1921, with the headline, "Dean Case Refuses to Stay in Limbo."

In fact, however, the Dean controversy did gradually subside to a low, simmering resentment that continued to be felt by Jaffrey residents for the next several decades. Despite appeals from concerned citizens, neither the state nor federal governments ever took new action on the Dean case. People on either side of the issue refused to discuss it openly, but continued to trade rumors, memories, and theories in hushed tones. More than half a century passed before the Dean murder found its next champion and reemerged from the shadows.

26

THE STENOGRAPHER

THE CLERK OF THE CHESHIRE COUNTY COURTHOUSE PULLED OUT THE storage drawer, read the label on the brown paper-wrapped bundle, and paused. The year was 1976, and a new addition was being added to the back of the old courthouse, which had been built over a hundred years earlier and was running out of room. The clerk, Stillman Rogers, was responsible for transferring a century's worth of records from the basement of the old building to the vault of the new addition, a massive job.

The court's documents had been kept in wooden drawers three to four feet wide, about 10 inches high and 10 inches deep. Rogers examined the label on the brown paper package: "Hearing by the Grand Jury on the Death of William K. Dean, April 11–22, 1919—Courthouse, Keene, New Hampshire." Inside the wrapping were twenty stenographer's notebooks, each filled with the arcane marks and squiggles that characterized the lost art of shorthand dictation.

As Rogers studied the notebooks, he recalled a man who had come to the courthouse some time earlier seeking information about the Dean murder. DeForrest "Bud" Sweeney was the son of Dr. Frederick C. Sweeney, Charles Rich's friend and personal physician. Bud Sweeney had grown up hearing stories of the Dean murder and the strife it caused in the town of Jaffrey. Now living in California, he had returned East to do research for a novel he hoped to write about the Dean case and had come to the courthouse seeking information.

Rogers thought that Sweeney would probably be interested in the notebooks. He wrote to Sweeney to tell him about them, but Sweeney replied he was unable to return to New Hampshire to inspect them. Even if he had been, the trip would have been futile; the notebooks were written in Pittman shorthand, about which he knew nothing. To the average person, it might as well have been Sanskrit.

Sweeney had another idea, though. In the course of his earlier trip, he had visited with Delcie D. Bean, Jr.—known to friends and family as Jack—the son of D.D. Bean. Jack had also grown up hearing stories about the Dean murder and had adopted his father's attitude to it. As a boy, Jack had known Charles Rich, but "He did not like Mr. Rich as a person," Jack's wife, Margaret, remembered. He described Rich as "very austere, not a friendly, warm, outgoing kind of person," Margaret said. "But for a number of reasons, he just didn't feel Mr. Rich was guilty."

Upon learning of the notebooks, Sweeney thought that Jack and Margaret might have some idea about what to do with them. He forwarded the letter from Stillman Rogers to them and asked, "Any ideas?"

It was a fortuitous connection. Margaret had been hearing about the Dean murder ever since she and Jack were married and was fascinated by the case. She understood that the notebooks could reveal a hidden treasure of information about the case. Nor was she put off by the fact that they had been written in shorthand, thanks to a lucky happenstance. "In my pre-marriage days I had worked on Wall Street and Pittman shorthand was my tool," she recalled.

Her interest piqued, Margaret contacted Stillman Rogers and asked if she might be allowed to transcribe the notes. As a rule, grand jury transcripts cannot be released to the public, but Rogers contacted the state's chief justice, who decided that because the case was so old and no indictment had been made, "a bit of deference was shown," as Rogers recalls.

Beginning in February, 1981, Margaret was allowed to borrow two notebooks at a time, and would have to return those before she could borrow more. She immediately set to work, thoroughly engrossed in the task. "It was the double thrill, of deciphering a code, and as it was deciphered, hearing the very words spoken by the people at the time," she said. Familiar names leapt from the pages, the ancestors of people she knew, most long gone, speaking words that no one had heard outside of the Keene courtroom in 60 years.

Almost immediately, however, she ran into trouble. "I was working on the first notebook, making progress but having some difficulty." Some of the shorthand signs were unfamiliar to her and difficult to translate. Accurate shorthand depends greatly on the skill of the stenographer, and she wondered if Lena Marsh had made mistakes in her transcription. "She occasionally wrote names in longhand," Margaret noted, "but sometimes her handwriting was more of a challenge than her shorthand."

Still, Margaret plugged away at the task. Busy with family life and social activities, she worked on the notebooks when she could, "like handwork," as she described it. When she and Jack took a month-long vacation to Jamaica, she brought the notebooks along, knowing she would have time to work on them uninterrupted. The trip led to another fortuitous connection, this one bordering on the miraculous.

One day, Jack was reading the local newspaper, the *Jamaica Gleaner*. "Hey, listen to this," he said. The newspaper's front page showed Samuel Fitz-Henley, a Jamaican and an expert in Pittman shorthand who had just been involved in a recent case in Florida. "The article told how Mr. Fitz-Henley had a worldwide reputation and was often called on to transcribe notes from many years before, in research projects, or even Congressional situations," Margaret said.

The coincidence was too good to ignore. Margaret arranged to meet with Fitz-Henley before she and Jack left Jamaica for home. The meeting was a milestone. Fitz-Henley explained that Lena Marsh was, in fact, an excellent stenographer; she had simply been using an earlier version of Pittman shorthand than the one Margaret had learned. "He showed me a teaching manual and a shorthand dictionary from the early 1900s, books Lena Marsh would have used, and pointed out the major points of change."

It was a turning point in the transcription. Margaret searched out copies of the out-of-print books that Lena Marsh had used, and now the work proceeded smoothly. "It was a little like doing a crossword puzzle," she said. "A definition would elude you and suddenly you had it."

Then, in 1983, the project hit a roadblock.

Stillman Rogers wrote to Margaret, "I have been instructed by Judge Contas to request that we hold up on the transcription of the Grand Jury materials relative to the Dean Murder Grand Jury inquest." The judge's decision involved a 1982 murder case in which the defendant had requested the transcript of the grand jury hearing before her trial. The New Hampshire Supreme Court denied the request and added, "this court will not sanction any future transcription of grand jury testimony."

Undeterred, Margaret continued to work on the notebooks in her possession and appealed to be allowed to work on the rest. Almost a year passed before the New Hampshire Supreme Court made an exception and allowed her to complete the transcription of the Dean murder grand jury.

There was one more surprise to come. As Margaret was dropping off completed notebooks and picking up new ones, Stillman Rogers asked her if she would like to see something interesting. He pulled out a large cardboard box and said, "This is the evidence from the Dean inquest."

Inside were William Dean's clothes, the bloody blanket that had been wrapped around his head, the ropes with which he had been garroted, the bloody doorknob to the barn, and even the calendar with the ominous words "Billee die" written on it.

"My reaction was an emotional one," Margaret said. "This was no longer an impersonal transcript, but the unfolding of a real and gruesome murder."

In the end, deciphering the notebooks took Margaret six years. In 1989, she published her transcription of the hearing, a massive 350-page tome that includes every word spoken at the hearing, along with an introduction to the case and photographs of the evidence. It comprises the testimony of 43 witnesses and written statements from several others, including businessmen and factory workers, socialites and shop girls, gossips and investigators, and even, surprisingly, suspects; both Lawrence Colfelt and Charles Rich were summoned to testify, although Mrs. Dean was not. "I had hoped Mrs. Dean could be brought here," County Solicitor Pickard said, "but her physical condition is such that it seemed best, by agreement of everybody, that she should not be brought." He did not say whom "everybody" included.

The publication of the transcript inspired renewed interest in the Dean case, along with a revival of the old arguments: was German espionage involved, or was that speculative nonsense? Was Charles Rich the culprit, or the victim of small-town gossip? Was Lawrence Colfelt a spy, or simply a rich ne'er-do-well caught up in war hysteria? Those arguments had lain dormant for decades but still simmered beneath the surface, and older members of the community still refused to discuss the case, recalling the bitterness and divisions it had caused in the past. Alice Lehtinen, who wrote the third volume of the town history, was rumored to know who the murderers were but refused to tell anyone. Archie Letourneau had been 17 years old and working at Goodnow's store when Dean stopped in on the night he died. Letourneau, too, claimed to know who killed Dean, but when asked who it was, said, "I'll let you know when I'm a hundred." Archie died at the age of 91.

27

THE WRITER

In the fall of 2017, I had just finished a major writing project and was taking time off, clearing the decks so I could concentrate on a number of other projects, including a thriller that I was sure would be a bestseller if I could only finish it. I wasn't looking for a true-crime story to write about. Then I got the email.

The message came from Rob Stephenson, with whom I had worked before. "I've got another project you might be interested in," Rob wrote. "Involves murder most foul!"

When it comes to murder mysteries, I tend to favor the cozy variety: amateur detectives in quaint villages uncovering the dirty secrets of their neighbors with a minimum of sex and violence, the actual mayhem occurring discretely off-screen. Too high a body count, too much delving into the troubled mind of a serial killer, and I don't sleep well.

Nevertheless, I called Rob and asked what was up. He explained that the Jaffrey Historical Society was planning to commemorate the 100th anniversary of the murder of William K. Dean. Would I be interested in writing a play about it?

My heart sank. For anyone who has lived in the Monadnock region for any length of time, the Dean murder is an iconic event, an unsolved mystery that resonates with small town scandal, intrigue, and even espionage. How could I say no? So much for my thriller.

I met with the members of the Dean Murder Research Group headed by Mark Bean—son of Margaret Bean and grandson of D.D.

Bean—whose fascination with the case rivalled that of his mother. We
came to an agreement and I went to work.

I began my research by reading Margaret Bean's transcription of
the grand jury hearing. It is not, frankly, an easy read, a bit like sorting
through a 1,000-piece jigsaw puzzle when you don't know what the picture is supposed to be, whether some pieces are missing, or if some of the
pieces belong to a different puzzle altogether.

After plowing through the transcript, I turned to the Bureau of
Investigation's reports on the Dean case, which Margaret Bean had
obtained under the Freedom of Information Act. These documents
comprise over 1,200 pages on the Dean murder, including reports from
dozens of agents, private correspondence, and other material related to
the case. I read every single page, in the course of which I realized that
some pages were missing. I filed another FOIA request, the first of dozens I would come to file with the FBI, Naval Intelligence, the National
Archives, and other government departments, requests that unearthed
still more documentation on the case.

I read everything in the Jaffrey Historical Society's archives on the
Dean murder, including hundreds of loose newspaper clippings and a
shirt box full of clippings that had come down to Bruce Hill, then president of the Historical Society, from his grandparents. When I opened the
box, I noticed a penciled inscription on the inside cover to the box: "M.R.
Garfield." It was, I realized, the personal collection of Martin Garfield,
Dean's nearest neighbor and an important witness in the case. It took me
a full week to simply arrange the newspaper clippings in chronological
order.

The Historical Society's archives also contained correspondence
between County Solicitor Roy Pickard and Jaffrey businessman George
Duncan, along with Duncan's personal recollection of the case and its
aftermath. Another file held correspondence between Margaret Bean
and David Kelley, a member of the Humiston family, whose members
had been key witnesses. William de Kerlor's report on the case was there,
along with his original notes.

Unfortunately, pieces of the puzzle were still missing, most importantly Pickard's file on the case, including the investigation by Pinkerton

Agent Harry Scott. Also missing was the transcript of Charles Rich's lawsuit against Edward Boynton, although the depositions taken before the trial were there. Over the months of working on a dramatized version of the Dean case I searched for those documents, hounding every local, county, and state department where they might have ended up. The officials I spoke with were unfailingly helpful but ultimately stymied; they had no idea where the records went either.

By the time I finished my research, I was certain of only one thing. A grave injustice had been done to William Dean and to his wife, Mary. That became the theme of the play, which ends with Bert Ford addressing the audience in the somewhat formal language of the time.

"How much time must pass before an injustice is no longer an injustice? Ten years? Twenty? Would fifty years suffice? Given such a horrific crime, a crime against a good, honest man, his community, and indeed against the very principles of decency and honor—given that, would the passing of a hundred years be enough to erase the stain of injustice? I don't think so. Do you?"

The play, performed 100 years to the day Dean was murdered, was a success, leaving me with feelings of both satisfaction and regret; the play had been able to cover only a small portion of the research I had done on the Dean murder. A definitive book on the subject had never been written, and I had more than enough material for one. But other projects beckoned, and I reluctantly put the idea aside. Perhaps someday I would find the time to work on it.

A year passed, and I was no closer to finding the time when a tragedy caused me to make the time. Almost exactly one year after the commemoration of William Dean's death, Mark Bean died suddenly while jogging near his home. He was 65 years old. Now, I felt, the book had to be written, to complete the work Margaret Bean and Mark had begun.

Thus, with the information now available to us from Bert Ford's articles, the slander trial, the grand jury transcript, FBI files, and my own research, we can revisit the events surrounding the Dean murder and perhaps, 100 years after the fact, grant a measure of justice to William and Mary Dean.

III

JUSTICE

28

THE STRANGER AND THE SIGNALS

JAFFREY'S CHIEF OF POLICE, GEORGE NUTE, WAS SUSPICIOUS. LIKE EVERY patriotic citizen during World War I, Nute had been on the alert for anyone behaving suspiciously, and Lawrence Colfelt fit the bill.

Even before America's entry into the war, Nute had been hearing reports of mysterious goings on in the Monadnock region: men on horses gathering at mountain retreats, large cars on lonely country roads at all hours of the day and night, signals being flashed from the hills. Then he began hearing complaints about a wealthy foreigner, Lawrence Colfelt.

Colfelt had first come to New Hampshire with his wife and stepdaughter in the summer of 1915. They had stayed at the Shattuck Inn, a popular resort hotel at the foot of Mount Monadnock. The Shattuck, like many resort hotels in New England, had begun as a farmhouse that took on summer boarders looking to escape the noise and heat of the city. The original farmhouse had been destroyed by fire in 1909 and replaced by a grand hotel that could accommodate up to 500 guests in comfort and luxury. Visitors arrived from all over the country and from other nations. Among those visitors was Lawrence Colfelt.

The Colfelts enjoyed their time so much that they returned in the summer of 1916 and rented a secluded hilltop home in East Jaffrey not far from William Dean's home. They became friendly with Dean and returned the next summer, renting Dean's large summer house. Then, to the surprise of locals, they stayed on through the winter.

In his free time—which, as a wealthy man, he had a great deal of—Colfelt liked "to mix with people in society," according to Charles Rich,

and the Shattuck Inn was where he would find them. He could also—
or so some worried—find people with pro-German sympathies. One
of these, a wealthy resident of nearby Dublin, had played host to the
German ambassador to the United States, Count von Bernstorff. Von
Bernstorff himself had even stayed at the Shattuck. As a frequent visitor
at the inn Colfelt could well have met von Bernstorff there, though there
is no evidence that he did.

A number of Jaffrey residents had spoken to Chief Nute about the
mysterious Colfelt. They said he was pro-German, owned an automobile in which he traveled all over, and told conflicting stories about his
background. Nute decided it was time to act. He contacted the Bureau of
Investigation, asking them to check into Colfelt. As it happens, agents of
the bureau were already in the area, investigating reports of signal lights
from Mount Monadnock and the surrounding hills.

In the summer and fall of 1917, a number of residents had reported lights
flashing from Monadnock and the surrounding hills, but federal agents
who investigated them found nothing substantive. Then, in the spring of
1918, new reports began coming in. Eva Sweeney, wife of Dr. Frederick
Sweeney, swore that she and her husband saw lights coming from the
Dean farm.

"One night during the month of March, 1918, Dr. Sweeney called my
attention to a big light at the Dean house where the Colfelts were then
living," she testified. "We both watched the light for some time, flashes
going toward Temple would glow out at intervals. This was between half
past ten or eleven o'clock and lasted for half an hour, I would say."

The reports of signal lights came to the attention of Norman L.
Gifford of the Bureau of Investigation's Boston office, who noted that
"many strange lights had been reported in the southern New Hampshire,
particularly in the neighborhood of Peterboro." Gifford may have focused
on Peterborough more than Jaffrey because "Peterboro has been for several years past a rendezvous of Germans whose residence there had been
considered to be somewhat due to their admiration for Edward McDow-
ell, the American composer." MacDowell's widow had founded an artists

colony in her husband's name to support artists, writers, and musicians, including some with "strong German sympathies," according to Gifford.

The bureau's investigations in 1917 had been unable to explain the lights. But by the spring of 1918, "some of the most prominent inhabitants of Peterborough were still most insistent that these lights continued to appear," according to Gifford.

Among those prominent citizens was Arria Frazier Morison, whose husband had worked in Washington and who had connections within the Justice Department—connections that she did not hesitate to make use of when she became concerned about the signal lights. Mrs. Morison made a call, the U.S. Attorney General's office alerted Norman Gifford, and Gifford decided the suspicious lights should be looked into again.

To assess the situation in Peterborough, Gifford called on Nathanial C. Nash, a Boston attorney with considerable outdoors experience. Given the rural nature of the Monadnock region, Nash seemed like the right man for the job. He was also, like many agents of the young bureau, essentially a volunteer.

Nash arrived in Peterborough on Friday, March 29, 1918. His instructions were to conceal his identity while looking for any signs of "flashing lights, aeroplane activities, German spy reports and other war matters," as he wrote in his initial report. Nash spent the weekend in the Peterborough area, maintaining a low profile while walking country roads, hiking trails, and taking note of the surroundings. On Monday, he returned to Boston and filed his report.

"The country surrounding Mount Monadnock, New Hampshire, and including Peterborough, New Hampshire, and Dublin, New Hampshire, has every facility for pro-German operations," Nash noted. "The terrain is so hilly that it would be very easy to establish a chain of signal points which could be seen only from given spots; it contains several prominent mountains which, if necessary, could be used to send signals with a minimum of relays from New York State to the coast of Maine. There is much wild land, abandoned farms and passable but disused roads, which could be utilized for secret communication. There are also excellent automobile highways connecting the important points. Lonely lakes from which hydro-aeroplanes might operate are numerous."

Nash also noted that residents' fears about espionage seemed to depend on their social class. "The farming population has not awakened to the dangerous possibilities, and as it does not travel around after dark there is nothing to hinder nightly communications or secret meetings. The city people, most of whom reside in this district only during the summer, are very much excited over the suspicious happenings."

Based on the preliminary report, Norman Gifford decided to send Nash back to Peterborough to conduct an in-depth investigation. He returned, checked into the Peterborough Tavern and began making contact with locals who had reported seeing signal lights. Chief among these was Mrs. Morison, who lived on the old Jaffrey-Peterborough Road, in an impressive estate with stunning views of the surrounding hills. It was less than a mile from the railroad station at Noone Mills in South Peterborough, a location that facilitated her frequent trips to Boston.

Mrs. Morison was intelligent, well-spoken, and not one to be intimidated by authority figures. She was also, like Mary Lee Ware, a force to be reckoned with.

29

THE MATRON

Arria Morison met Agent Nash, who told her he had yet to see any lights. She immediately insisted he relocate from the Peterborough Tavern to her home, where she was certain he *would* see them.

Nash did as he was instructed and transferred his belongings to Mrs. Morison's home. That evening, he went to town to meet up with another agent. Upon his return, Nash found Mrs. Morison highly excited, claiming that he had just missed seeing a signal light. As they watched together, the light appeared once more, briefly, and Nash fixed a telescope on the spot so as to identify its source in the light of day.

The next morning, he found the telescope to be pointing at a house two miles away to the east. As it happens, George Clement—president of a Peterborough company that produced windshield wipers—lived in that direction and happened to call on Mrs. Morison the same day. Nash asked Clement if the house in the telescope was his and he said it was not, but he did not know whose it was.

Nash suggested that Clement call his wife and ask her to hang a red cloth from a window of their home. She did, and the cloth was clearly visible in the telescope. Clement conceded that it was his home and remembered that they'd had houseguests the night before who had been moving around in an upper room, passing back and forth in front of a large oil lamp as they packed their bags.

The episode was typical of Nash's attempts to locate any signal lights, which were invariably fruitless. He walked country roads, lay out in fields at night, tramped through the woods, and never found any real evidence of signaling. On one excursion, he did find an old pair of wooden skis that had been abandoned in the woods, and although he did not find them particularly suspicious, he nevertheless included a detailed description of them in his daily report.

Despite the disappointing results, Nash's supervisor Gifford—after consultation with an expert in signaling—concluded that "there was considerable likelihood that some system of communication by lights was being at least experimented upon in southern New Hampshire."

On April 19, Gifford sent Nash back to Peterborough once again, accompanied this time by another volunteer agent, Harry Marshall. Nash and Marshall checked into the tavern and spent the next few days exploring the region. They began with a farm not far from Mrs. Morison's home that belonged to a family named Moore. Signal lights had allegedly been seen there, and the agents took turns staking out the farm at night.

One night while Nash was laying out in the field, he "saw a man come from Moore's farm with a lantern to a chicken house, where he remained for one minute and then locked up and returned to the farm." Nash watched the man closely for several minutes but saw nothing suspicious. "It has since been suggested that he may keep a bottle of liquor in the chicken house," he reported later.

On another evening, Marshall reported a light "which looked flashing at first but I soon discovered that this flashing effect was caused by an intervening branch or pole which made the light appear to flash as I moved my head."

On yet another occasion, a light that both agents thought was the flashing of dots and dashes of Morse code turned out to be simply an electric light swinging at the end of a cord.

Thus far, the results of their investigation were disappointing. Then, on April 24, Nash received instructions from Norman Gifford to contact the chief of police in nearby Jaffrey about a resident who had been behaving suspiciously and had been reported by the manager of the Shattuck Inn: Lawrence Colfelt.

30

THE AGENTS

AGENTS NASH AND MARSHAL, ALERTED TO LAWRENCE COLFELT'S SUS-picious behavior, began seeking information about him from Jaffrey residents. They learned that Colfelt was an avid horseman and spent entire days—and sometimes nights—riding on trails in the area, or taking late-night drives on back country roads in his large Marmon automobile. Colfelt and his wife, Margaret, were reported to make frequent trips to New York by train, as many as two or three times a week, for reasons that were unclear at best. The Colfelts were alleged to have made unpatriotic statements and were guarded about their mail and telephone communications.

On the other hand, neither Colfelt nor his wife appeared to be German or had a German accent. "They resemble New York society people," Agent Nash reported, and a worker who had been in the Colfelts' house a few days before speaking with Nash saw nothing suspicious there.

When not investigating Lawrence Colfelt, the agents continued to explore the surrounding countryside looking for signal lights or other suspicious activity. On one occasion they came upon three men in the woods cutting trees and eyed them warily. The loggers returned the favor; given the setting, they probably had more cause to wonder what the agents were up to than vice versa.

Perhaps because of that, the agents began to worry that their continued presence in the area might cause talk. To that end, they came up with a cover story; they were visiting the area to fish. They bought fishing licenses, tackle, and worms, and spent time angling on the Contoocook River in Peterborough, in plain sight of main roads where they were sure to be seen. In his report of April 25, Nash noted that "there being nothing particular to investigate during the afternoon, Agent and Volunteer Operative Marshall went fishing and caught one trout, two perch, and four dace"—a better result than their other, more official fishing expedition had produced thus far.

The next day, Nash and Marshall scouted the local golf course under the pretext of gathering mayflowers. In the evening, they returned to Moore's field and watched until 10 p.m. but saw nothing suspicious. As they walked back to their hotel, they passed Mrs. Morison's house and saw that she was at home. Nash decided they should let her know what they were up to, lest she come to the hotel looking for them and blow their cover.

The agents spoke with Mrs. Morison, who was convinced that the lights were certain to appear over the next few nights because there was a full moon, providing enemy agents with light by which to make their way around unfamiliar countryside. She was also certain that her home was the perfect place to observe the signal lights. "She was very anxious for one of us to stay at her house," Marshall reported, adding that "it was arranged that Agent Marshall should spend the week-end at her farm." Agent Nash, having had the privilege of lodging with her before, apparently decided to pass.

The relationship between Mrs. Morison and Agent Marshall must have been an interesting one. In one of his daily reports, Marshall noted that he had helped Mrs. Morison with her housework and in her garden. After lunch, he inspected her farm and made supper for her in time for her to catch the evening train to Boston.

That night, while Mrs. Morison was away, Marshal watched at Moore's field for a light that she claimed to have seen in the direction of Pack Monadnock to the east, a light she described as large, with a very dull glow "such as would be produced by a Japanese lantern." Marshall watched until 3:45 in the morning but saw nothing.

A few days later, he spoke with former New Hampshire governor Robert P. Bass and another man who had been at the Morison home on the night she claimed to have seen the "Japanese lantern" light. The men were certain that the light was simply the Dog Star, Sirius, rising in the east behind Pack Monadnock. They had tried to convince Mrs. Morison of that fact, but as Marshall noted drily, "They were unable to do so."

At this point, it appears that Marshall, at least, had seen enough. In his report for May 1, 1918, he wrote, "Unless further instructed, Agent will consider this matter closed." Ten days later Agent Nash, using almost the exact same wording, came to the same conclusion.

Despite their vigilance at Moore's farm, the agents never saw anything conclusive in regard to signal lights, although their initial description of the farm includes this telling notation: "Not far to the West of Moore's Farm and connected by a good road is a farm occupied by one Colfelt who has been complained of as a German spy. From Colfelt's house an excellent view is obtained to the West of high hills south of Monadnock Mountain. Lights have been reported from these hills. It would seem therefore, that Colfelt might easily receive signals from the West and walk to Moore's farm and relay the signals to the East which would thus eventually reach the seacoast."

31

THE PLAYBOY

"Playboy" seems an apt description of Lawrence Colfelt, a man who appeared to do no work but nevertheless lived comfortably and spent freely. According to Robert Hamill, who owned a livery business in town, "Colfelt was a man who always seemed to have plenty of money and he wasn't stingy with it either."

Colfelt's only paid occupation appears to have been as a young man, when he worked for a stock brokerage in New York. It was a career that did not last long. Colfelt had hoped to buy his own seat on the exchange, but he did not have the $60 to $80 thousand dollars that seats were selling for at the time, and his mother declined to bankroll the project. Also, Colfelt said, "my health wasn't any too good in the office, so I dropped out." Perhaps coincidentally, the company for which Colfelt worked was suspended from trading in December of 1908 for involvement in illegal trading, and later went out of business. At any rate, it may be that Lawrence Colfelt was not temperamentally suited for business; one associate described him as a "very erratic young fellow."

Following his brief career in the stock market, Colfelt appears not to have been gainfully employed, nor needed to be. His income came from his mother, who had inherited $4 million upon the death of her father, millionaire industrialist and political boss "King" James McManes.

Lawrence's mother continued to take care of him even into adulthood. Case in point: she engaged Dr. Robert J. Carlisle of Manhattan to attend to Lawrence's frequent illnesses, telling the doctor that "he was to call and see him at any time Lawrence requested, and all of his bills for his services were to be sent to his mother," according to Dr. Carlisle. Carlisle's wife, who knew of Lawrence only by hearing others speak of him, said that he had a reputation of being "feckless, dissipated and wild, not of good moral character."

Compared to Lawrence's privileged upbringing, Margaret Colfelt had much more humble origins. She was born Mary Margaret Reid in Brooklyn, New York, in 1897, the first of seven children in a large Irish family. Whereas Lawrence's father was a renowned minister and his grandfather McManes a millionaire whose portrait hangs in the National Gallery, Margaret's father was a grocer's clerk and later the bookkeeper in a fish market.

From infancy Margaret was known to family and friends as Daisy. At the age of 18 she married Francis B. Roberts, a New York real estate broker. A year later, their only child, Natalye, was born. The marriage dissolved not long after. Margaret ran off with Lawrence Colfelt while she was still married to Roberts, taking Natalye with her. She divorced Roberts and married Lawrence Colfelt in 1904, although she appears to have stayed in touch with Roberts over the years, even staying in an apartment building that belonged to him when she visited Manhattan.

It appears that Lawrence's mother did not approve of his relationship with Margaret, a divorced woman with no money and a seven-year-old child. "Colfelt's mother was doing everything she could to effect a separation between them," Dr. Carlisle said. She refused to include Margaret in her will, meaning that Margaret would be penniless if Lawrence were to die. "When Mother dies I will get an income," Colfelt said, but added that "if anything happens to me, my wife and daughter get nothing."

For Margaret, not having her own money seems to have been an overarching concern. She was opposed to Lawrence entering the service for fear that, should he die in the war, she would be left with nothing. At one point, she asked her mother-in-law to provide an income for her apart from that of Lawrence. "I said if she would give me $3,000 a year then he, Lawrence, could join any regiment," Margaret said. "She wouldn't. My husband told his mother and she wouldn't agree to my having anything."

Despite this worry, the Colfelts appeared to be well off, purchasing whatever they felt like, tipping generously, and giving frequent gifts to friends and associates. Even the size of their grocery orders drew the attention of locals, who wondered why three people would need so much food.

Beyond their extravagant spending, locals also found it curious that the Colfelts continued to live in the Deans' drafty summer house year round; most summer people departed the region at the first sign of cold weather. Everett Bingham, who lived about a mile from the Dean place, said, "I have worked for wealthy people a lot in my life, and I thought it was strange for a wealthy man to want to live out in a place like Dean's in the middle of winter, and the going as bad as it was. Very bad winters we have out there, especially the last year. That's the only thing that passed through my head. It was funny a man would want to live out in that part of the country."

Charles Linek, who worked for the Colfelts and lived at the Dean place with them, agreed. "The house where the Colfelts lived in was built for warm weather and it was impossible to heat it in the winter as we didn't have any coal to burn, wood only," Linek said. "The house was so cold that when I brought the milk in, it froze before you could get to it."

Locals also wondered about Margaret's frequent train trips to New York. "She makes trips about twice a week of one or two days duration each," Agent Nash noted, adding that she "has given many different contradictory reasons for her trips to New York." While on the train, Margaret was often seen writing in a notebook according to Frank Humiston, who had worked for the Colfelts and noted, "when Mrs. Colfelt went on the train to Boston or New York she would be writing all the way down."

On occasion, the Colfelts would take the train from Winchendon, Massachusetts, some 12 miles away rather than the Jaffrey station, which was only two miles from their home. Perhaps this was because they didn't want to leave their car at the depot; Selectman Edward Boynton noted that Colfelt seemed protective of his automobile and said, "when he came to the village one of them, either he or his wife, would always stay with the car."

The Colfelts were fond of driving their car around the region at night, another habit that drew the attention of locals. "I knew he was driving around nights a good deal," said Martin Garfield, one of their closest neighbors. Another neighbor, Everett Bingham, testified, "I've seen them go by my house as late as eleven o'clock," although he admitted, "He isn't the only one, of course. I've seen other people out late."

Frank Humiston said that they "seem to be exhausted and out of sorts in the morning as if they had been traveling late at night."

The Colfelts' protective attitude toward their auto was also reflected in their communications, where they displayed a degree of caution bordering on paranoia. To make long-distance phone calls, they would travel to the telephone exchange office in Jaffrey or Peterborough rather than calling from their home. "They told me they could get better services here than if they called from their home," the Peterborough operator said. Admittedly, the home phone was on a party line, notoriously bad for private conversations. But neighbors wondered what the Colfelts could possibly have to hide.

Even when making calls from the telephone office, the Colfelts seemed to be circumspect, to the point of using what sounded like code. Grace Leighton, the operator of the Jaffrey exchange, reported that Mrs. Colfelt several times called New York and said, "The cook is gone. Come on quickly. It is urgent." But according to Agent Weiss, "As a matter of fact, they only had two cooks working there in all and yet these telephone calls were repeated many times."

On another occasion, Lawrence Colfelt received a telegram that advised him "not to buy no more candy because they were putting ground glass in it," according to Frank Humiston, who believed that to be some kind of code.[8]

Grace Leighton remembered an occasion on which Margaret engaged her in conversation while Lawrence was making a long-distance call so that she could not overhear what was being said. "Miss Leighton is positive that this was Mrs. Colfelt's object," according to Agent Weiss.

Margaret perhaps had reason to guard their privacy. Grace Leighton also testified she had overheard Lawrence Colfelt telephoning his mother after reading some good news for the Germans in the paper. "We had good luck," she recalled Colfelt saying. "I see by the papers that the Germans have captured a British fort."

Another time, Lawrence was speaking to Margaret over the phone and, according to Leighton, said that "their work for their government in that vicinity was about over, that they could do no more there." However, Leighton reported the conversation several times and the wording varied slightly from report to report. She told Agent Nash that Colfelt talked about moving back to New York, "where he could do good for their government," which leaves open the question of which government he was talking about.

Perhaps to prevent her conversations from being overheard, Margaret asked another operator, Catherine Priest, to teach her how to run the switchboard. According to Priest's sister, Mrs. George Hart, "She told us that Mrs. Colfelt visited her frequently and asked her many times to teach her how to operate the switchboard." Margaret had been generous in her attempt to befriend Catherine and her family. "Mrs. Colfelt called upon us and was forever giving Catherine gifts for my children," Mrs. Hart said. "She gave them money, books and other things." But on the advice of another sister, Priest refused Margaret's request. The sister "told not to allow anybody to use the switchboard while we were at war," said Hart.

The Colfelts' handling of their mail was equally guarded. They sent most of their outgoing mail from the Peterborough post office, where they had a box. In Jaffrey, they received a great deal of mail, according to George Duncan, who was postmaster up until May of 1918. But Colfelt refused to allow mail to be delivered to his home even though he lived on an RFD route, preferring instead to pick it up in town. "He had a private box for his mail and gave strict orders that no letters should ever be given a carrier to take to his house," Agent Nash reported.

In fact, as a rule, the Colfelts didn't seem to want people around their house. Frank Humiston reported that the Colfelts raked the walkway to their house every evening "so that they could tell if anybody would come near the house during the night so that they could see the tracks."

Those who had dealings with the Colfelts often found them peculiar. "They could be kind of funny, and I thought several times he appeared to be very nervous at times," said Martin Garfield. "I went up there and he was very nervous when I went up to spray out his horse stalls, very nervous indeed, and pretty cranky. And when I got up there, he was swearing a blue streak, something about his automobile, and I thought he made a good deal more fuss about it than there was any need of."

When anyone asked the Colfelts where their sympathies lay in regard to the war, they loudly proclaimed their loyalty to America and the Allied cause. But testimony from those who knew them paints a different picture.

Lester Ellsworth, an East Jaffrey resident, told of a conversation he had with Colfelt while delivering wood to him. "On the second trip to the place with a load of wood, [we] were in the cellar, Colfelt and I, throwing the wood back of the furnace and there was something said about the war by me. He said that President Wilson was no good; that he was a fool and not fitted for the chair."

The talk turned to Germany and Ellsworth said, "I don't see why Germany should want to kill off so many of her own people and so many others."

"If you raised a lot of fighting cocks and spent a lot of money to train them up, you'd like to see what they could do," Colfelt replied. "That's the way it is with Germany; they raised a lot of soldiers and spent a lot of money."

"Yes," Ellsworth said, "they showed what they could do by the way they handled women and children in Belgium."

"After that," Ellsworth told federal agents, "he didn't have any use for me."

Another local who found Colfelt to be suspicious was Hugh Churchill, brakeman at the train station in Greenville, New Hampshire. "I never spoke to him but once, that was down at the blacksmith shop," Churchill said. Churchill's route took him to the train station in Ayer, Massachusetts, where Camp Devens was located. According to Churchill, "He asked me if the 76th Division had left Ayer, and asked if there were very many men in camp, and I told him yes."

"What do you mean by 'very many'?" Colfelt asked.

"A whole lot," Churchill replied circumspectly.

"By a whole lot, do you mean 5,000, 10,000, or 20,000?"

Churchill, well aware of the danger of loose talk, refused to give Colfelt a straight answer. "I never talk about the things I see in there," he assured the agents.

32

THE HORSEMAN

Much of the talk about the Colfelts' unpatriotic statements appears to have originated with Frank Humiston, a young man who worked for them until he entered the service. "I went there because he had some fine colts he raised and did not know how to take care of them, so he hired me for the job," said Humiston, who was an expert horseman and who probably got to know the Colfelts better than anyone else in Jaffrey. He and Colfelt spent a good deal of time together, riding and training the horses, and Humiston came to believe that Colfelt used him as a sounding board to find out what people in town were talking about.

"He said one day, 'I heard there has been lights in the mountain. What do people say about it in the village?'" Humiston recalled. "He always wanted to know anything that was going on around the village and I was to tell him always what the people were thinking about it, if they saw anything."

During one conversation, Colfelt bragged to Humiston that he'd had German military training. "I don't know whether it was private training or official, but anyhow he assured me that it was very excellent German military training." In fact, Colfelt had simply attended The Hill School, a private prep school in Potsdam, Pennsylvania, that had a Cadet Corps, as did many such schools at the time.

Colfelt then asked Humiston to show him how Americans did the manual of arms—instructions for handling a rifle. "I illustrated with a broomstick, and he showed me a different way to shoulder a gun, saying that was the way he had trained."

Later, Humiston asked Margaret what kind of German military training her husband had received. "I told her what he had said to me and she said that I must be mistaken," Humiston recalled. "That started an argument between her and me."

As far as pro-German remarks were concerned, "He certainly has praised the Germans," Humiston told federal agents. One time, he overheard the Colfelts say they thought the Kaiser was sure of victory, "and upon their discovering Humiston's presence, they spent an hour and a half in talking to him to overcome the impression they thought this remark had made on him," Agent Nash reported.

It is possible that the Colfelts, both of whom had an Irish heritage, were not so much pro-German as they were anti-English. Lawrence Colfelt "hated the English the worst possible way, and he called them all kinds of names that he could think of," Frank Humiston said. Even before the Dean murder, Agent Nash noted, "The suspect and his wife are anti-English and anti-Wilson. They have been overheard to say that 'they hoped there would not be a single Englishman left.'"

At one time, Frank Humiston had worked as a mounted guard at the Remington Arms factory in Bridgeport, Connecticut. He facetiously told Colfelt that he had caught some Germans in Bridgeport and had come to the Dean farm to catch him. "Mr. Colfelt actually turned white in the face," Humiston recalled. "He could not say anything for a minute or two, and then he asked how I did it."

Humiston laughed and Colfelt, realizing his error, backpedaled. "I haven't got any German in me," he sputtered. "I am Irish as near as I can make out, and I have been buying Liberty Bonds to help the thing along."

According to Humiston, at about the time Agent Nash was conducting his initial investigation into them, the Colfelts became nervous and short-tempered. "He was a pretty nervous man along the last," Humiston said. "He could not sleep night or day. He got nervous and could not sleep. He was on the jump all the time."

Agent Nash reported, "So marked was this change that Humiston was afraid to work around the place without carrying a gun." Humiston had seen Colfelt with a Colt revolver, and he became convinced that, on one occasion at least, Colfelt wanted to shoot him. "We were riding out into the woods and Colfelt said to me, 'What do you say if we shoot at a target?' He was going to shoot first and get me to look at the target to see where he made a mark. I saw right through it and that he would shoot me, and it would be a nice little accident if I was hit."

Humiston suggested that it wasn't a good place to target shoot and that perhaps they should find another spot. "Then he made up an excuse for me to ride ahead of him, but I kept on the right side of him a little bit in the rear, about two paces behind him all the time. He is a pretty smooth boy, but I was where I could put my hand on the hardware all the time."

Humiston left Colfelt's employ when he entered the army on April 25, 1918. It took Colfelt a month to find someone to replace him, a man named Frank Romano who had worked for Colfelt at his home in Harrison, New York, and again in East Jaffrey during the summer of 1916. Romano was a Lithuanian Russian whose wife and children were still in Russia. When he began working for Colfelt at the Dean farm, rumors quickly spread in town that the dark-complected Romano was German, Austrian, Polish, or some other nationality. Typical of the local attitude was that of Rosanna Deschenes, who lived near the Dean farm and said, "I did not like his expression. I did not like that man to look at." Reverend Enslin described Romano to federal agents as being of "sinister and desperate appearance."

"He was a pretty hard looking ticket," Frank Humiston recalled. "He stood in military fashion, and I think that if any dirty work would have to be done he would be the fellow to do it for Colfelt."

33

THE LANDLORD AND THE TENANTS

LAWRENCE AND MARGARET COLFELT FIRST MET WILLIAM DEAN IN 1916 when they rented a house not far from the Deans. "We liked them very much," Colfelt said.

The Deans were easy to like. William Dean was careful in his appearance and his conduct, with dark eyes that could switch from intensely studious to wryly amused in an instant. He was not one to act in haste, and a measured calm seemed to define his actions. At five-foot six-inches, he was of average height for the time, generally cheerful, and as friendly with his working class neighbors as he was with his more affluent acquaintances. Mary Dean, four years older than her husband, was universally acknowledged to be kind and generous, with a fondness for children and animals. According to a neighbor, she "looked like Martha Washington," with soft grey curls framing her face.

According to Lawrence Colfelt, the Deans came to dinner at his house several times in the summer of 1916. After returning home to New York that fall, the Colfelts kept up a correspondence with Dean, "particularly my daughter and he," Colfelt said. The families were close enough that Dean offered to rent the Colfelts the large house on his property the next summer. Lawrence, Margaret, and daughter, Natalye, arrived on August 12, 1917, almost exactly a year before Dean's murder.

The Colfelts enjoyed their stay and at summer's end, decided to stay on through the winter; Natalye was enrolled at Radcliffe College in Boston, and they felt it would be easier for her to visit them in New Hampshire than in their home in New York.

As fall turned to winter, William Dean gradually became unhappy with the arrangement with the Colfelts. The rent he charged them had been, in his mind, for the summer house only, not the barn; Dean used the barn for his horse and carriage along with his turkeys and a few other animals. But Colfelt had begun using the barn as well, keeping his horses and his auto there.

Dean expressed his frustrations to his friend Margaret Robinson. "In renting the house he had expressly stated he couldn't let them use the barn as he needed it for his own animals," Robinson said. "Nevertheless, they actually took possession, made themselves very troublesome, using his implements, freely admitting to breaking them."

The barn became an ongoing source of tension, according to Charles Rich. "Mr. Colfelt had to put his automobile in where the hens ran and he must have objected to that," Rich said. "Mr. Dean must have objected to having the automobile there for he couldn't get his horse or his buggy out very well."

For his part, Colfelt claimed that he was doing Dean a favor by staying on into the winter and renting the house from them, as he knew Dean needed the money. "He was so bad off financially I asked to lend him money," Colfelt said. "I would have done it, but he was such a proud man, you know, I couldn't get to him at all."

Despite whatever friction there may have been over the use of the barn, the Colfelts claimed that their relationship with the Deans was entirely amicable. According to Margaret Colfelt, "They were always pleasant and agreeable and we were very, very fond of them."

True, Lawrence Colfelt occasionally argued with Dean, but it was nothing serious according to Natalye Colfelt. "They sometimes used to get angry about little things," she said. "Oh, whether they would put the turkeys in one place or another, or something of that kind, or the turkeys got on top of the automobile and scratched it. But it was nothing at all serious, that is, they always made it up afterwards and I think he liked Father very much."

Colfelt acknowledged that his wife and Mr. Dean argued a great deal, but this was just playful banter. "They were very friendly," he said. "Mr. Dean could argue about anything. The first thing you knew, you would be talking about something and he would take the other side. He was a very charming man to converse with."

Margaret felt the same about her disagreements with Mr. Dean. "He used to argue with me and have fun with me," she said. "I think he enjoyed it. He was teasing all the time." As to her husband's relations with Dean, "They were always pleasant," she said.

But what the Colfelts described as playful banter seemed more serious to others, like Frank Humiston. "I thought when I left there would be something doing between Mr. Dean and the Colfelts because they were continually arguing, and especially Mrs. Colfelt," Humiston said. "I always thought they would come to blows right away at one time." And while Lawrence Colfelt always claimed to have nothing but respect for Dean, Humiston recalled things differently. "He didn't like Mr. Dean," Humiston said. "He tried to impress me that I should not have anything to do with Mr. Dean, that he was an old crab and all kinds of other names that he called him, most anything he could think of."

By the spring of 1918 it was clear to those who knew Mr. Dean best that his relationship with the Colfelts had soured. Dean told his friend Mrs. Robinson that it made him uncomfortable to be around Lawrence and Margaret Colfelt. According to Robinson, "Each aired their marital grievances to him, especially Mrs. Colfelt, and this was a great trial to him. At times she would declare she couldn't possibly go on living with Colfelt, that he was always going off on these trips without telling her where he was going, that she had seen him with other women, that she believed he was crazy, that he had been at one time in a sanitarium for mental derangement, that she ought to have left him when Natalye was a baby, and would have done so but for the fact that she had no means of support."

Dean's neighbor, Martin Garfield, was also aware of the increasing tension. "In the Spring, that April, I began to realize that Colfelt and Mr. Dean seemed to be out of tune," Garfield said. It had been a typically muddy spring, and one day Colfelt's auto got stuck on a waterlogged road, so Colfelt called Garfield to come help him out. "I asked him about Mrs. Dean," Garfield said, noting that he did not see so much of her as he used to.

Colfelt replied, "Dean is a damn brute to bring a woman like her to a place like this, for it is a living death for a woman who was so fond of society and life to come to such a wilderness." He went on to grumble, "I've got to get out of this place. I might as well get out, everything is going wrong. This is a beautiful place, but when you say that, you've said it all."

Even Charles Rich—who had not visited with Dean very much that winter—heard the rumblings. "It must have been the first of May when I first heard that he couldn't agree with the Colfelts," Rich said. Rich asked what the trouble was and Dean indicated there wasn't room for them. "And there wasn't," Rich said. "They both had stock enough to fill the barn and there had to be an agreement."

Another area of disagreement had to do with the use of the farm itself. Dean wanted the fields to be cultivated to produce some useful crop to support the war effort because the need was so great. Mrs. Dean's infirmity and his own declining health left him unable to work the land, but he had hoped that Lawrence Colfelt would step up to the task, all the more so as the planting season approached. In this, he was to be greatly disappointed. Colfelt may have been many things, but he was not a farmer. To him, horses were for riding, not plowing.

"I gave him every chance to make good on this farm," Dean told a friend. "I didn't have the money myself to run it during these war times, but I gave him every chance to use the land and do anything he wanted with it. But he never had the slightest interest to raise anything of any kind."

Colfelt's excuse was the Dean didn't have the appropriate equipment to farm the land. Furthermore, he argued, there was a shortage of labor because of the war. "Who is going to cultivate this place when a man can go to a factory and make from five dollars to ten dollars a day?" he said. "Who would be willing to cultivate a little place up here?"

In any event, Colfelt suspected the real reason for Dean's dissatisfaction with him was Colfelt's hired hand, Frank Romano. Dean and Romano clashed over the use of the barn, a situation that appears to have been a case of too many cooks in the kitchen. Romano complained that when he cleaned up after Colfelt's horses, Dean would come along and clean up after his own horse, tossing the manure where Romano had just cleaned. The situation infuriated Romano, according to Natalye Colfelt, who recalled a time when Romano stormed in from the barn and threw his hat on the kitchen table.

"What is the matter, Frank?" Margaret asked.

"That old man is getting the place all dirty again," Romano grumbled, "and some time you will find him hanging up in the barn."

"Or something to that effect," Natalye noted. "I don't remember the exact words."

34

THE MOVE

FINALLY, COLFELT DECIDED HE'D HAD ENOUGH OF DISAGREEMENTS over the barn and Frank Romano's run-ins with Mr. Dean. In an effort to keep Romano from quitting, Colfelt told him, "We'll be going the first of May," and he set about looking for a new place to live.

The decision came as a relief to Dean, according to Martin Garfield. "Mr. Dean told me sometime about the middle of April, 1918, that Colfelt was going to leave his place May 1," Garfield said. "He seemed pleased and relieved. I think that he felt that he didn't want Colfelt around there."

The Colfelts' initial efforts at finding a new place were unsuccessful. Then a solution occurred to them: they would buy the farm from Dean. They approached banker Charles Rich about the possibility of getting a mortgage to buy the farm because, despite his lavish lifestyle, Colfelt does not appear to have had the ready cash for that kind of purchase. In any case, Dean was not interested in selling the farm, at least not to the Colfelts. According to Margaret, he told them, "What, do you think I would sell the farm to the likes of you?"

Fuming, Margaret vowed that they would have the farm one way or another. Frank Romano recalled, "Mr. Colfelt liked the place and wanted to buy it, but Mr. Dean wouldn't let him have it. Mrs. Colfelt said that her husband would someday buy it from the bank, which it seemed had a mortgage on the property."

By now, Colfelt's standing with Dean had done a complete reversal, according to Charles Rich. "He changed from a friend to a man he had no use for."

The Colfelts, who claimed that they never spoke disrespectfully or disparagingly of Mr. Dean, were now overheard to vilify him. "Colfelt was very bitter towards Dean and called him some very terrible names which I am ashamed to repeat," Helen Ellison said. The prim Mrs. Ellison wrote the words on a piece of paper for the federal agents: "Pay no attention to that old crab. He is a damn son of a bitch."

Frank Romano felt no such compunction about reporting Colfelt's words. "Colfelt said to me that Dean was a son of a bitch, and a dirty bastard, and was no good," Romano said. "Mrs. Colfelt said that Dean was no good and he beats his wife and that she would like to kick his bottom."

In addition, Colfelt complained that he heard hollering at night coming from the Dean bungalow. "Once I called him up and he said, perhaps it was a screech-owl." Given the location, that was a distinct possibility; the shriek of a screech owl would certainly unnerve the average city dweller who had never heard one before.

Colfelt also told investigators, "Frank Humiston, who used to work for me and is in the service, said Dean used to drink." There is no confirmation that Humiston ever made such a remark, or if he did, that he intended it to mean that Dean drank to excess. At any rate, it was an allegation that no one else ever made.

Affairs between Dean and the Colfelts continued to deteriorate. At one point, Margaret telephoned Dean and asked him to come up to their house. According to Margaret Robinson, to whom Dean related the incident, "He didn't want to go and tried to excuse himself but she insisted and so he went. She met him at the door, didn't invite him in, but began a tirade of abuse, mostly about people who were trying to injure them, that is, the Colfelts."

"Mrs. Colfelt, do you mean me?" Dean asked.

"Yes, I do," Margaret Colfelt said, "you have been telling things about us that aren't true."

"I don't remember ever having told anyone anything about you."

"Yes, you did. You said over the telephone that Mr. Colfelt's mother never came to see us. We told her about it and she is very angry that you should say such a thing."

Dean searched his memory. "I do remember how that someone asked me whether Mr. Colfelt's mother had visited you and I said no, that you had said that her children all went to see her but that she didn't go to visit them. You told me that yourself, so I supposed there was no harm in saying it." It then occurred to Dean that there was only one way Margaret would have known what he'd said in that private conversation. "But may I ask, Mrs. Colfelt, if you have been listening at the telephone?"

"Yes, I have," she answered.

It was, to Dean, simply more evidence that the Colfelts were "the most undisciplined, irresponsible people he had ever known," as he told Mrs. Robinson.

By the end of May, the Colfelts had not found a new place to rent, and Dean decided he'd had enough. "I asked him to go," he told his friend Mary Lee Ware.

Ware replied, "I thought you found them very pleasant neighbors, Mr. Dean. What is the trouble?"

"Well, I didn't care to have them," he said simply.

Lawrence Colfelt, on the other hand, said the move was his idea, as he testified at the grand jury.

PICKARD: How was it you happened to leave eventually?

COLFELT: I just realized. He said there was no hurry to get off, the only thing was I was interfering with his turkeys.

PICKARD: Did he tell you he wanted the place, that he wanted you to vacate, he wanted the place?

COLFELT: No, he didn't say that in so many words.

PICKARD: How did you come to the understanding you were going to move, and how did he know you had reached that conclusion?

COLFELT: Well, I told him, I said I realized I was in the way there.

Colfelt told a different story to Robert Hamill, who helped him move, saying that he left Dean's because Dean wanted more rent than he was willing to pay. Colfelt's realtor, Mrs. D.M. White, offered yet another explanation, that the Colfelts left because Mrs. Dean's "ravings" affected Margaret's nerves. "Mrs. Dean, widow of William K. Dean, is almost crazy," White said. "She has been so for many years and should have proper medical care." In contrast, White called Lawrence Colfelt a fine man with whom she'd had successful business dealings and through whom she expected to do business with his wealthy connections in New York. As the federal agent who interviewed White noted, "Informant is a clever business woman who guards her interests first and last."

35

THE BOX

FINALLY, IN THE FIRST WEEK JUNE 1918, THE COLFELTS LEFT THE Dean farm and moved to Greenville, some fifteen miles away. The new home, owned by a family named Sterling, sat on a high hill and had an extensive view of the surrounding mountains, just as the two houses that Colfelt had rented in Jaffrey did.

The Sterling property consisted of two summer houses, one closer to the peak. The Colfelts moved into the lower of the two houses, though they would have preferred the one at the top of the hill, according to Bert Ford.

Colfelt hired liveryman Robert Hamill to move his belongings, beginning with trunks and boxes, one of which gave him pause. "There was a box that had attracted my attention, to speak plainly," Hamill said.

The box was roughly two and a half feet square by five feet tall, constructed of plain spruce boards. It had already been nailed shut when Hamill arrived, so he did not know what it contained. The box weighed, Hamill estimated, between 400 and 500 pounds. "It was so heavy that we had to load it on to our automobile truck by sliding it on metal piping."

Colfelt kept a close eye on the men as they loaded the box on to the truck, insisting that it be kept upright at all times. "Mr. Colfelt wanted it placed just so," according to Ralph Davis, who helped Hamill with the move. "He was very particular about it."

Colfelt explained that the box contained a Victrola, a very expensive one. "It may have been," Hamill said. "But I never saw a graphophone yet that weighed as much as a piano, or that I couldn't handle with ease myself." Hamill had moved Victrolas before, and he had an idea of how much they weighed. "Now I claim I can lift 200 pounds, and I could not lift that box and the young man who helped me couldn't lift it either."

When the truck was fully loaded, Colfelt reiterated that the box not be tipped at all in transit. Driving his own car, he followed the truck from Jaffrey to Greenville, keeping a close eye on the box the entire way. When they arrived at the new house, the men unloaded the box on to the porch, again using the metal pipes. "It was heavy enough so we didn't lift it, we shoved it around on the piazza and put some scratches there," Hamill said.

Colfelt was concerned about leaving the box on the porch and asked Hamill if he thought it would be safe there. Hamill assured him it would be, but told investigators, "If he hadn't been so very particular, I never would have been so suspicious."

Later, when asked about the box, both Lawrence and Margaret Colfelt claimed that it contained a phonograph. "It's a Victrola, a two hundred dollar machine," Lawrence said. "I don't think they make them anymore."

"It was in a great big box," his wife said, adding that, "we always kept it in the box we bought it in."

But Ralph Davis was doubtful. "That box was so heavy that when I went home that night, I asked several persons how much they thought a Victrola ought to weigh, and when I told them the one owned by Colfelt must have weighed about 500 pounds, everybody thought there must have been something else in it."

Davis shared his doubts with Hamill, who said, "We talked the matter over the next morning about this box and we both decided it must be something different from a Victrola on account of its weight."

In fact, the Colfelts did have a Victrola, according to Frank Humiston, who remembered seeing it in their house in Jaffrey. "It was a small Victrola worth $50," he said. "I picked it up once and played it and it would weigh about 25 pounds."

Before the Colfelts left Dean's summer house, workers who had occasion to be in the cellar reported seeing large wooden boxes there. "I saw quite a large box there," Martin Garfield said, though he didn't think too much about it at the time. When asked how it would compare in size to a Victrola, Garfield said, "Well, I don't hardly know. It seems to me it was larger."

After having been in the cellar and seen the large box, Garfield thought the Colfelts seemed more guarded around him. "After that Mrs. Colfelt used to come into the cellar while I was working there and talked with me for an hour and a half at a time," he said. "That made me think that there was something funny going on. It looked as though she wanted to know where I was and what I was doing."

Lester Ellsworth, who had delivered wood to Colfelt, also remembered seeing large wooden boxes in the cellar, "one about six feet long and about two feet wide made out of ordinary unpainted wood. The other was about two and half feet square and about three and a half feet in height." Ellsworth had been allowed unfettered access to the cellar until the day he decried how the Germans had treated women and children in Belgium. After that, Ellsworth said, "He never let me in the cellar again."

The most intriguing report, however, came from Charlie Bean. In March of 1918, Colfelt asked Bean to come dock a puppy's tail. When Bean arrived, the Colfelts were not at home, though Frank Humiston was. Bean entered the house and saw a wooden box in the living room. "And being nosy, I opened the cover of the box and was surprised to see apparatus in that box that looked very like a flashlight or wireless with a keyboard."

Bean described the device as being "like a telegraph operator's apparatus" with "two cylinders here, and this little knob up here to press down, and then there were wires connected, as if there was a battery in here somewhere." Bean admitted that he had never seen anything like it before. He closed the cover and left quickly, afraid the Colfelts might return and find him snooping around.

Rumors about Lawrence Colfelt being a German spy—which were widespread in Jaffrey by now—made Robert Hamill and Ralph Davis even more suspicious of the heavy box they had moved for him. "We were so suspicious, that Mr. Hamill reported the matter to the Board of Selectmen," Davis said. Unfortunately, the selectmen never had a chance to check into the box. The day after Hamill moved it to Greenfield, according to Bert Ford, Colfelt had it shipped from the Greenville station. The destination, Ford said, was "some point in New York."

36

THE LETTER

ALTHOUGH FEDERAL AGENTS HAD FAILED TO FIND ANY CONCRETE EVI-
dence of German espionage in the Monadnock region, they continued to
be concerned about the possibility. The Bureau of Investigation appealed
to citizens in a newspaper notice that appeared across the region on June
12, 1918: "Your patriotic duty: To report disloyal acts, seditious utterances
and any information relative to attempts to hinder the United States in
the prosecution of the war . . ."

The appeal undoubtedly increased the vigilance of Jaffrey's residents,
already on alert for spies and signal lights. William Dean, given his patriotic nature, would have taken it quite seriously. Soon after the publication
of the notice, Dean received a letter that troubled him greatly. The letter
was left in his R.F.D. mailbox, unsigned and unstamped. At about that
time, he received a visit from his friend Mary Lee Ware. They were talking
about the Colfelts and the signal lights reported around the mountain
when Dean seemed troubled and said, "I have had a threatening letter."

Surprised, Ware asked, "Have you got any enemies, Mr. Dean?"

"I didn't know I had."

"Where did it come from?"

"I don't know," he said, explaining that the letter had no postmark
and had simply been left in his mailbox.

Ware's recollection of the letter's contents was hazy, but she said, "the
only thing I can recollect about it is that it made some allusion about
dropping him down a well."[9]

Dean would not say any more about the letter, telling Ware, "I don't want to get you into trouble."

She knew, however, that the letter worried him. "He had a look in his eyes as though he realized he was up against something new, something he did not know how to gauge." She tried to ease his concerns, telling him the letter was probably just tomfoolishness.

"What would you do about it?" he asked.

"I would pay no attention and see what further comes of it," she said. But when Dean brought the matter up again she said, "I tell you what I would do. I would take it to Jaffrey and show it to the police, or somebody there, and see what they think of it."

Dean appears to have taken Miss Ware's advice. On a Tuesday evening not long after, while in town running errands, Dean approached officer Walter A. Lindsay of the Jaffrey police force. Lindsay was the town's truant officer and wore a large police badge, of which he was perhaps inordinately proud and which amused some townspeople.

Dean noticed the badge and asked Lindsay if he was still on the force. Lindsay said he was and Dean told him, "I have lived on the farm for 28 years and I have never been molested in any way, shape or manner, but if I wanted police protection, where would I telephone to?'

"Either the station, Duncan's, or Fred Stratton's livery stable," Lindsay replied.

Dean did not say why he was asking and Lindsay didn't pry because, as he said, "I thought he was a man who didn't discuss his affairs." Nevertheless, Lindsay noted, "He looked solemn as though he had some dread."

Later, some suggested that Dean was just joking about needing protection. Attorney General Young asked acting police chief Perley Enos if much attention was paid to Dean's request at the time. "There wasn't," Enos said, "because some kind of thought Mr. Dean was quite a hand to joke, and some took it as a joke."

Martin Garfield was more inclined to take the story seriously. He spoke to Sheriff Walter Emerson, detective Harry Scott and game warden George Wellington, all of whom said there was nothing to the story of Dean asking for protection. Garfield told Lindsay, "Wellington said it isn't so."

"Tell Wellington he is a damn liar," Lindsay replied.

37

THE NAVAL OFFICER

ON JUNE 25, WILLIAM DEAN WROTE ON HIS CALENDAR A SINGLE WORD: "Information." He may have been referring to the threatening letter left in his mailbox, or he may have been thinking about a visit he had received.

Earlier that year, in the course of his investigation, Agent Nash had visited the Portsmouth Naval Shipyard in Portsmouth, New Hampshire. The navy yard, tasked with overhauling and repairing ships, had recently begun building submarines as well, its workforce swelling to nearly 5,000 people during the war.

The navy yard was also the home to the New Hampshire division of the Office of Naval Intelligence. The ONI was formed after the Civil War with the goal of modernizing America's navy and bringing it up to the standards of European nations. In 1916, as conflict was brewing in Europe, the U.S. Congress authorized a major increase in the ONI's personnel and budget, broadening its mandate to include domestic security operations. The goal was to ensure that the country's ports, harbors, and marine facilities were safe from enemy infiltration and sabotage.

Among the personnel the expanded ONI brought on board was Bernard A. Bradley. Before the war, Bradley had been a U.S. Marshall assigned to round up "slackers and alien enemies." Now he was assigned to head up the ONI's office in Portsmouth. Bradley was not in the office on the day Agent Nash visited, but Nash nevertheless "went through their files and arranged that a list of reports dealing with subjects in hand be mailed at once to the Boston office," he reported. Among those subjects was Lawrence Colfelt.

As Bradley reported later, "Approximately six weeks prior to the date of the Dean murder, I received instructions in writing from the naval Intelligence Office in Boston to proceed to East Jaffrey as early as may be practicable, to investigate one Colfelt of that town, who was reported to the Boston office as being a German suspect and as one who had information regarding the movements of our warships."

Bradley was accompanied in his investigation by fellow Naval Intelligence Officer Albert O. Shaw. The agents began in Greenville, New Hampshire, where Colfelt was living by then. They arrived at Colfelt's house unannounced, and he was not at home. The Colfelts had gone to Boston for the day, according to Frank Romano, whom the agents came upon in the barn.

It was a fortuitous meeting. Romano showed the agents around the barn and the stable. He told them that Colfelt rode his horse every day and many evenings, and that he often had guests who arrived in automobiles and would stay until after dark.

Bradley and Shaw examined the grounds of the house, looking for indications of a wireless transmitter, but found nothing. They proceeded to Jaffrey, where they spoke to the manager of the Shattuck Inn, garage owner Robert Hamill, and a few town officials. Finally, they visited Charles Rich at his home.

Rich confirmed that there had been much talk in town about signal lights on Monadnock, though he personally had not seen them. He had noticed strangers in town and "had heard talk of how they had been seen with Coldfelt [sic] outside the town sitting by [the] roadside talking," according to Agent Shaw. Rich himself had seen Colfelt two miles from town on the road to Peterborough, speaking with a man who turned his back as Rich passed so that his face could not be seen.

Rich told the agents about Colfelt's finances, explaining that he appeared to live on a monthly check from a Philadelphia trust fund. As to Colfelt's standing in town, Rich told the agents that people in general did not like him, but that he did.

Several times during the conversation, Rich suggested that the agents speak with Colfelt's former landlord, William Dean, whom Rich described as "a nice old man, rather peculiar, funny notions and a man that some people would not get on with." The comment is only noteworthy because there is little evidence of anyone other than Colfelt that William Dean could not get on with.

In his daily report, Shaw noted that, "Of the people interviewed this day, all seemed to be straight forward and not evasive, but both Mr. Bradley and myself were not [sic] struck with the attitude of the manner of talk by Mr. Rich, nothing direct but so different from others we had interviewed that it was noticeable and each of us, at different times referred to it."

The agents left Rich's house and proceeded to Dean's farm, where Dean invited them on to the stoop of his house to talk. According to Bradley, "I found Dr. Dean to be an intelligent and extremely patriotic American. It was a pleasure to interview him, he was so sane and sober in his opinions."

Bradley approached the subject of Lawrence Colfelt circumspectly. He began by explaining that he was with naval intelligence and had been sent to look into the reports of signal lights. Dean seemed surprised and told the agents they were the first government officials of any kind to interview him. (Earlier that year, Agents Nash and Marshall had scoped out Dean's farm and noted that it was an excellent location from which signals could sent and received, but they apparently had not felt it necessary to speak with Dean.)

Bradley asked if Dean had seen any signal lights and Dean replied that he had heard about the lights, but he hadn't seen them himself, nor had he spoken to anyone who had. The agents then got to the real purpose for their visit and asked him about Lawrence Colfelt. According to Bradley, Dean "stated emphatically that at no time did he ever see actions on the part of any individual in East Jaffrey that could be considered pro-German."

Dean did say he consider the Colfelts to be rather "stuck up" and noted that "they act funny at times." Asked what he meant by that, Dean replied, "Oh, they seem to want to keep in the house and then when they come out go down out of sight beyond their house and not come by my house for days at a time." Dean also admitted that he'd had trouble with Colfelt over money matters, an area that did not interest Bradley.

The agents asked Dean if he had seen automobiles calling at the Colfelts' residence. He told them that at times he had seen a large car with two or three men pass by his house on the way to Colfelt's, but he had paid little attention as he did not want to appear nosey. However, he did recall that Colfelt had had one fairly regular visitor, a man Dean did not recognize who came every other week or so in a one-horse buggy. He had not gotten close enough to be able to describe the man, "but should say that he had dark whiskers on chin." Asked to describe the horse and buggy, Dean described the horse as dark brown and full of life, the carriage a top buggy with its top usually down, and wheels painted a light color.

Had Colfelt had received any shipments in large boxes? Dean said the only large boxes he recalled were several long boxes, perhaps 10 or 12 feet long, with iron pipe that Colfelt planned to use as water pipe. Dean thought Colfelt had not actually used the pipe and he didn't know what became of it.

"Dean then arose and asked us to step in front of the house and pointed over the Temple Hills and showed us the house that he said Coldfelt [sic] occupied," Shaw reported.[10]

Dean told the agents that Colfelt had stopped by some time after moving to Greenville and pointed out that one could see the new house from Dean's farm. Colfelt had said, "Why don't you try and see if you can see my house over in Temple, some night when you go out to milk, there might be a light then, and tell me when you see me." That seems like odd request, given all the rumors about signal lights. At any rate, Dean had looked but never saw any light from Colfelt's new home.

The agents went into the house and met Mrs. Dean but did not interview her because, according to her husband, "she is a sick woman and will do it when she is feeling better." It seems likely that he did not want to give his wife one more thing to worry about.

As the agents prepared to leave, Bradley said, "Don't you think that so many boxes and that long pipe coming to Coldfelt [sic], and those men coming at all hours of the night, looks funny?"

Dean thought for a moment and said, "I don't know but what it does." He told the agents he would talk it over with his wife to see what she thought. In the meantime, he would be on the lookout for anything suspicious. "I have plenty of time to watch and I shall be only too happy to be of whatever service I can to my country," he said.

Dean asked whom he should call if he saw anything. "I told Dr. Dean that he if discovered anything he ought to notify Superintendent George E. Kelleher of the New England bureau of the Department of Justice in Boston," Bradley said. He did not tell Dean to get in touch with him personally, having decided based on what they'd learned about Colfelt that this was not a matter for naval intelligence.

As the agents left, Dean asked who sent them to him. They told him it was Charles Rich and asked if he knew Rich. "Yes," Dean replied, "we used to be warm friends but I don't go in town much now."

Later, Charles Rich would ask Dean about the agents' visit. "I asked Mr. Dean what he had told them and what they asked," Rich said, "but he didn't tell me anything."

38

THE CONFIDANT

SHORTLY AFTER THE VISIT FROM THE NAVAL INTELLIGENCE OFFICERS, William Dean visited friends in Jaffrey Center, Margaret C. Robinson and her husband, Harvard botanist Benjamin L. Robinson. The Robinson first came to Jaffrey from Cambridge, Massachusetts, in the summer of 1895. They fell in love with the area and proceeded to build the first of three summer homes, each of which boasted a splendid view of Mount Monadnock. Outside of Jaffrey, Mrs. Robinson was well known as a patroness of humanitarian efforts and passionate activist for conservative causes. In Jaffrey, she became active in efforts to preserve and beautify Jaffrey Center, serving as president and guiding light of the Village Improvement Society for 20 years.

It was through the Village Improvement Society and its annual social events that the Robinsons came to know the Deans. Over the years the two couples became great friends. The Robinsons exchanged visits with the Deans, lent them books they had enjoyed, and sent them records to play on their phonograph.

That summer of 1918, the Robinsons arrived in Jaffrey at the very end of June, later than usual, and Dean came to visit them. "I've had the strangest experience of my life," he told them. "I don't know what to make of it." He asked if he could tell them about it, but then hesitated.

"I could see that he was uncomfortable, feeling that he was gossiping or talebearing," Mrs. Robinson said. But she urged him to go on, and he did.

Dean explained that he'd had a visit from federal agents asking him about Lawrence Colfelt, about whom he'd previously had no suspicions, although he had been distressed by Colfelt's contemptuous remarks about his patriotism.

Dean recalled Colfelt saying, "It's all very well for you to talk patriotism. You know you are safe as you are too old to fight, and you are poor so you won't have to pay war taxes. American people don't care anything about this war." He had argued that one didn't hear patriotic talk in New York and Philadelphia. "Everybody is making all the money he can out of it, and that's all they care about it."

The Robinsons were shocked by this conversation and asked Dean if he thought Colfelt was a spy. Dean declined to answer at first, then smiled and said, "He doesn't seem to me to have brains enough."

39

THE NEW TOWN

GREENVILLE, NEW HAMPSHIRE, THE TOWN WHERE THE COLFELTS HAD moved, had roughly the same population as Jaffrey, about 1,300 people. Like East Jaffrey, a water-powered mill was at the heart of the town, along with a branch of the B&M Railroad. And just like in Jaffrey, the behavior of Lawrence and Margaret Colfelt aroused suspicion.

In the same way as they had in Jaffrey, the Colfelts came to the telephone exchange office to do much of their telephoning despite having a phone in their new home. The Greenville operator alleged that the Colfelts sent and received telegrams from New York, "partly in English and partly in code or numbers," according to detective Harry Scott. The same operator told federal agent Feri Weiss that the messages "were absolutely code words as they had no sensible connection when given to her."

People who worked for the Colfelts in Greenville also found them suspect. Henry Ash, caretaker of the rented house, noted that they were often out late at night on horseback or driving in their auto. On one occasion they stayed away all night, leaving the house unlocked, and the two young women they had hired as servants complained that "as they were alone in the house, they weren't going to stay if such conditions continued," according to Ash.

"Another morning they told me that an officer in American uniform visited the Colfelts the night before and remained closeted with Mr. Colfelt behind closed doors for a long time," Ash said. "The girls told me that while the American soldier was talking with her husband, Mrs.

Colfelt walked up and down the hallway in front of the room, the door of which was closed."[11]

"The thing that struck me most of all was that the Colfelts never seemed to be settled in their home," Ash said. "They did not live like other people who occupy such places. They kept strange hours and their household effects looked as if they were ready to move on short notice."

Ash's most startling interaction with the Colfelts occurred one day when he was working in the rental house at the top of the hill. "I received a telephone call from Mrs. Colfelt, who asked me to hurry right down to the other house," he said. "When I reached there I was astonished to find Mrs. Colfelt with a revolver in her hand in the living room. I didn't know what to make of it. She seemed excited. I didn't know but that she might have heard something, and might try to take it out on me. I thought perhaps she might have heard the talk from the servants."

"It was such an odd situation that I was going to be on the safe side, if she tried to pull anything. I made sure that the door was open and looked to see what I could defend myself with, and before she could say anything to me, there was a knock at the door. She put the revolver away, and the owner of the property and his wife came in. That ended the affair. She never said anything to me afterward, and I never learned why she had a revolver in her hand that day."

Later, at the grand jury, Margaret Colfelt would deny that she had ever handled a revolver. "I'd be terrified to use it," she told County Solicitor Pickard, although she admitted that they did own a revolver.

Frank Romano had moved to Greenville with the Colfelts and continued to care for their horses, but the relationship became increasingly strained. "When I worked for him the first time, he acted all right," Romano said, "but the last time he was very irritated and nervous." Before, Romano had found Colfelt to be kind and generous, but by the time he came to work on the Dean farm, Colfelt had become "a changed man, very excited and cool, always finding fault."

Like the other employees, Romano was bothered by the Colfelts' frequent, unexplained absences. "The Colfelts used to go away for a week at a time and I was the only one working on the place and I didn't have anything to eat as there was no one to do the cooking," he said. "They would say they were going away for a few days and stay away a week."

Romano had worked for the Colfelts longer than others, and perhaps had greater insight into the couple's relationship, telling federal agents that the Colfelts did not seem to get on well except for short intervals. "Mrs. Colfelt is the one who is making him do all the things," he told Agent Nash. "She was the one who was causing the trouble." Several times, Romano had heard Margaret threaten Lawrence, who would then "be nice to her for a while." He believed that Margaret Colfelt held a club over her husband and "had something on him."

Within two months after the move to Greenville, Romano decided he'd had enough of Colfelt's abuse and Margaret's temper. He left them on July 28, 1918, a little more than two weeks before Mr. Dean's murder. According to caretaker Henry Ash, "Romano said he guessed he'd get out before things got too hot."

40

THE ARGUMENT

AFTER LAWRENCE AND MARGARET COLFELT MOVED TO GREENVILLE, their relationship with William Dean became marked by petty bickering. They had, in their haste to move, inadvertently taken a couple of items that belonged to Dean: a small green rug for the floor of his buggy and a tie chain with snaps on each end used to secure an animal's stall. Meanwhile, the Colfelts claimed that Dean had a saw that belonged to them.

There were financial squabbles as well. Dean owed Colfelt for milk that they had provided when Dean's cow ran dry, and Colfelt owed Dean for hay that he needed for his animals. Letters and telegrams were exchanged, culminating in a terse telegram from Dean to the Colfelts on August 8: "Please send back my things. Send a check for hay."

Colfelt was undoubtedly feeling other pressures as well. The First Draft had only included men up to age 30, but the War Department had asked Congress to expand the draft to include all men between the ages of 18 and 45. Colfelt was 39, and nervous about the possibility that he might be called up, according to brakemen Hugh Churchill. "He seemed to be anxious about the draft bill, just to find out whether they were going to pass that or not, the 45 age limit, and I told him there was no question but it was to be passed," Churchill said.

Faced with the possibility of being called up, Colfelt decided his only alternative was to find work in some defense-related industry. He applied to the Columbia Mills dyeworks in Greenville, which was doing work for the government. According to the mill's foreman, "He said he had to get work somewhere, under the 'work or fight' law." But the foreman called game warden George Wellington to check up on Colfelt and, "On account of the village talk, we decided not to employ him," he said.

No one, it seemed, was interested in hiring Lawrence Colfelt. Finally, however, he found work with the help of Rev. Myron L. Cutler of the Universalist church in Jaffrey. Cutler, himself too old to serve in the armed forces, traveled every week to the navy yard in Portsmouth, New Hampshire, where he worked at the Atlantic Shipbuilding Company, returning on weekends to serve his church. Cutler was a close friend of Charles Rich, who attended his church, and recommended Colfelt to the shipbuilding company. Colfelt applied on Thursday, August 8, only a few days before William Dean's death.

"I went up there, as an ordinary applicant would," Colfelt said, "and they asked me what I could do and I said I didn't know what I could do, but I knew there was something I could do."

Colfelt was hired on the spot, to begin work the next week.

To the people of Jaffrey, the idea of Colfelt going to work was surprising. "It looks very funny that Colfelt having unlimited wealth should look for a job as a laborer," Margaret Robinson said.

Colfelt, when asked why he had taken the job, attributed the decision to good citizenship. "Well, everybody was doing something and that seemed to be the only thing I could do." His wife, Margaret, backed him up. "He wanted to do something worthwhile, he didn't want to have just a little government job sitting around doing nothing," she said.

On the other hand, Colfelt's physician, Dr. Carlisle, took a more cynical view, saying "Colfelt's wife had him go into this work for the purpose of evading the Selective Draft Act."

On the evening of the day Colfelt was hired, the Colfelts went to the Shattuck Inn to make reservations for the next Wednesday night, for an indefinite period of time. Colfelt spoke to another regular guest—a traveling salesman named Mayo—who told the Inn's manager, "Soak them good, they say they got to break up housekeeping. Colfelt just said they could not get help and had to break up house, and he is going in the service."

Apparently, Margaret was expecting a house full of guests within the next week—friends from New York and friends of her daughter's—and was worried about accommodating them. "Natalye expected all these guests, and I was almost frantic," she said, undoubtedly because they were having such a hard time keeping servants. "Well, I could hardly keep any help, from the stories that were going around that town."

Lawrence also blamed their domestic problems on the gossip in town. "We had so much trouble with help," Colfelt said. "The help got to taking up this German spy business." Apparently, it had not occurred to him that the help left simply because they were impossible to work for.

At any rate, the Colfelts claimed they made the arrangements with the Shattuck Inn simply as a contingency, in case they should have a need. However, the inn's manager considered it to be a firm reservation. "Colfelt said he would let us know Sunday night whether they were coming Wednesday night or Tuesday night, but he did not let us know," the manager reported. "I really expected they were coming and held a couple of rooms ready for them for Tuesday night."

On Saturday, August 10, Lawrence Colfelt stopped at the Monadnock Savings Bank to withdraw some cash in preparation for starting work in Portsmouth on Monday. He told Rich he had received a letter from Dean which disturbed him immensely, probably referring to the dunning telegram Dean had sent about the hay.

From the bank, Colfelt went to Goodnow's store and purchased a pair of khaki pants (cost, $2.48), two khaki shirts ($.98 each), and a pair of innersoles ($.10)—his new job required work clothes, which he had never had occasion to own before.

On Sunday, Colfelt drove his Marmon to Pollard's Garage in Nashua, New Hampshire, to have it serviced. Two of the garage's mechanics rode with him to the Rockingham Hotel in Portsmouth, then drove the car back to Nashua. "You see," Colfelt said, "I had no use for the car up there," meaning at the shipyard.

Colfelt arrived at the Rockingham Hotel in Portsmouth at 6 p.m. He registered and ate dinner at the hotel, ready to begin work at the Atlantic

Shipbuilding Corporation the next morning, Monday, August 12, one year to the day that he had moved to the Dean farm.

That Sunday evening, Mr. Dean visited his friends the Robinsons at their Jaffrey home. "He came in bringing a bottle of cream," Mrs. Robinson said. "He always brought something to his friends if he could, and he began talking about the future life."

Dean told the Robinsons he had been reading some books about the afterlife and was very much interested in the subject. "I can hardly wait, I am so anxious to see what is going to be on the other side," he told them. At some point in the conversation, Dean began to speak of the signal lights and related matters, then stopped himself. "But I must not burden you with my troubles," he said.

Mrs. Robinson pressed him, but he would not discuss the subject further. She told the grand jury, "You see, he didn't want his friends to be mixed up in such things, so he didn't want them to know anything of it. Our conversation was rather personal and hardly worth telling."

It was also her last conversation with Willian Dean.

On the morning of Monday, August 12, as Lawrence Colfelt began work at the shipyard in Portsmouth, Dr. Frederick C. Sweeney left his home in Jaffrey, headed for Fort Oglethorpe in Georgia. Sweeney had enlisted in the Army and would serve in France after his training.

That afternoon, the first of Margaret Colfelt's houseguests arrived, a college friend of her daughter Natalye's. Margaret also received a telegram from a friend named Ethel Potter, telling her in the clipped telegraphic style of the day that they would arrive the next day: "Will take five nine Tuesday so glad you want us."

William Dean also wrote to Margaret that day. He thanked her for returning his missing items and proceeded to detail what they owed him for hay, what he owed them for milk, and a few smaller items. He ended with a personal note about his wife, Mary, whom he often addressed by the affectionate nickname Polly. "Polly is pretty comfortable just now. I can't say she is any better. I am well enough except that it is rather cool to walk and now both arms are poor. I hope you and Natalye are having a delightful summer."

As far as we know, it was the last letter he ever wrote.

William K. Dean in 1908, about 10 years before his death. Dean appreciated music, literature, a good joke, and the company of women as well as men.

Although William Dean considered himself a farmer, he sometimes treated his animals—especially the strays and aged stock he took in and cared for—as pets. Apart from the cutting of hay, the only profitable aspect of his farm was his white turkeys, for which he was locally known.

Mary Dean was remembered by her friends and neighbors as a kind woman, a gracious host, and a gentle soul who could never have murdered her husband.

The summer house at the Dean farm provided stunning views of the surrounding countryside, but little protection from winter's harsh weather.

When the Deans' summer house became too expensive to maintain, they renovated this small bungalow and moved into it. To the right of the porch is the uncovered well that Martin Garfield suggested William Dean might have tripped and fallen into, a suggestion that would have unfortunate consequences for Mary Dean.

NO CLUE TO MOTIVE FOR MURDER AT EAST JAFFREY

Milking Pail Dean Carried With Him on Night of Crime Missing—Threatening Letter Said to Have Been Sent to Victim Some Time Before

SCENE OF MURDER OF WEALTHY FARMER, WILLIAM K. DEAN, AT EAST JAFFREY, N. H.

At the left is the barn where Dean is thought to have been struck down as he went to milk his cow near midnight Tuesday, arrow indicating where bloodstains were found on the portico. At the right is the cistern in which his body was found, indicated by cross. Peering into the cistern are, left to right, Cagetan Deschenes, employee of Dean many years; Attorney-General Oscar L. Young and County Solicitor Roy M. Pickard.

Early newspaper reports noted that there appeared to be no motive for the murder of William Dean, a man well-liked and respected by everyone. His body had been dragged from the porch of his barn to a cistern by his large summer house. *Boston American, August 16, 1918.*

The evidence from the Dean murder investigation included, among other items, the blanket that was wrapped around his head, the burlap sack placed over him, bloody doorknobs, his shoes and socks, and the ropes with which he was strangled and bound.

The Deans' kitchen calendar held notes about the weather, temperature, and the ominous message "Billee die" on the date of Dean's murder.

Banker, businessman, and political boss Charles Rich was among William Dean's closest friends. But mysterious cuts and bruises on his face caused locals to suspect Rich knew more than he would say about Dean's death.

William de Kerlor was an author, lecturer, newspaper reporter, psychic investigator, and, above all else, a self-promoter. His involvement in the Dean murder case was welcomed by some and decried by others.

A *Boston Post* article lauded William de Kerlor's work on the Dean murder case, noting that his "deductions are so like those of Sherlock Holmes in their uncanny shrewdness."

Two weeks after William Dean's funeral, his body was exhumed at the request of William de Kerlor, shown here center, holding the rolled paper he would use to trace the cuts on Dean's head. Charles Rich (far right) was also present, little knowing the use to which de Kerlor would put that paper. (Photo courtesy of the Historical Society of Cheshire County.)

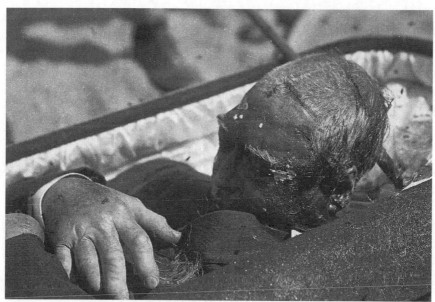

Upon exhumation, William Dean's body had already begun to decompose, but the cuts and bruises on his head were still evident, cuts that William de Kerlor was convinced would match those of Charles Rich. (From the collections of the Historical Society of Cheshire County, Keene, NH.)

The only known photograph of the elusive Lawrence and Margaret Colfelt, pictured in front of William Dean's summer house with their prize Marmon automobile.

PROMINENT FIGURES IN THE STORY OF DR. DEAN MYSTERY

Cheshire county solicitor Roy Pickard (left) and Attorney General Oscar Young (right) suspected Mary Dean of murdering her husband, to the chagrin of Mrs. Dean's friends, including Boston socialite Margaret Robinson (center). *Boston American, October 27, 1919.*

Wealthy neighbor Arria Morison spoke to William Dean on the day before his death. Dean told her he had information for the government, information that was too dangerous for a woman to know.

Mary Lee Ware maintained homes in Boston and New Hampshire, where she became a close friend of William Dean and a witness in the murder investigation.

Father Herbert Hennon provided support to Jaffrey's selectmen, federal agents, and others investigating the Dean murder, earning him the ire of some who later tried to implicate him in the murder.

Who Murdered
DR. DEAN?

Yankee Patriot Victim of German Spy Plot

Von Bernstorff Was There--- What Was HE Doing?

Expose of International Murder Mystery

> DR. WILLIAM K. DEAN, Scholar and Gentleman Farmer, of East Jaffrey, New Hampshire, discovered evidence proving that light signals were being flashed from New Hampshire mountains to German submarines at sea, giving information on United States transport sailings. He immediately reported the fact, and, on the following day, was found at the bottom of a well on his estate—foully murdered. Investigations started, but the case was suddenly and unaccountably hushed up.

After months of investigation the Boston American publishes FACTS that will startle all New England

THE EXCLUSIVE EXPOSE STARTS IN TOMORROW'S

BOSTON AMERICAN

A year after William Dean's murder, *Boston American* reporter Bert Ford began a series of sensational articles that reignited the controversy over the case.

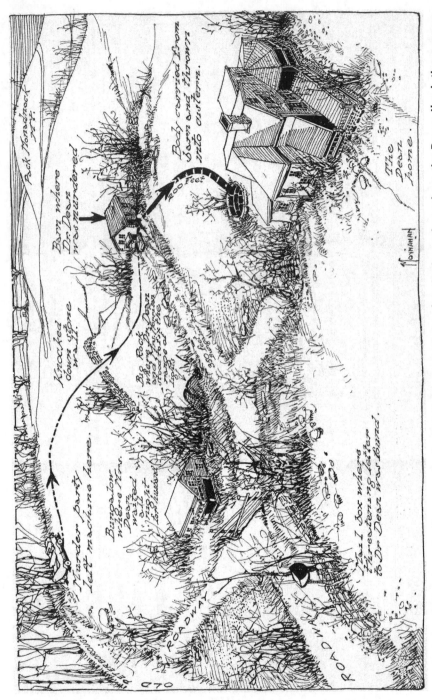

Bert Ford's articles about the Dean murder included this sketch showing the bungalow where the Deans lived, the summer house Dean rented to Lawrence Colfelt, and the barn where the murder took place.

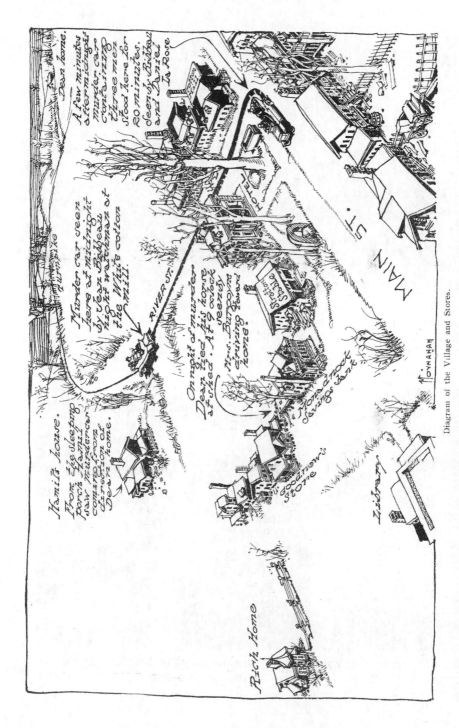

Diagram of the Village and Stores.

Another Ford article depicted the downtown of East Jaffrey, where witnesses saw a large car coming and going in the direction of William Dean's farm on the night of the murder. Note that North Street is inaccurately labeled "River St."

On the night of his murder, William Dean stopped at the post office and Duncan's drugstore, which shared this building. The car seen coming from the direction of Dean's farm later that night parked by the watering trough across the street.

Dean also stopped at Romolo Vanni's market, where he bought some currant buns that later helped to establish the time of his death.

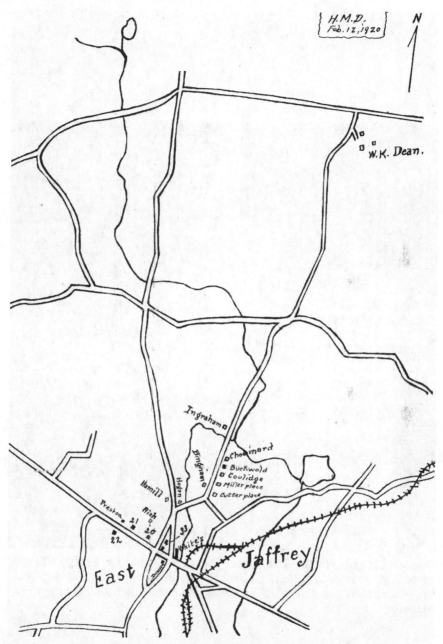

Detail of a map showing the homes of witnesses who saw William Dean drive home on the evening of his murder. Dean's cousin Henry Dean prepared the map for a meeting with Governor Bartlett, a meeting that quickly collapsed into vituperation and hardened opinions.

Five months after William Dean's murder, medical expert Dr. George Magrath performed a complete autopsy on Dean's body in the frigid vault of the East Jaffrey cemetery and confirmed that Dean had been suffocated, his neck broken.

NEW PROBE OF DR. DEAN TRAGEDY IS DEMANDED

Will Gov. Brown Help "Lift the Lid?"

Jaffrey, N. H., Officials Win Vindication at Town Election;
Many Disclosures at Capacity Hearing in
Rich's Slander Suit

In March of 1921, the *Boston American* newspaper accused Jaffrey's businessmen—the so-called Soft Pedal Squad—of keeping a lid on the Dean case and asked if new Governor Albert O. Brown would take more of an interest than had his predecessor, John. H. Bartlett.

Count Johann von Bernstorff, German ambassador to the United States, visited the Monadnock region of New Hampshire around the time of William Dean's murder. Von Bernstorff was later found to have funded a German spy ring involved in sabotage operations against American military and industrial sites.

Jaffrey resident Charlie Bean told stories related to the Dean murder—including one about meeting Count von Bernstorff—that some found hard to believe and that earned him the nickname "Crazy Bean."

41

THE MESSAGE

On Tuesday, August 13, Arria Morison and two other ladies visited Mr. Dean at his home, seeking items for a rummage sale to benefit the Peterborough Hospital. They arrived at about 11:30, chatted with Mrs. Dean, and explained to the Deans the purpose of their visit.

Dean told the women, "I would like to give you a good big check but I can't afford to." Instead, he took a valuable bronze from his mantelpiece and gave it to them, along with some of this best books. "Can you suggest anything else?" he asked.

Mrs. Morison asked if he had any antiques and Dean replied, "I haven't any here, but over at the other house I have a few and if you will come over with me perhaps you can find something that would interest you."

Dean and Mrs. Morison left the other ladies to keep Mrs. Dean company and walked to the summer house. Along the way they passed a few of Dean's turkeys, and Mrs. Morison asked Dean if he might spare a turkey for them to raffle as a fundraiser.

"I would like to, Mrs. Morison, but I haven't any at all."

"What has happened to them?" she asked. "Have they died?"

"They're being killed, or at least, they have disappeared."

"Foxes?"

"Well, I think this one is probably a two-legged fox," Dean said, suggesting that someone was stealing his turkeys.

Dean and Morison proceeded to the summer house, where he chose some dishware, an antique spinning wheel, and a wool winder to donate to the sale.

As they headed back to the bungalow, Dean stopped. "Mrs. Morison, Miss Ware told me that you had seen lights up in this part of the country. Have you seen them lately?"

"Yes, Mr. Dean, I saw them last night."

He asked her to point out where she had seen the lights. When she did, he said, "Yes, that's just about where I've seen them." He marked the spot with some stones and then hesitated, as if he had something he wanted to say. "Mrs. Morison, are you ever in communication with anyone who could be of any help with the lights?"

"Yes, I am in constant communication with the Boston office of the Justice Department."

"Can you do something for me?

"Yes, I'd be very glad to."

"Can you get a message to send me up one of the best men they have? I want the very best, not just an ordinary man who doesn't know his work."

His tone of voice told her this was a serious matter. "Mr. Dean, couldn't I do better than that? Couldn't you tell me what it is and I will get the message to them at once? I'll telephone as soon as I get home."

"No. I don't want you to telephone. I can't give you the message." She pressed him, asking why not, and he said, "Because what I know is too dangerous for a woman. I have no right to tell you."

"Why, Mr. Dean, if it is so serious as that why haven't you sent for someone before?

"Because I wasn't ready." He explained that two government men had spoken to him earlier, but he hadn't been ready to say anything at the time. "I wanted to be perfectly sure. Now, the quicker someone comes the better."

She asked why he didn't simply contact the federal agents himself, immediately.

"I can't telephone because it isn't wise," he said, perhaps not trusting the privacy of his party line. "I can't write for the same reason." It seemed to Mrs. Morison that he suspected his mail was being watched or tampered with.

Dean gave her another reason for not going to the authorities him-self. "I can't leave home on account of my wife, and also because I don't want anyone to know that I was leaving her, and that's the reason I'm asking you to do this for me."[12]

Morison tried again to get him to tell her the substance of his mes-sage. "I think you can trust me, Mr. Dean. If you could tell me I think I could give the message sooner."

Again Dean hesitated, as if he was about to tell her, then changed his mind. "No. I haven't the right to. You are a woman." To modern ears this sounds like rank chauvinism, but it was probably genuine concern for her safety, not without reason given what happened later.

They began walking back to Dean's house when he stopped again. "What do you know about the Colfelts?" he asked.

"Why, I don't know anything about them," Mrs. Morison said with a laugh. "I think you know more than anyone else as they are living on your place."

"I did, Mrs. Morison. I knew just a little too much. I gave them 24 hours to get out."

"What do you mean, Mr. Dean? What was the matter?"

"Well, I needed the rent very much, but I am too good an American to keep people of that kind on my place." Beyond that, Dean would not elaborate on his reasons for asking the Colfelts to leave.

They continued on to the house and Dean asked, "How late can I reach you on the telephone tonight?"

She assured him that she was always up late and he could reach her at any time. "You needn't hesitate to call me. Why?"

"Well, if I come out here tonight and see the lights, I'll call you up."

"Why, Mr. Dean, would that be safe?" she asked, remembering his concern about using the telephone.

"Yes, I think so," he said, and suggested that they could use a code to talk about the lights. "I might say something about bringing the turkeys over and you would know what that meant. Then, if you will look out and see what you see from your place, we can compare notes afterwards."

Mrs. Morison agreed with the plan and told him to call her at any time. She never heard from Mr. Dean again.

42

THE VISITORS

THAT EVENING, MARGARET COLFELT'S GUESTS, HOWARD AND ETHEL Potter, arrived at Greenville station on the train from Boston. Station agent Robert F. O'Brien happened to be on the train, and took note of an unfamiliar couple.

"A man sat across the way on the train," O'Brien said. "I knew he was a foreigner." O'Brien had nothing against the stranger on that account, "But somehow I noticed that fellow and a woman who sat directly ahead of him. Occasionally she had her arm back of the seat"—a gesture that seemed odd for a woman. The woman made a distinct impression on O'Brien, who described her as "homelier than hell."

Hugh Churchill, brakeman on the train, also recalled the couple and described the woman as "very distinguished looking." When asked if she might actually have been a man disguised as a woman, he replied, "It could have been."

The train arrived at Greenville, the couple got off, and O'Brien gave little thought to them until later, after hearing of Mr. Dean's murder.

That same evening, the East Jaffrey Brass Band held a concert at the common in Jaffrey Center. According to Margaret Enslin, "Jaffrey has no band but the East Jaffrey Band can certainly make enough noise for both."

Later, it was rumored that Mr. Dean was seen talking to Mr. Rich at the concert, but there were no credible witnesses to this.[13] Furthermore, a

Jaffrey resident named Margaret Costello reported seeing both Mr. Dean and Mr. Rich in downtown Jaffrey at the time the concert was going on.

According to a timeline developed by federal agents, Dean left home in his buggy at around 8 p.m. He was seen driving to town by Mrs. Clara Ingraham, Mrs. Emma Chouinard, and a boy named John Bryant, who was playing outside at the time.

Everett Bingham, who lived about a third of a mile from downtown Jaffrey, was in a swing on his porch at about 8:20 p.m. when Dean came by, headed toward town. "He drove up to the yard and was talking with me," Bingham said. Dean asked about Bingham's brother and brother-in-law, both of whom were serving in France. They spoke for about 15 minutes, then Dean said good night and went on his way.

Dean's first stop in town was Goodnow's store. As he pulled up to the store he saw Charlie Bean, with whom he spoke briefly. Dean asked, "What time is it, Mr. Bean?"

"By my time it is 8:30," Bean said, then pointed to the town clock, "but by that clock up there, it's 8:35."

Dean replied, "I must hurry along because the stores close at nine and I've got some purchases to make."

Dean hitched up his horse and went into the store through the back door. He bought a few items, then left through the front door, where he ran into liveryman Fred Stratton. They bid each other good evening, then as Stratton continued into the store, Dean called to him, "Have you an automobile now?"

"Sure," Stratton said.

"Bring me 100 pounds of sugar, will you?"

It was a facetious request, especially given the wartime rationing, and Stratton knew it. "Yes," he said. "I'll be right over with it."

Dean laughed and headed out, seeming to be in his usual good humor as far as Stratton could tell. In contrast to others who saw Dean that evening, Stratton said, "I never saw him in better spirits in my life than he was that night."

The time was about 8:45. Dean walked to Duncan's drugstore and asked George Duncan if he had a battery that would fit his flashlight. In all probability, Dean wanted to use the flashlight that evening while watching for signal lights from the farm. Duncan did not have a battery in stock, but told Dean he would have one later.

While at the drugstore, Dean met his friend Georgina Hodgkins, sister to Mrs. Lana Rich. They spoke briefly, then Dean went next door to the post office—located in the same building—to check his mail. Perhaps he was hoping for a check from Lawrence Colfelt, but there was no mail for him.

Dean then crossed the street to Meyers dry goods store, still seeking a battery for his flashlight, but that store did not have one either. Meyers did provide laundry service and Dean dropped off a bundle, then crossed back over the street to Vanni's market. He bought some currant buns and headed back to his buggy at Goodnow's. It was now a little past 9 p.m.

According to Georgiana Hodgkins, Mr. Dean gave her a ride in his buggy to the home of Charles and Lana Rich, who lived very close to downtown. But the only people who confirmed this were the Riches, who may have had a vested interest in the matter. Miss Georgia Lynch, who was at the drug store with her sister that evening, did overhear Dean and Hodgkins talking. According to Lynch, "Mr. Dean asked her if she was going right to home, and he said, 'I'll drive you up.'" However, neither Lynch nor her sister actually saw Hodgkins take Dean up on the offer.

In fact, other witnesses stated that Mr. Dean was alone when he rode home that evening. Mrs. Weltha Crouteau was at the drug store getting ice cream and said that when Dean drove off, "He was all alone by himself."

Charlie Bean, who had been walking his dog after speaking to Mr. Dean, also said that when Dean drove off, he did so alone, although he acknowledged that Dean could have picked Miss Hodgkins up later on.

Helen Chamberlain, whose house was on Dean's route home, said, "I knew nothing about the murder, the only thing I know that Dean passed by our way going home alone."

Likewise, Mrs. Alfred Burgoyne told the town's selectmen "that she saw Mr. Dean leave Goodnow's store about 9:00 alone in his carriage for home and that he was not accompanied by Miss Hodgman [sic] as Rich's people claim."

What difference does it make whether Dean gave Miss Hodgkins a ride to the Rich home or not? It would make no difference, except as it relates to another question: Did Dean actually stop at the Rich house at all?

43

THE VISIT

According to Charles Rich and his family, William Dean stopped and visited with them before driving home on the evening of August 13. Rich told Pinkerton agent Harry Scott that Dean drove into his yard with Miss Hodgkins at 8:40 that evening. But later, at the grand jury, the Riches and Miss Hodgkins all stated that Dean arrived at 9 or "a little after." Still later, in a deposition taken as part of his slander suit, Rich stated that Dean arrived between 9:15 and 9:30; it seems that the later the story was told, the later Dean arrived.

Just before Dean arrived, according to Charles Rich, he had been injured by a kick from his horse in the barn. When Dean and Hodgkins entered the house, Rich and his wife were in the kitchen heating water to put on his injured eye. They also had a preparation with alcohol in it, which prompted Dean to joke, Rich said, "that I needed the alcohol more inside than outside."

Mr. Dean and Miss Hodgkins passed through the house to the front porch where they sat and talked, while Rich stayed in the kitchen bathing his injuries. Mrs. Rich went back and forth, alternately visiting with Dean and tending to her husband.

According to Georgiana Hodgkins, she and Dean talked about the war and the fate of the young men who had lost their lives in battle. They discussed the afterlife, a subject about which Dean found Hodgkins's views to be too pessimistic. "He said he hoped, when I told him what I thought, he hoped more for himself than that," Hodgkins said. Apart from that discussion, she did not find Dean to be particularly somber or worried that evening.

In the course of the conversation, Dean mentioned his disappointment that he had not been able to buy a battery for his flashlight. Mrs. Rich and Miss Hodgkins attributed his distress about the battery to not wanting to drive home in the dark. The moon had set by the time Mr. Dean left, they said, and Mrs. Rich remembered him saying, "Oh, I hate to go home in the dark."

The solution, Miss Hodgkins suggested, was for Dean to borrow their lantern for the ride home. Dean agreed and they went to find Mr. Rich, who went out with Dean to get the lantern. "It was hot, and I went with him to the barn and put my lantern on his buggy and lighted it," Rich said.

Rich then put a cigar in Dean's mouth and lit it. According to Rich, "He said he didn't know but what he preferred his cigarettes, but he said he would do the same as I did when I went to his house. He went away smoking that cigar."

Lana Rich confirmed that her husband gave Dean a cigar, but Georgiana Hodgkins remembered the story differently when questioned by Attorney General Oscar Young:

YOUNG: Were there some cigars passed there or something?

HODGKINS: Yes. Mr. Dean said, "Now, Mr. Rich, when do you want this lantern back?" and Mr. Dean said, "about midnight?" And he said, just as he went away, "Would you have a cigar?"

YOUNG: Who said that?

HODGKINS: Mr. Rich. And Mr. Dean said, "No," and we tried to think afterwards what he did say, just about his cigarette, and as nearly as I can recall he said, "I'm going to light a cigarette after I've started," but he already was lighting his cigarette.

YOUNG: Didn't he light a cigar, as a matter of fact?

HODGKINS: No, I don't remember that he did. I think he said, "I'm going to light a cigarette." He might even have lighted up. But I remember his making that remark. It's hard to remember a conversation exactly if you didn't know it is going to be reported."

The question of whether Dean was smoking when he left would only become significant later.

Just before Dean left, Mrs. Rich put a box in the back of his wagon. In it were some empty cans that had held sour milk, which Dean had brought to them on a previous visit. She also put in a small bunch of sweet pea flowers and, Charles Rich said, some canned fruit—although by the time of the grand jury he appears to have forgotten about the fruit.

According to Rich, Dean left his home at about 10:30. Rich repeated that time to federal agents and at the grand jury, where Georgiana Hodgkins corroborated his account. Sometime later, Rich reiterated that time to a bank examiner he spoke with about the murder. However, at the slander suit two years later, Rich said Dean left "very near 11 o'clock" and denied that he'd ever said it was 10:30.

Outside of the Rich family, there were no witnesses to confirm the story of Dean's visit to their house that evening. The Riches' neighbor Mary Hutchinson did provide a detailed account of Dean's visit to the Rich home—the injury from the horse, the alcohol joke, the visit on the piazza—but she had no first-hand knowledge of the visit, as she was not there, and the information could have come only from Charles Rich.

44

THE JOURNEY HOME

OTHER WITNESSES TOLD A DIFFERENT STORY OF DEAN'S DEPARTURE from town that evening. Everett Bingham heard a rig pass by about 9:45 or 10 and thought it was Dean's.

A few hundred yards beyond Bingham's house was the home of Emma Chouinard, whose children were playing in the street that evening. At 10 p.m., she went out to call her children just as Mr. Dean passed by in his buggy. The children had been playing under a streetlight, the sun was setting, and a crescent moon shone just above the horizon, providing more than enough light for Chouinard to recognize Dean as he passed by.

A number of other villagers saw Dean driving home while it was still light enough for them to recognize him, including Fred Croteau, Mrs. Alice Burgoyne, Mrs. Fannie Howard, and Helen Chamberlain. Chamberlain was asked if it was dark at the time Dean passed by her house. "No," she said, "how could it be, or I wouldn't have seen him." The moon set at 10:37 p.m. that evening, which means that according to all those witnesses, Dean must have passed by on his way home before that.

Apart from the Riches and Miss Hodgkins, the only witnesses who stated that Dean drove home later than 10:30 or so were the Riches' neighbors, Alfred and Mary Hutchinson. The Hutchinsons lived only a few hundred feet from the Riches, on a knoll that provided a view of the Riches' driveway as well as the road Dean would have taken home, the Old Peterborough Road. (Another road, usually called the Railway Road because it followed the train route north, would eventually become the main road to Peterborough, U.S. Route 202.)

The Hutchinsons were in the habit of sleeping on a side porch facing the Rich home, where evening breezes provided relief from the oppressive summer heat. That evening, Alfred Hutchinson had retired to the porch, leaving his wife indoors to read a magazine. "I seen a horse and buggy drive down the walk right here coming from Mr. Rich's barn," Alfred Hutchinson said. The moon was on the increase at the time, he stated. "It was bright moonlight that night, and I could see quite plainly."

But there are problems with Hutchinson's testimony. To begin with, his statements about the time he saw the buggy are inconsistent. Very soon after the murder, he was interviewed by federal agents who asked whether Mr. Rich had mentioned anyone driving out of his barn that night. "Yes," Hutchinson replied. "Mr. Rich said it was Mr. Dean, and that he left about half past ten."

Hutchinson's wife, Mary—who did not see the buggy herself—told a federal agent that she and her husband spoke to Mr. Rich the next day and Rich said Mr. Dean had been at his house that evening.

"Did he mention the time?" the agent asked.

"I won't be sure about that, but I think he said Mr. Dean went away at half past ten or a little later. He did not mention any positive time, but just as I said in a general way spoke about it."

Note that in both cases, it was Charles Rich who first said that the buggy left at 10:30 p.m., not the Hutchinsons.

Later, at the grand jury, Alfred Hutchinson stated that he couldn't be positive about the time that he saw the buggy. When County Solicitor Pickard suggested that it was half past ten, Hutchinson replied, "I would judge so, yes. I couldn't say positive because there's no way of knowing. I didn't look at the clock."

Still later, Alfred Hutchinson gave testimony that was reported in the *Keene Sentinel.* "Alfred Hutchinson testified he could see anything that happened at Rich's house from his piazza, on which he slept during the summer of 1918. He said that between 9:30 and 10:30 on the night of August 13, 1918, he saw a horse and wagon begin driven out of the barn, the driver smoking a cigar. From what Mr. Rich told him the next day he said he was certain the man was Dean starting for home."

Note that the time Hutchinson reported has now shifted, from 10:30 to "between 9:30 and 10:30."

There is another problem with Hutchinson's testimony. He insisted to federal agents that the moon was shining brightly when the wagon came down the Riches' driveway. But the Riches and Miss Hodgkins all said that the moon had *set* by the time Dean left their house, which puts it sometime after 10:30.[14]

If the Riches are to be believed, all the witnesses who said that Dean traveled home between 9:30 and 10:30 were wrong. If we believe the other witnesses, the Riches were, at the very least, wrong about the time Dean left their home. Perhaps Dean did visit them that evening, but left before they said he did. The other possibility is that the Riches made up the story of Dean stopping at their house entirely.

There are other discrepancies between the Riches' testimony and that of others regarding Mr. Dean's drive home. In the aftermath of the murder, the Riches made a point of telling others that they had lent Dean a lantern for his buggy. According to Mary Lee Ware, "I heard Mrs. Rich say that Mr. Dean had trouble with his lantern and that they loaned him a lantern." Lewis Davis, the executor of the Dean estate, also reported that Rich told him he had loaned Dean a lantern to see his way home.

But no one outside of the Rich family reported seeing a lantern on Dean's buggy that evening. And if Dean traveled home at twilight, while the moon was still up, he would not have needed a lantern.

Similarly, none of the other witnesses who knew Mr. Dean and saw him driving home that evening mentioned him smoking a cigar or cigarette, as the Riches testified that he had. Alfred Hutchinson, who did not know Dean, described the driver of the buggy he saw leaving the Riches' as a middle-aged man in a coat and hat, smoking a pipe, cigar, or cigarette.

Examined closely, the Riches' testimony and that of other witnesses conflicts in a number of areas: the timing, the state of the moon, whether Mr. Dean had a lantern on his buggy, and whether he was smoking. The only way to harmonize the testimonies is to conclude that some of the witnesses were wrong or lying.

Or that a second buggy left the Riches' house that evening.

45

THE BUGGIES

AT THE TIME OF HIS DEATH, WILLIAM DEAN HAD IN HIS POSSESSION two buggies (or wagons, as some called them). The wagon he had used most often—and which most people in town remembered—was a small, rubber-tired buggy with dark wood coloring. But according to Fred Stratton, who ran the local stable, Dean had acquired another buggy about a month before his death. That wagon belonged to his friend, Mrs. Robinson, who was no longer using it as she preferred to travel about in her automobile. It was a larger, buckboard-style buggy with steel wheels, which Mrs. Robinson had given to Mr. Dean in hopes that he might be able to sell it for her.

This steel-wheeled wagon, according to Charles Rich, was the one that Dean had been driving lately and had used on the evening of August 12 when he came to town. Everett Bingham, sitting on his porch swing that evening, also testified that Dean drove into town in an old buggy with iron tires.

Later, at the grand jury, a great deal of attention was given to the question of what buggy Dean had driven that evening. Why? Because although many witnesses saw Mr. Dean driving home between 9 and 10 p.m. that night, none of them could confirm what kind of buggy he was driving. Those who heard a buggy passing later, between 10:30 and 11 p.m., said it had steel tires. But this could not have been Mr. Dean, the first group argued, since his buggy had rubber tires.[15]

Of all the witnesses interviewed, only two gave direct testimony about a buggy leaving Mr. Rich's yard that evening. The first was Rich's neighbor Alfred Hutchinson, who said he did not know Mr. Dean and did not recognize the driver of the buggy. It was not until the next day when he spoke to Mr. Rich that he decided it must have been Mr. Dean.

The other witness was Charlie Bean, who saw Mr. Dean heading home in his buggy shortly after 9 p.m. Later, at about 10:40, Bean was smoking his pipe in front of Stratton's livery stable on Main Street. He heard a wagon drive down Rich's driveway, which would have been behind him, to his right. "The sound came from a rig with steel tires," Bean said. "I recognized from the sound of the horse and buggy that it was Rich's."

How could Bean be so certain it was Rich's horse and not Dean's? "It went down with a fast trot," Bean said. "Rich's horse has life in it—it's no dead beat. Dean's horse you could not stir up unless you put dynamite under its tail."

The conflicting testimonies appear to be irresolvable, one group insisting that Dean drove home earlier in a buggy with rubber tires, the other that Dean left later in a steel-tired wagon. Alfred Hutchinson said the buggy that left Rich's yard was not Rich's; Charlie Bean insisted that it was.

The testimonies contain one crucial piece of information, however. Everett Bingham, who had spoken with Dean as he drove into town that evening, testified that Dean's buggy had no top to it. Similarly, both Emma Chouinard and Mrs. Fanny Howard saw Mr. Dean as he drove home and said his buggy had no top to it. And Charlie Bean was insistent: "There was not that night a top on Dean's team. I know that positively."

On the other hand, Alfred Hutchinson told federal agents that the buggy he saw driving away from the Rich home "was a top buggy, and the top was up"—an assertion that he repeated twice. If so, then whoever Hutchinson saw leaving Rich's yard later that evening was not William Dean.

Who *did* Hutchinson see driving from Rich's yard? Charlie Bean, from his vantage point on Main Street, could not see the buggy, although he did see a flash of a light coming on at Rich's barn, as if someone had turned on the electric light just before the team drove out. From the sound of the buggy's tires and the quick gait of the horse, Bean was quite certain that it was Rich's horse and buggy. When asked where the buggy was headed, Bean replied, "It was going towards the Dean place."

46

THE NIGHT

ACCORDING TO THE RICHES, THEY STAYED UP LATER THAN USUAL THAT night, continuing to apply hot cloths to Charles's injury. The women helped him bathe his face, then retired to prepare for bed. According to Rich, "They went upstairs and then I stayed and kept up the application until I heard them leave the toilet room, and then I followed and went to bed."

At some point, according to Rich, he went to the barn to look for his pipe, which he'd lost when the horse kicked him. Rich, his wife, and his sister-in-law all testified that he did not otherwise leave the house again that night, and all were in bed by a little past 11.

But others disputed their testimony. Margaret Costello lived across the street from Charles Rich, two doors down from Goodnow's store. That evening, she had gone to the post office with her sister Annie at about 9:30 to mail a letter through the overnight slot. The girls walked home and sat on their porch, talking.

At roughly 9:45, the sisters saw Charles Rich walk by, headed to town. They knew Rich well and their porch was a mere 10 feet from the sidewalk, with an electric streetlight illuminating the way, so they were positive of their identification.

As Rich passed, the left side of his face was toward the sisters, and although they did not pay any particular attention to it, they did not notice any marks or discoloration on his face. "He was walking along at rather a hard gait," Margaret said, and recalled he was wearing a light shirt and no jacket, appropriate for a warm summer evening.

Rich was also seen by Camille Bruneau, who had attended the band concert at Jaffrey Center that evening. Bruneau came back to East Jaffrey with friends and got out of the car in front of Vanni's store to walk home. "Just as I was getting ready to start for home, I noticed Mr. Rich standing in front of the post office steps," Bruneau said. "It was then between 9:30 and 10."

Just before 10 p.m., Margaret Costello went into the house, but her sister Annie stayed on the porch a bit longer. The town clock struck 10, and soon after Annie saw Charles Rich walking by again, headed toward home.

At about 10:45 p.m., Daniel LaRose was walking from his boarding house on River Street, not far from downtown, intending to mail a letter at the post office. According to LaRose, "Just as I turned the corner of River Street onto Main Street, in front of the post-office, I saw an automobile. It was coming down Main Street toward River Street. I noticed that it didn't have any lights. There was a shifting of brakes, and as the car got near me it almost came to a stop. It seemed as though the car wasn't running all right and I was about to start toward it to help them, because I always did that, having had some experience with automobiles. When I got within ten or twelve feet of the car, I saw Judge Rich at the wheel. It was a right-hand drive car which brought him on my side of the car.[16] It was a bright night and there was an electric light right on the corner. I could take my oath that it was Judge Rich at the wheel of the car. He had on a light cap which I had seen him wear before. We both glanced at each other and as soon as he saw me, he turned the wheel and put on more power and the car turned the corner into North Street, going north. I noticed that the tail light was not lighted. I also noticed there were two men in the back seat who appeared as though they knew me but didn't want me to see them. They shielded themselves from view and they tried to draw their coats up around the faces."

At the time, LaRose didn't notice anything wrong with Rich's face. "His face looked plain to me," LaRose testified. "I knew the man and his face looked the same as my face now."

LaRose watched the car till it passed out of sight over a rise in the road that made it impossible for him to tell whether it continued on

North Street toward Dublin, or turned right on the road to Peterborough and William Dean's farm.

At first, LaRose did not report the incident to anyone because, "I wasn't looking for trouble," he said. But two days later his landlord Louis Cournoyer mentioned that Charles Rich had gotten a black eye the night of Dean's murder, "and then I told Mr. Cournoyer it was very funny because he didn't have it when I saw him in the automobile," LaRose said.

When Cournoyer was interviewed by federal agents, he mentioned that LaRose had a story they would be interested in. The agents interviewed LaRose, and his reluctant testimony became part of the public record.

At about the same time LaRose saw the automobile go by—roughly 10:45 p.m.—Charlie Bean also saw an auto heading out of town on North Street. "I heard it toot twice," Bean said. Then, a light came on in front of Charles Rich's barn, "and I heard a carriage drive out and pass down the road." This was the horse and buggy Bean identified as Charles Rich's, headed toward the Dean place.

Everett Bingham, who lived a short distance up the road toward the Dean farm, also heard a team go by, followed by a touring car with an engine that was "heavier than that of a Ford," a car that he described as "Going very fast."

Max Buckwold, who lived a few houses past Bingham, heard the vehicles pass and told William de Kerlor, "a quarter of eleven, as he was about to go to sleep, that a team with a horse went by at a very good rate, and a few minutes behind it, perhaps two or three, he heard a rather large automobile."

Slightly less than a mile further, at the turn to Mr. Dean's home, Charles Deschenes was in his kitchen, rinsing his mouth because he'd had teeth pulled that day. "I was bathing my face, when I heard a team and an automobile go by," Deschenes said. "They were pretty close to each other. I went out to see which way they were going but could not see anything. It was pretty near 11 o'clock."

Deschenes thought at first that it was the Turner family returning from the moving pictures in Jaffrey. But the Turners lived two miles away and from the sound of it, the drivers had not gone that much farther.

Also, the Turners generally took a different route home, which made Deschenes wonder, "Who the dickens can it be up this time of night?"

Elizabeth Bryant, who lived near the Deschenes, did not hear anything, but her brother heard a team go by the house at 10:30. "My brother said that right after the team went by, an auto went right after the team," Bryant said. The car was a Ford, he told her, but it turned around before it reached them. Then a second, larger car went by, "about quarter past eleven."

47

THE AUTOMOBILES

According to Mary Dean, her husband returned home that evening at his usual time, 9:30, about the time one would expect if he left town shortly after 9:00 o'clock. "He told me when he got home that he had seen the Riches at their house," she stated. If so, he could not have stopped for very long, and certainly not as long as the Riches said he did.

She told authorities that William brought in his purchases from the store, then took his horse and carriage to the barn. He came back to the house and changed out of his good clothes into his barn clothes. He drank some milk and ate one of the currant buns he had bought in town, then smoked a cigarette. At 11 o'clock, he headed to the barn to do the milking, telling Mary he would be back in an hour or so and asking her to have some supper ready when he came back.

Dean's final meal helps to establish his time of death. The examination of his stomach after his murder showed that it contained a little milk and some partially digested currants. Given that Dean ate his final meal between 10 and 10:30 that evening, it can be estimated that he died sometime between 11:15 p.m.—Bert Ford's reckoning—and 1 a.m., the latest possible time according to federal agents.

At about midnight, Selectman William Coolidge was asleep in his home a half mile from the center of town on the Old Peterborough Road. "I was sound asleep, but there was a peculiar kind of noise and it woke me up instantly, and I recognized it because I run a car myself, and it was the shifting of the gear going downhill," Coolidge said. He got up and saw the back of a car as it headed out of town. "Just a few minutes afterwards I heard a team going the other way, and a car," he said. A few minutes after that, the first car came back.

Robert Hamill, who lived only a few houses away from Charles Rich, also heard an auto around midnight. "On the night that Dr. Dean was killed I decided to sleep in a porch hammock where I often slept, as it was a very hot night," he testified. "I soon fell asleep. I don't know how long I slept, but it must have been in the neighborhood of midnight that I was awakened by the sound of an automobile coming down the old Peterboro road toward the village. My house is on an elevation close to the junction of River street and the Peterboro turnpike and a few minutes' walk from Main street. The automobile had its dimmers on. I noticed that in particular. It was headed in the direction of Main street, but I don't know whether it went that far."

Up to road, at the White Brothers Cotton Mill in the center of East Jaffrey, night watchman Jean Bibeau began making his hourly rounds. At the stroke of midnight, Bibeau walked out of the boiler room to the corner of Main Street and North Street. "While walking on North Street, carrying my lantern about five minutes past twelve, I noticed an automobile, coming toward the square coming from Peterboro way," Bibeau said. "They slowed up when they saw my light. I got that impression strong."

Bibeau entered a small wooden outbuilding, "and when I came out to go into the brick building, the car had passed and was stopped at the corner right near the watering trough with the front facing up Main street toward the bank." He noted that the car didn't have a tail light by which he might have seen a license plate.

"I went into the main part of the mill, and that automobile must have stood there fifteen minutes," Bibeau said. "It takes me about fifteen or twenty minutes to make my rounds. As I came along each floor, starting from the top, I could see through the windows that it was still there."

The car had not moved as he returned to the boiler room, and Bibeau recalled seeing that there were three men in it, two in the front and one in the back. "I was not near enough to see their faces," he said, although, "I think they were from around the village."

The men were talking low, and he did not pay enough attention to recognize their voices or listen to what they were saying. "After I heard of the murder, it all came back to me, and I wished I had walked nearer to the car in returning to the boiler room," Bibeau said. By the time he began his rounds again, the car was gone.

In summary, the automobile reported by a number of witnesses was a dark-colored vehicle that was not running smoothly, whose occupants did not wish it to be seen or heard, traveling with no lights on or with the lights dimmed. It was likely a touring car, larger than a Ford Model T, but not one of the largest tourers. Daniel LaRose, the person with the clearest view of the auto, said, "The automobile looked to me like a Buick or an Overland."

As it happens, a car fitting that description spent much of its time parked in Charles Rich's barn. It belonged to Susan Henchman, assistant cashier of the Monadnock National Bank.

Susan Henchman was born in 1872 in Worcester, Massachusetts, the youngest of five children. In 1889, the Henchman family moved to East Jaffrey, renting a farm on Thorndike Pond in the shadow of Mount Monadnock. The ensuing years were tragic ones for Susan. One year after the move to Jaffrey, her mother died of kidney disease. Three years later, her father died of a sudden, massive heart attack. At her father's funeral service, music was provided by a quartet that included Charles and Lana Rich. Charles Rich was 40 years old at the time; Susan was 21.

Susan worked as teacher until 1907, when she was given a job at the Monadnock National Bank, where Charles Rich was head cashier. She began as a bookkeeper, and later became a cashier. She led an active social life, performing in theatrical productions, visiting and receiving friends, and attending functions such as the Governor's Ball in March of 1911 with a party that included Mr. and Mrs. Rich.

In the aftermath of William Dean's death, rumors were rife that Charles Rich's relationship with Susan Henchman was more than that of a protective friend and guardian. Charlie Bean said as much to Alice Humiston, who acknowledged that she wasn't always sure whether to believe Bean. "However that may be, he had known for some time that Mr. Rich had been spending quite a considerable amount of his time with a woman who works in the bank," Humiston said. "He had seen them out riding or walking in the country, several times." Bean told Humiston that on the night of the murder he saw Rich driving away from his home late and night, and his first thought was, "Well, there goes Rich out to the farm to see Susie." (It should be noted that Alice Humiston was not a fan of Charles Rich. "I had always despised the man and perfectly hated to have anything to do with him in the bank," she said.)

Still, the rumors of an affair did not all come from people who disliked Rich. Herbert Sawtelle, a fellow Mason and banker who described himself as a good friend of Rich's, said Rich and Miss Henchman were very intimate. "You know what I mean," Sawtelle said. "Rich has one bad fault. He is very sweet with the fair sex and will go out of his way when he sees a nice face."

Charles Rich did not own an automobile, but he allowed Susan Henchman to store her car, a Buick that he occasionally drove, in his barn. Susan Henchman described the car as "small, four passenger," with four cylinders.

Rich, when asked at the grand jury what kind of car Henchman owned, replied similarly. "A small one. 1912 model. Five passenger." There was, perhaps, a reason that both Henchman and Rich described her car as "small."

In 1912, Buick made two types of cars: smaller, two-passenger roadsters, and touring cars with two bench seats. The most popular style was the dark blue Model 35, a right-hand drive, four-cylinder touring car that could hold four or more people. This matches the description of Susan Henchman's car perfectly. It also matches the automobile that most witnesses reported heading in the direction of the Dean farm at about 10:45 and returning at midnight.

48

THE LONG WAY ROUND

AT THE TIME THAT WITNESSES REPORTED SEEING A CAR HEADED IN the direction of Mr. Dean's home, Arria Morison was entertaining company at her home, about two and half miles past the Dean farm. Her company left at about 11 p.m., after which she sat at her writing desk to do some work.

The Morison home was on the Old Jaffrey Road, the opposite end of the Old Peterborough Road where Mr. Dean lived. (In New England, roads are often named for where they are going, so the same road may have more than one name—a feature not intentionally designed to confuse outsiders, but which serves the purpose.)

Mrs. Morison's writing desk faced a window looking out to the road and beyond that to the Railway Road, which ran alongside the Boston and Maine railroad tracks, about 700 yards away. As she sat writing, Morison heard a high-powered auto coming from Jaffrey on the Railway Road. Generally speaking, cars on that road continued north to Peterborough. "Very rarely a car turns up our road, and this one turned up, and it went past our house at a high rate of speed," she said. This meant that the car, which had come from the direction of Jaffrey, was now headed back toward Jaffrey—unusual, given that any point beyond Mrs. Morison's home, such as the Dean farm, could be reached more easily and quickly by way of Old Peterborough Road. The time, as best she could estimate it, was between 11:50 and 12:10.

"I went on then with my work at the desk and got interested and forgot about the time until I was recalled to it by the same car coming back at a tremendous speed," Mrs. Morison said. "It came so fast I could hear it just simply roaring, don't you know, and I put up the shade because I wanted to see who it was going by so fast." She was too late to get a good look at the car, but she noted the time: 1:15 a.m.

Mrs. Morison prepared for bed, anticipating her trip to Boston in the morning and remembering that Dean said he would call her if he saw any lights. "Why, Mr. Dean hasn't seen anything evidently," she thought. "I know he would have called me up, and now it's too late."

Then it occurred to her that perhaps Mrs. Dean was ill and that Mr. Dean had sent for a doctor. But that couldn't be, because the car had not come from Peterborough, and any doctor coming from Jaffrey would not have taken such a roundabout way to get to the Dean home.

It did not occur to her that a car might have taken the long way around—a route that was largely uninhabited—because the driver did not want to attract attention. Mrs. Morison did not see the car, so there is no way to know if it was the same car that Jean Bibeau had seen near the mill. If it was the same car, why was it returning to a place it had left only a short while earlier?

49

THE PHONE CALLS

On the morning that Mary Dean discovered her husband missing, she asked Arthur Smith to look for him. As she told investigators, "I then called up Mr. Rich by the telephone but he said he didn't know where he was. I told him my husband was lost last night and that I felt he had died."

It is not surprising that the first person Mrs. Dean thought to call was Charles Rich, given their closeness over the years. But Rich declined to respond, so she called Martin Garfield. According to Garfield, Mrs. Dean called his house at "about eight o'clock in the morning," which means she must have called Mr. Rich before that.

But Charles Rich denied that Mrs. Dean called him that morning, as did his wife. Rich's sister-in-law Georgiana Hodgkins also backed him up, despite evidence to the contrary that federal agents appeared to have:

Q: Are you sure that Mr. and Mrs. Rich did not receive word over the telephone?

A: I am sure that they didn't receive word over the telephone.

Q: Then the records in the telephone office, calling Rich's house from the Dean house are wrong.

A: I don't know. I am sure that the first we all knew about it was about 10:30 a.m. August 14.

Arthur Hatch, who worked at Goodnow's store, also contradicted Rich, testifying that he spoke with Rich at the store between 8:00 and

8:30 in the morning. The men greeted each other and Hatch asked, "What's the news?" Rich told Hatch that Dr. Dean was missing, and Hatch asked him how that happened.

"I guess that's all I can tell you," Rich replied.

Later, Rich denied saying anything to Hatch about Dean being dead or missing that morning. But Archie Letourneau was there and remembered, "I worked in the store and Arthur Hatch, he got mixed up in it too, because he saw him too, that morning."

Despite this, Rich claimed that he knew nothing of Dean's disappearance until later in the morning, when young Elizabeth Henchman—Russel Henchman's daughter—called her aunt Susan at the bank with the news. Apparently, Mrs. Dean had called the Henchmans to ask Russel to come get their cow, but he was not at home, so his daughter called her aunt at the bank.[17] Susan Henchman had arrived late that morning, having dropped off her car at Charles Rich's home, where she spoke to Rich briefly, then rushed to the bank. It was not until after 11 a.m. that Elizabeth called and said, "Do you know what Mrs. Dean is saying? That Mr. Dean is dead."

Here again, Rich's story was contradicted, this time by undertaker William Leighton. According to Leighton, he had gone to his shop that morning and was reading the paper when Charles Rich came in between eight and nine o'clock.

Rich asked, "Have you been called up to Mr. Dean's?"

"No," Leighton said. "Why?

"Oh, they're telling around that he is either dead or lost," Rich said, and asked if Leighton knew anything about it.

"No," Leighton replied. "I haven't heard a thing about it."

Later, Leighton would say that Rich came into the office at about 9 a.m., and he repeated that time at the grand jury. But two years later, at Rich's slander trial, Leighton seemed less certain. "Well, that I am not very positive about, more than I can say that I think it was between the hours of 8 o'clock and 10 o'clock in the morning." When reminded of his earlier statements, Leighton said, "Why, it was certainly after 8 o'clock, that is the only thing I can tell."

As Rich related the incident, he went to see Leighton soon after hearing that Dean was missing, at around 11 o'clock. Rich asked Leighton if he would take his car up to the Dean place, but Leighton demurred. "I said I never have run after a job and I don't intend to, but if I was called I would go."

Rich told him, "Mrs. Dean ain't responsible and we don't know what to think."

Leighton suggested that Rich call Mrs. Dean to ask for Mr. Dean. Rich agreed and used Leighton's phone. When Mrs. Dean answered, she told him that her husband wasn't there and she hadn't seen him since last night.

At this point Rich left the undertaking parlor, and Leighton did not see him again until around 11:30 when he went to the post office. There, Leighton began talking with George Wellington when Rich came in and said, "they want some help up to the Dean farm to find Mr. Dean."

Leighton agreed to help, but as it was close to the lunch hour, he wanted to stop home and eat something first—apparently not too worried about Mr. Dean's situation. He went home, ate lunch, then called Rich to see if he had rounded up any searchers. "I haven't anybody but my wife and I, and my wife's sister wants to go," Rich said.

Leighton agreed to take them to the Dean place and they arrived just after Mr. Dean's body had been found, to the surprise of selectman William Coolidge who was in the process of calling Rich at the bank. The timing was perhaps coincidental, but it struck Coolidge as suspicious. At the grand jury he testified, "What I want to impress upon everybody that's here is that nobody had occasion to telephone after we found that he was dead but myself."

50

THE NEWS

AT THE TIME WILLIAM DEAN'S BODY WAS FOUND, ARRIA MORISON WAS
in Boston, meeting with officials of the Bureau of Investigation. She
had arrived that morning and stopped at the Chilton Club, an exclusive
women's club in the Back Bay named after the first woman to step foot
on Plymouth Rock from the Mayflower. Morison called Norman L.
Gifford, second in command at the Boston office, but he was out, so she
decided to have lunch at the club before heading to his office.

The Boston office of the Bureau of Investigation was located at 45
Milk Street, an historic Beaux Arts building in the financial district not
far from Boston Common and Government Center. Morison arrived at
1 p.m. and related her conversation with Mr. Dean, passing along his
request that the bureau send someone to speak with him as soon as possible. "Knowing Mr. Dean as I do, I know this thing is serious," she told
Gifford. "He wouldn't have spoken in the way he did unless it was and I
have the feeling he needs some help at once."

"I'll send a man up on the five o'clock train, but he won't be the man
I want," Gifford said. His best man was on another case and would not
be available immediately. But he had a "thoroughly good man" and would
send him up right away.

Satisfied, Mrs. Morison left and headed to North Station to catch
the afternoon train home. At the station, she picked up a copy of the
Boston Evening Transcript. Perusing the paper, she was horrified to read

the news of Dean's brutal murder. As soon as she arrived home, she telephoned Norman Gifford and gave him the news.

"Ah, my God," Gifford said, a fairly strong expletive for the times.

As Arria Morison was meeting with Norman Gifford, William Dean's body had been found but not yet removed from the cistern, as the searchers were waiting for the county authorities to arrive.

Arthur Smith was there and heard Charles Rich remark to Martin Garfield that Dean had probably put himself out of the way. "Mr. Rich was there while the body was in the cistern and said out loud in front of everybody that it was a suicide and everybody laughed," Smith said.

Peter Hogan also overheard the conversation and confirmed that Rich said to Garfield, "I guess it's a case of suicide, isn't it?"

Later, Rich tried to explain his comment. "We all felt Mr. Dean had been so tired out and discouraged and hardly himself that it might be suicide," Rich testified. Which might make sense, except that no one but Rich ever made the suggestion that William Dean had killed himself.

As soon as Dean's body was removed from the cistern, it became obvious that Dean could not have killed himself. Also, most impartial observers recognized that Mrs. Dean could not have deposited her husband's body there; the cistern was perhaps 200 feet from the barn where Dean had been murdered, uphill, and the absence of any tracks made it clear the body had been carried, rather than dragged—a physical impossibility for the frail Mrs. Dean.

It also seemed clear that more than one individual had been involved. In a lengthy analysis presented at the grand jury, Dr. George Magrath explained his reasoning for believing this. "You had the weight of the dead man and the weight of the stone, and take into account the one hundred foot distance [sic], assuming the preparation for placing it in the cistern to have been done at the barn, and it is quite a task for one man to accomplish." It strains credulity to the breaking point to imagine that Mrs. Dean was capable of such a feat.

Other evidence indicated that more than one person had murdered Dean. Although his hands and knees had been bound, the rope around his neck had not been tied or knotted. To William Leighton, this suggested that two men had been pulling on opposite ends of the rope. At the grand jury, a juror asked Leighton, "What gave you the impression that two men were pulling on the rope?"

"Because the rope wasn't tied but left with two good long ends to work with," Leighton said. "I saw the rope around there and it was for that purpose. It wasn't tied to choke him to death." At least, it wasn't intentionally designed to do that.

Mr. Dean's physical condition also argues against the idea of a lone assailant. Despite whatever ailments he might have had, Dean was not the weak, helpless individual some made him out to be. Dean's nephew William Dean Goddard noted that "Mr. Dean was not what we call 'sickly,' but on the contrary, was remarkably muscular."

According to Charlie Bean, Dean was a boxer, and the two had often sparred together. "Mr. Dean was a man that understood the art of self-defense," Bean said. "He had a crack at my nose several times." Asked whether Dean would have put up a good fight at the time of his death, Bean said, "I would hate to tackle him then. I think Mr. Dean could defend himself with me all right, to be that age." He admitted that Dean was older, but added, "He was a great man to exercise with dumbbells and in his life he was a man of fine physique."

Also, it was clear from the murder scene that Dean had put up a serious fight against his attackers. Arthur Smith, the first person to arrive on the scene, said, "we noticed everything mussed up in the barn"—an indication that a real fight had taken place there.

In the aftermath of the fight, the murderers had wrapped a blanket around Dean's head, apparently to stem the flow of blood from his head wounds. One tantalizing rumor held that the blanket belonged to Charles Rich—a damning piece of evidence if it were to be proven true. But the majority of witnesses identified the blanket as Dean's own, one that he kept in the back of his buggy to throw on his horse on cool nights. One witness did claim that the blanket had Rich's initials on it, but this was hearsay, and another merely said that it "might" have been Rich's blanket. Among the officials investigating the case only one, Agent Valkenburgh, believed it was Rich's blanket, and even the credulous detective de Kerlor thought him wrong.

Rich himself denied giving Dean a blanket, declaring that he was "too stingy to give away a blanket." (Although it should be noted that he did claim to have lent Dean a lantern—an arguably more expensive item.) Oddly, Rich also testified that he had joked with Dean about putting a blanket on his horse before driving home that night. "I suggested to Dean in a joking manner that he had better blanket his horse while being hitched up at the back of the house." This was a joke because it was a sultry August evening and the last thing a horse would need was a blanket.

When testifying at the grand jury, Rich's sister-in-law, Georgiana Hodgkins, recalled some banter about a blanket, though she seemed unclear about what had been said. And Rich's wife, Lana—the only other person who would have been there—recalled nothing about a blanket. Selectman Peter Hogan spoke with Rich after the finding of Dean's body, and Rich brought up the subject of the blanket unsolicited. "I was looking around the barn and this wagon was there that Mr. Dean used the night before," Hogan said, "and Mr. Rich spoke about there being a blanket in the wagon when he drove up to his place the night before." Rich went on to tell Hogan that he had joked with Dean about putting a blanket on the horse to keep it from cooling off.

If the blanket belonged to Dean, then Rich's remark to him was simply a poor attempt at humor that becomes macabre given the use to which the blanket was put a few hours later. On the other hand, if the blanket was Rich's, how did it come to be at Dean's farm on the night of the murder? In that light, Rich's supposed jest sounds like the nervous chatter of a guilty man trying to deflect suspicion.

51

THE FIRST EXAMINATION

By 3 P.M. THAT AFTERNOON, WILLIAM DEAN'S BODY HAD BEEN REMOVED from the cistern and taken to the kitchen of the summer house. Among those present at the examination of the body were the medical examiner Dr. Dinsmore, Dr. Childs, undertaker William Leighton, and Arthur Smith.

They began by removing Dean's clothes, and in so doing found the initialed snuff box, which Oscar Dillon described as "one of the old-fashioned snuff boxes that Dean used as a match case."

William Leighton did not remember what the box looked like but testified, "I am pretty sure I fished in his clothes and found [a] tobacco box and that is all."

Arthur Smith remembered that the box came "out of the right hip pocket." But at the grand jury, Dr. Dinsmore denied that anything was taken from Dean's pockets.

"Absolutely nothing found in his pockets except one or two sheets of folded toilet paper in one hip pocket," Dinsmore said. "Absolutely nothing in his pockets, absolutely nothing."

It is unclear who took charge of Dean's cigarette case, but at some point it came into the possession of Deputy Sheriff Walter Emerson, who would tell a different story about where it was found.

While Dean's body was being examined, local and state officials continued to search for clues. Upon climbing into the hay loft in the barn, they noticed an impression in the hay, as if someone had lain there for a time. The imprint was the size of a full-grown man, according to Sheriff Emerson, and George Wellington said that it "looked as if somebody was lying there with his hands over his head."

Emerson asked Arthur Smith, who had recently done the haying, to look at the impression. Smith testified, "It must have been done recently because we had put hay there a day or two before." Still, he admitted, "We might have done it ourselves when we were haying."

The searchers also found footprints on an unused trail off the Old Peterborough Road. According to the *Boston Post*, "Broken twigs, a footprint here and there, and a disturbed stone or two on a wall, all of which, Wellington and other men familiar with the woods agreed, were made from four days to a week ago, left faint yet convincing traces of someone having traversed the road to or from the Dean estate within that time." The paper noted that road had not been used for years, and was overgrown with brush and grass. "It furnishes an ideal way for a stealthy approach to the Dean estate from a side road a short half mile off towards the mountains in the rear."

Sheriff Emerson also saw tire tracks where one or more cars had pulled off of the road just past the Dean farm, but he admitted those could have been caused by something unconnected with the murder. At any rate, whatever evidence the footprints and tire tracks might have provided was largely destroyed by the thunderstorm that struck that afternoon. "Probably washed away everything, did a great deal of damage," George Wellington recalled.

Along with the more obvious clues—the bloody door knob, blood stains on the door and porch, the items with which Dean's body was bound—searchers found a few items that may or may not have been significant, including the tortoiseshell hairpin found near the cistern.

To County Solicitor Roy Pickard, the hairpin immediately suggested one suspect. Mary Lee Ware recalled, "On the first day Mr. Pickard had asked us to see if Mrs. Dean had any big colored hairpins, that a woman's hairpin had been found near the well." The implication was clear; if Mrs. Dean had a matching hairpin, that placed her at the cistern where her husband's body was found.

Detective William de Kerlor also believed that the hairpin was a significant piece of evidence. "I had, prior to this time, made up my mind that a woman had been present at the scene of the murder," he said. "You will remember that a hairpin was found near the cistern in which the body was thrown." But that woman could not have been Mrs. Dean, according to de Kerlor. "To my mind no one like Mrs. Dean could do it," he said.[18]

Another incident took place at the cistern that day. Ralph Baldwin was walking by the summer house when he saw Charles Rich kneeling next to the cistern as if he were looking for something. Baldwin approached Rich, noticed the bruises on his face, and asked, "How did you get that black eye?"

Rich looked startled, but explained that he had gone to the barn to feed his horse the night before. "I had a basket with some pea pods in it. There was no light in the barn, the horse didn't hear me and when I touched him he kicked the basket and it hit my face."

It was another hot August day and Rich pulled the collar of his shirt to loosen it, at which point Baldwin noticed bruises and scratches on his neck. "Well," Baldwin said, half joking, "the basket might hit your eye but I can't see how it could make the bruises on your neck."

At this, Rich jumped up and doubled his fists "as though he was about to strike me," Baldwin said. Rich then turned and strode quickly away. Nothing more was said about what he might have been looking for by the cistern.

52

THE LANTERN

EARLIER THAT DAY, ACTING POLICE CHIEF PERLEY ENOS HAD ASKED Mrs. Dean where her husband's lantern was.

"Lantern? Lantern?" Mrs. Dean asked, confused. "What is that?"

"What he goes with in the night time," Enos replied.

"Oh, this is what you mean," she said, and took him to a hallway where she had put the lantern after retrieving it from the barn.

Later, according to Lana Rich, when she and her husband arrived at the farm, Mrs. Dean brought them the lantern they had lent Mr. Dean the evening before. "Here's the lantern that Mr. Rich let Billy take last night," Lana Rich reported Mary Dean as saying. "Now, remember to take this home."

No one else heard this conversation, which credits Mrs. Dean with a fair degree of clarity given her mental state. Earlier, Mrs. Dean couldn't even remember what a lantern was. But when it came to the Riches' lantern, according to Mrs. Rich, she knew what it was, whose it was, and how and when it came to be in her house.

Mrs. Rich testified that she took the lantern from Mrs. Dean and put it on a table on the Deans' back porch, but forgot to take it when she went home. It was not until the next day that her sister, Georgiana Hodgkins, brought the lantern home, according to Mrs. Rich and Hodgkins.

However, this story conflicts with Charles Rich's testimony about how he got his lantern back. At the grand jury, Attorney General Young asked Rich, "Did you ever get it back?"

"I brought it back," Rich replied, then seemed to correct himself. "Mr. Butler—I don't know but that the ones who took possession of it put it in Mr. Butler's car." (Fred Butler was a local chauffeur and deliveryman.)

William de Kerlor, in the course of his investigations, asked Rich when he got his lantern back, but Rich was evasive and avoided the question. In the end, de Kerlor came to believe that the entire story of Rich lending Dean a lantern was a fabrication. "I don't think it's true," de Kerlor said. He was never able to find anyone else who saw Rich's lantern at the Dean farm or who could confirm that the Riches recovered it later.

If the Riches did not lend Mr. Dean a lantern on the evening of his murder, why invent the story? Perhaps because the buggy that left Mr. Rich's house at 10:30 that night had a lantern, which the Riches felt they needed to account for. Or if Rich's lantern was found at the scene of the murder, perhaps the story was intended to explain how it got there.

Unfortunately, none of the investigators apart from de Kerlor seems to have cared enough about Rich's lantern to have looked into it more closely. At the grand jury, de Kerlor challenged Attorney General Oscar Young on the matter of Rich's lantern. "At any rate, if Rich did get that lantern back the day after the murder," de Kerlor said, "I think it was the business on the part of the officers who were looking after the goods of the murdered man to know Rich got that lantern back. It was a gross piece of inefficiency because the goods of the murdered man's should never be touched."

Young tried to argue that Rich had every right to retrieve his own lantern. "It was Rich's lantern, it wasn't the goods of the murdered man, was it?"

"If it were Rich's lantern, it was something that Rich should not have handled," de Kerlor countered. "Rich should not have handled anything that the murdered man had handled."

"You understand, really," Young said, "that any property of your own that happened to be in the—"

"I understand, for the purpose of safeguarding, nothing that applies to the murder case should be handled by anybody outside of that case," de Kerlor said, demonstrating that despite his occasionally questionable methods and conclusions, he could be dead right at times.

53

THE EVENING VISIT

THAT AFTERNOON, THE SEVERE THUNDERSTORM DREW A HALT TO FUR-ther investigations at the Dean farm. Nurses came to care for Mrs. Dean while men stood watch at both houses in case the murderer should return.

In the evening, Sheriff Emerson drove to Greenville to see what the Colfelts might know about Dean's death. He was accompanied by Ralph Davis, the young man who had helped move the Colfelts' belongings to Greenville.

To conceal the real reason for their visit, Emerson drained water from his car's radiator and sent Davis to the house under the pretext of needing water to refill it. Margaret Colfelt recognized Davis, gave him some water, and followed him out to speak to Emerson, leaving her guests—the Potters and her daughter's friends—in the house.

"She was very nervous," recalled Emerson, who did not identify himself to Margaret, but asked where her husband was.[19]

"He's away," she replied.

"Has he gone over to the other side?"

"I hope not," she said, and explained that her husband had "gone to work for the government." She told Emerson he had been gone for "a month or six weeks." In fact, he had been gone for only a few days.

Emerson and Davis left her and drove the car down to the barn, hoping to speak to the coachman, Malcolm Carlson. They asked where Colfelt's car was, and Carlson said Colfelt had taken it when he left. The men had not spoken long when Margaret came from the house, trailed by her guest Harold Potter, whom she had asked to come along, perhaps because he was the only man in the house. As she recalled, Potter did not take the matter seriously. "They're probably young men, heard you have a lot of pretty girls here and they came over to see them," he said.

Margaret stormed up to Emerson, insisting on knowing why he and Davis had stopped at the barn and what they wanted. At this, Carlson fell silent, and Emerson realized he would learn nothing more that night, so he and Davis left. According to Margaret Colfelt, she had no idea at the time that Emerson was investigating the murder of William Dean.

54

THE DEPARTURE

THE NEXT MORNING, AUGUST 15, WALTER EMERSON SENT THREE MEN to watch the Colfelt house and see who came and went. The watchers saw the Potters being chauffeured to the Greenville station with their bags and followed them there.

At the station, the Potters were seen by station agent O'Brien, who had seen them arriving two days earlier. "Thursday morning the next morning after the murder, the man and woman were at the station in Greenville again," O'Brien testified. "The man was anxious to get a morning paper and I said we don't have them here, you will get them in Ayer."

The brakeman Hugh Churchill also saw the Potters, and remembered that they did not sit together, either when they travelled to Greenville or when they left. "I thought it was rather funny they did not talk with one another, when they left together and returned from Colfelts together," Churchill said. "I remember that."

Later, federal agents investigated the Potters, suspicious that they might not be who Margaret Colfelt said they were. Agents spoke with Robert Potter, brother to Mrs. Ethel Potter. (Ethel's husband, like William Dean, had married his first cousin.) Robert Potter described his sister as "medium height, about 5 feet, 5 inches, and is very slight in build. Howard M. Potter is about 5 feet, 9 inches in height."

But Robert O'Brien described the couple he had seen at the Greenville station as follows: "Woman: about 5 ft. 10 in., very powerful and very masculine; might be a man, dressed as a woman. Man: Short and stout, and looked like a foreigner."

The idea that a man might be disguised as a woman to escape detection might seemed far-fetched, but at least one German spy is known to have used just such a cover to enter the country and carry out sabotage operations.

Unfortunately, federal agents appear to have confused the Potters with another couple that O'Brien saw passing through the Greenville station at the same time: a short foreign-looking man and a tall, blonde woman. According to O'Brien, "She was a dolled up old bird between 45 and 50, powdered up and sprayed and all that kind of stuff . . . a hell of a big woman."

She was, in fact, Maud von Lilienthal, "a tall, masculine-looking woman with a blonde wig," according to Agent Feri Weiss. Her companion was Carl Behr, a musician and conductor who had done work at the Plymouth Theatre in New York. They were an unlikely pair to have been brought in as assassins to dispense with Mr. Dean.

As were the Potters. Howard Nott Potter was a well-known and highly respected architect who had designed churches and homes for a number of wealthy clients. The Potters were prominent members of New York society and were members of Mrs. Astor's 400, the list of everyone who was anyone in society at the time. Mr. Potter had built a house for Lawrence Colfelt in Harrison, New York, where the Potters also owned a home.

In all likelihood, the presence of the Potters at the Colfelt home at the time of William Dean's murder was coincidence and nothing more. Hugh Churchill, the brakeman at the Greenville station, was undoubtedly right when he responded to Robert O'Brien's suspicions with, "they had more of a refined look than to be mixed in a thing like that."

55

THE FIRST REPORTER

By Thursday, word of Dean's murder had gotten out and curious spectators flocked to the scene. According to one eyewitness as many as 150 people were at the Dean farm that afternoon. A.J. Daniels, a freelance stringer for the *Boston American*, arrived on the scene and began taking pictures of the Dean bungalow until, as he reported, "a women who declined to give her name appeared to be in charge and angrily refused to allow any pictures of the building to be taken."

The woman was Mrs. Rich, and she ordered Daniels to leave the premises. "Although she wished to interfere with me, nothing was done to a crowd of spectators who roved wherever they wished," the reporter noted.

He ignored Mrs. Rich and drove up to the summer house, where he was confronted by an unnamed official in overalls and hip boots, who demanded to know his business. Daniels explained that he was a reporter and the man told him to speak to County Solicitor Pickard.

Pickard gloomily informed Daniels that nothing in the way of a clue had been found, aside from some blood on the barn doorknob. He gave the reporter permission to take pictures of the summer house and cistern, but as he did Lana Rich rushed up from the bungalow, out of breath and still incensed. She demanded that Daniels stop taking pictures, arguing that they would hurt Mrs. Dean's feelings. Pickard acquiesced to Mrs. Rich's demands and told Daniels to refrain. Daniels readily complied; he had already used all the film in his camera anyway.

Daniels recalled that curiosity seekers roamed freely, snooping around and handling evidence, including the bloody doorknob. None of the officials present tried to prevent onlookers from disturbing the murder scene or touching potential evidence; forensic science at the time was in its infancy and the concept of a "crime scene" as we understand it today—taped off, with latex-gloved investigators bagging evidence—was unknown. Still, the handling of the investigation seems slipshod even for the times, perhaps because those searching for clues were at best amateurs. According to Daniels, the man leading the search would scan the ground in front of him and, upon spotting a stone or a small stick, gently pick it up, examine its underside closely, and carry it to a small pile of evidence he had already accumulated. "The other constables were engaged in a like manner, but the leader had by long odds the biggest pile of evidence," Daniels stated drily.

At around 10 a.m., Russel Henchman arrived to take away the Deans' cow and young bull. Henchman milked the cow and then helped Will Cleaves load the animals into a truck for transporting to Mary Lee Ware's farm in Rindge. That done, Henchman swept the floor of the barn, in all likelihood destroying any evidence like bloodstains that might have been there.

Later, federal agent Valkenburgh challenged Henchman about cleaning up the barn. "Who asked you to go there to do that?"

"No one," Henchman replied, insisting that it had been entirely on his own initiative.[20]

In fact, there was no one there to stop him. The selectmen and the country authorities had not yet arrived that morning, and Sheriff Emerson was engaged elsewhere on the farm. The only person who might have questioned Henchman was police officer Lemire, who had spent the night guarding the big house and came down to the barn when he saw Henchman arrive. Lemire spent only 10 minutes at the barn, but he was there long enough to see blood spots on the floor, "within 8 or 10 inches from the door," he said. Later, when asked if he spoke to Henchman about the blood on the floor, Lemire said, "Yes, he and I were looking at it." Nevertheless, when Henchman started sweeping the floor, Lemire saw no reason to object, and returned to his post at the big house.[21]

Henchman would later claim that he merely swept up some manure that the bull had left in front of the door. It didn't occur to him, he said, that it might be improper to clean up a crime scene until the proper authorities had given the OK.

After finishing at the barn, Henchmen went to the summer house, where he turned off the water and drained the pipes, another action that came in for criticism. As Agent Valkenburgh demanded of him, "Who ordered you to go to the house where Colfelt lived, where possibly the murderers of this deed had gone in and washed their hands and possibly left some trace of blood in the kitchen or somewhere, who ordered you to draw the water off those pipes and out of the tank?"

Henchman explained that he had shut the water off to prevent the pipes from freezing. And later, at the slander trial, Rich's attorney Orville Cain waxed facetious about the objections to Henchman draining the water pipes. "You didn't think the murderer was concealed in the pipe, I suppose?" he asked Henchman. "And therefore it didn't occur to you to keep him there by not letting the water out?"

But as Alice Humiston said, "Do you suppose anyone in his right mind could have any such idea in his head as that pipes would freeze in that terrible hot spell we had last August?"

56

THE SEARCH FOR CLUES

WHILE RUSSEL HENCHMAN WAS ABOUT HIS CHORES IN THE BARN AND at the summer house, Mary Lee Ware kept company with Mary Dean, who was fitfully going through old letters and papers, intending to burn them. Ware became concerned that in her confusion, Mary might burn something valuable, so she alerted the selectmen and asked them to send someone to supervise Mrs. Dean.

They decided to send Peter Hogan, as the one who knew Mrs. Dean best. Hogan found her at her desk, which he described as "packed full of letters."

She told Hogan, "I want to get rid of all this old stuff."

Hogan had heard about the threatening letter Mr. Dean received and worried that this important clue might be in the papers she intended to burn. He told her, "I have a place for burning up this old rubbish and I'll carry them down when I go down to the village and burn them all up for you and save you the bother."

Mrs. Dean agreed and Hogan helped her box up the letters, a process that took a couple of hours. As they worked, Georgiana Hodgkins kept a close watch on them the entire time, which struck Hogan as strange.

When the papers were boxed up, Hogan took them to the summer house, where he and Ware went through the letters. They hoped to find the threatening note, but they did not.

Later, the letters came into the possession of Lewis Davis, Mrs. Dean's guardian and executor of the Dean estate. When William de Kerlor and Frederick Dean first visited the farm, they came upon Davis going through Dean's papers and de Kerlor asked him if he had found the threatening letter. "I question your authority," Davis snapped, leading de Kerlor to suspect that Davis might have stolen the letter, though this seems unlikely. There was ample opportunity for others to come across the letter before he did, especially those who were with Mrs. Dean in the bungalow. Federal agents suggested that Mrs. Dean might have inadvertently burned the letter before Ware and Hogan were able to intervene. But when they questioned Mrs. Dean about the letter she said, "I never heard or saw a letter that threatened to do him any harm. If there were such a letter," she added, "he didn't show it to me, or speak about it."

While Mary Lee Ware wasn't able to find the threatening letter, she did find something else at the summer house. "I was up in the house which had been occupied by the Colfelts and I was looking around to see if I could see anything, any trace of anything," she said. In the Colfelts' bedroom, she saw a hairpin lying in the middle of the bedspread. Recalling the hairpin that had been found by the cistern the day before, she alerted Sheriff Emerson, who took the hairpin to Roy Pickard, who confirmed that the hairpins matched.

The evidence suggests that the hairpin found at the cistern did not belong to Mrs. Dean, but to another woman who would have had more occasion to be around the cistern by the summer house: Margaret Colfelt.[22]

That afternoon, Margaret Colfelt drove to Peterborough with Natalye and her friends, intending to play golf at the Peterborough Golf Club. At this point, she still did not know about Dean's murder, she stated. She stopped to borrow some golf clubs at the real estate office of her friend Mrs. D.M. White.

"Did you hear of the thing that happened to Mr. Dean?" White asked, and proceeded to give Margaret the news.

Margaret hurried to the golf club, dropped the girls off, and immediately drove to the Dean farm. As she did, she was followed by George Wellington, who had shadowed her from Greenville to Peterborough and then to the Dean farm.

Mary Lee Ware was at the summer house when Margaret Colfelt arrived to see Mrs. Dean. Ware alerted Sheriff Emerson, who spoke with

Margaret Colfelt and noticed that she "showed symptoms of nervousness in her voice," according to Mary Lee Ware.

Margaret spent only a few minutes with Mrs. Dean and went off in such a rush that she left behind a fur boa, a silk scarf, and some packages. She did, however, give Mrs. Rich a ride home, then returned to Peterborough to pick up the girls. She never returned for her belongings; Lana Rich retrieved them later and delivered them to her.

57

THE CIGARETTE CASES

THE INVESTIGATORS WERE SEARCHING FOR THE MILK PAIL AND THE weapon that had been used to bludgeon Mr. Dean. On a hunch, County Solicitor Pickard instructed Sheriff Emerson to drain the wells and the cistern on the Dean to see if they might be there.

Emerson was assisted in the pumping operation by Frank Patterson and George Baldwin, who had worked for him before. They pumped the cistern until only a foot or two of water remained. There, shining at the bottom of the cistern, they found a silver cigarette case. Patterson handed the case up to Emerson, who put it in the sun beside the cistern to dry out. It lay there for perhaps a half hour before Emerson put it in his pocket to hold as evidence.

A number of witnesses saw the cigarette case and described it as a thin, flat case with square edges that opened like a book. There were no obvious decorations on it.

"It was flat and square, about four by three inches," Walter Lindsay said. "It was made of German silver and was marked 'Made in Germany' on the outside." Lindsay's description was confirmed by Edward Boynton, Joseph Lemire, and Charlie Stratton, the man who first climbed down into the cistern when Dean's body was found.

Later that afternoon, Oscar Dillon met Sheriff Emerson near the Catholic parsonage in town. Dillon asked if they had pumped the cistern and found anything, and Emerson showed him the cigarette case. "It was an old silver cigarette case about three and a half by two and a half inches, to the best of my recollection, and not much thicker than a cigarette,"

Dillon said. "It had square edges. There were some cigarettes in it which had been wet and were pulverized." Later, Emerson would deny showing Dillon the case. But when pressed specifically about whether he showed it to Dillon near the Catholic church, he replied, "I wouldn't say any one way or the other."

Now there were two cigarette cases in circulation: the one found in Dean's pocket, and the one pulled from the cistern.

That evening, yet another cigarette case was found, this one in the Dean bungalow. Marie Hiller, who had returned to the house with Elizabeth Bryant, said, "I saw a silver cigarette case on the kitchen table, which Mrs. Dean claimed she never saw before. Then someone said it was found in the cistern after the water was pumped out."

Hiller described the case as being "made of silver or nickel, very thin, just room for one layer of cigarette, and had a portrait of a woman on the front side." Inside were monogrammed cigarettes that appeared to be Russian or Turkish. The cigarettes were, to all appearances, completely dry and in new condition.

The women asked the men who had been assigned to stand guard over the farm where the case came from and were mistakenly told that it had been found in the cistern. "Well, that's funny," Bryant replied, noting the store-bought cigarettes in it. "Mr. Dean made his own cigarettes."

The next morning, Bryant asked Mrs. Dean who had left the case on the table and if it was anything that belonged her husband.

"No," Mrs. Dean said. "You may have it if you wish."

A short while later, George Wellington came to the bungalow and asked what had been found in the cistern. "We found a cigarette case," Mrs. Bryant said. She produced the case and handed it to Wellington, who took it to hold as evidence. At some point, the case—which had never been near the cistern—was labelled as "taken from the well," though by whom is unknown.

Later, Wellington showed the case to Charles Rich, who explained that the case with the woman's portrait was actually a chocolate candy cigarette holder and that he "had one just like it at home." Mr. Dean had received several of the candy cases as a gift and had passed them along to friends, including Charles Rich. "It wasn't very good," Rich said. "I've had mine seven years and there's still some candy in it."[23]

Now there were three cigarette cases to keep track of: the initialed snuff box found on Dean's body, the book-style cigarette case recovered from the bottom of the cistern, and the portrait candy case discovered in the bungalow.

According to Walter Emerson, he took the cigarette case found in the cistern to Mrs. Preston's boarding house in Jaffrey where he was staying. Frieda Preston recalled that Emerson left a case on a shelf in the kitchen, despite the fact that it was clearly an important piece of evidence. "It was nothing but an old-fashioned snuff box, with some initials on it," she said. Inside were wet papers and loose tobacco, the kind used to roll one's own cigarettes. Despite Emerson's claim that it had been found in the cistern, this was clearly Mr. Dean's case, the one given to him by his uncle and which others had seen taken from his pocket.

At some point, Mrs. Preston decided the case was not safe on the shelf, "as so many people were coming in here, and I was afraid they might pick it up." She put the case in the pocket of her dress and kept it there for a couple of days before returning it to Sheriff Emerson. "I never asked him where and how he got it," she said.

Emerson's handling of the case continued to be remarkably lax. Upon retrieving it from Mrs. Preston, he loaned it to William de Kerlor, who kept the case for two or more weeks before returning it. From this time forward, Sheriff Emerson would refer to the initialed case as the one found in the bottom of the cistern. He would deny knowing anything about a cigarette case found in Mr. Dean's pocket.

Meanwhile, the portrait/candy case—still marked "taken from the well" passed from the hands of George Wellington to Sheriff Lord at the Keene jail for safekeeping. Agent Valkenburgh went to Keene and was given permission to photograph the case.

According to Valkenburgh, "I took it out and put it on the mudguard of Oscar Dillon's car, who had taken me to the County, and as I was photographing this box, front and side view and open, he asked me what I was photographing that box for." Valkenburgh identified the case as the cigarette box found in the cistern after the water had been pumped out.

"Like hell," Dillon replied. He argued that the case on the mud-guard—with a woman's portrait on it—didn't look anything like the ini-tialed snuff box that Chief Nute had showed him, or the square cigarette case that Sheriff Emerson showed him.

Based on Dillon's comments, Valkenburgh began to question the handling of the various cigarette cases, which in turn led County Solici-tor Pickard to address the matter. Pickard instructed Sheriff Emerson to obtain affidavits from the men who had pumped the cistern regarding the cigarette case they had found in it.

Emerson took the initialed case to Parker's store in Fitzwilliam, where he met Frank Patterson and George Baldwin, his helpers at the cistern. Francis Parker, owner of the store, was also a justice of the peace and prepared the affidavit: "Then personally appeared Frank Patterson and George A. Baldwin, under oath before me, with the box attached to this affidavit as the same identical box which they removed from the bottom of the cistern at the Dean homestead in the town of Jaffrey, N.H. Francis R. Parker, Justice of the Peace."

Later, both Patterson and Baldwin testified that the initials on the case were "W.K.D." In fact, the initials on Mr. Dean's snuff box were "H.W.D.," which suggests that they had similarly faulty memories or that they had been coached to say the initials were those of Mr. Dean.

Emerson then gave the initialed case and the portrait case to Sheriff Lord in Keene for safekeeping before the grand jury. Both cases were dis-played at the grand jury, where several witnesses identified the initialed case as belonging to Mr. Dean. Sheriff Emerson declared it to be the case found at the bottom of the cistern and presented the affidavit signed by Patterson and Baldwin. "This is the one statement by the Justice of the Peace that I had those two men make before the Justice of the Peace, in that solemn setting, that's the box they found in the well." The solemn setting he referred to was Frank Parker's general store.

Emerson gave no explanation as to why an affidavit was presented at the grand jury rather than having the two men appear in person to identify such an important piece of evidence. "Just what was the reason, I don't recall now," he said.

At the grand jury, Emerson's testimony about the cigarette case concluded with Attorney General Oscar Young asking, "Well, I guess there's no dispute about the box, is there?"

"No," Emerson responded. "I guess not."

But there was.

Edward Boynton, when shown the two cases at the grand jury, stated repeatedly that neither of them, the initialed case nor the portrait case, was the one he saw removed from the bottom of the cistern.

"Neither one of these is the case that came out of the well?" Attorney General Young asked.

"I would say not."

Young held up the initialed case. "Is this the case?"

"No, sir," Boynton replied.

"That isn't the case that came out of the well?"

"No, sir, it isn't."

Young then showed Boynton the portrait case. "Is that the case that came out of the well?"

"No, sir, I would say not."

"Neither one of these is the case that came out of the well?"

"I would say not."

"Will you describe the one which did come out of the well?" Young asked.

"I think the one that came out of the well was a larger case than those. It opened in the same way that those open. I think it was, instead of round corners, it was square."

"Have you ever seen it since?"

"No, sir."

"Do you know who took it away that day?"

"Only from hearsay."

"Who did you understand took it away?"

"I understood Mr. Emerson took it away."

In response, Sheriff Emerson denied that he ever had in his possession any other cigarette box than the two presented at the grand jury and the slander trial.

At this point, trying to determine what happened to the cigarette case found in the cistern is like following the pea in a shell game. The situation was summed up by attorney Robert C. Murchie. "The evidence indicates that there was found in Dr. Dean's pocket an old cigarette case that he had used, and in the cistern, another cigarette case of a design peculiar enough to be remembered by those who saw it and which was carried away by the authorities."

It was clear, Murchie said, that at some point the case from the cistern had been swapped for Dean's case. "If the cigarette case was exchanged, that fact itself is evidence that someone was interested in having the original case disappear, and if that is so, it must be that the cigarette case would have furnished an important piece of evidence against the real perpetrators of the crime."

As it happens, the grand jury transcript contains mention of one more cigarette case, one that Mr. Dean had given to Mr. Rich 25 years earlier. According to Agent Valkenburgh, "I interviewed a party in Manchester who had been employed in the Rich family at the time and remembers the incident of Mr. Dean presenting Mr. Rich with a cigarette case." This was not the candy cigarette case that Dean gave Rich later. "No, nothing like that," the witness told Valkenburgh. "I'm talking about a cigarette case." It was, according to Valkenburgh, a plain cigarette case of German silver, matching the description of the case found in the bottom of the cistern, which disappeared and has never been seen since.

58

THE BANKER

IN THE DAYS FOLLOWING MR. DEAN'S MURDER, TOWNSPEOPLE BEGAN TO notice that Charles Rich's behavior seemed odd, even erratic.

Alvin Parker owned a small grocery in East Jaffrey. "On the morning following the finding of Mr. Dean's body, Mr. Rich came into my place," Parker said. "I said good morning and he didn't answer. He told me what he wanted and went out of the store." According to Parker, Rich seemed as if he had been under a strain. "He looked as though he hadn't rested very well. He looked like a man who had been on a journey."

Louis Cournoyer also thought that Rich seemed to be absent-minded and preoccupied. Two days after the murder, Cournoyer went to the bank. "I had a check for $128 to cash and I wanted the money," he said. "Rich took the money and put it in a drawer, then he put it back on the counter and, to make a long story short, he changed the money six times from one place to another and then asked me if he had given the money to me."

That same day, Mabel Enslin saw Rich's wife at the bank. "Mrs. Rich was very nervous," Enslin said. "She was typewriting—she had to move her lips to keep track of what she was writing, she would watch me and when she thought I was not looking she lost control of herself."

As time went on, locals were also puzzled that Rich showed so little interest in finding the murderer, especially given his friendship with Mr. Dean. Frieda Preston noted, "The only thing that ever looked suspicious to me was that Mr. Rich has always been a citizen of this town, and he went after everything with a great deal of vim, but when this murder came about, he seemed to have no interest in it, to hold back."

Edward Boynton also wondered about Rich's attitude. "I was surprised of the little interest Mr. Rich took in trying to discover the murder of his intimate friend," Boynton said. "This was not in keeping with his conduct on other occasions."

Even those who supported Rich, like Dr. E. Channing Stowell, found it troubling that he didn't try harder to clear up the mystery. "That is the way a normal man reacts," Stowell said.

Then there was Rich's black eye.

On the morning of Thursday, August 14, town barber Silas Christian was in his shop when Charles Rich came in. "He got into my chair and I saw that his left eye was blackened," Christian said. "I asked him how the other fellow looked."

Rich did not reply, and Christian asked him how it happened. "He told me that he went out to the barn and that he did not snap the light on, and he had a board in his hand," Christian recalled. "Then he said he stooped down, and the horse kicked him in the stomach and the board flew up and struck him in the eye."

Christian was doubtful but said nothing. "It looked to me as though Mr. Rich's eye had been struck by the blow of a man's fist."[24]

Later that morning, when Charles Rich came to William Leighton's undertaking parlor, Leighton noticed immediately that he had a black eye. "I saw he had a pretty bad looking eye on him, and I asked him how the other fellow looked," Leighton said. (Jaffrey residents were droll, if not very original.)

"I haven't seen him this morning," Rich replied.

"No joking, how did you do that? It looks pretty bad."

"Well, I really can't tell you, Bill," Rich said, and went on to explain, "I was smoking and I went in behind my horse and some way or other he struck out with his foot and broke my pipe and caused my eye to be swollen like that."

At about noon that day, when Rich arrived at the Dean farm, both Arthur Smith and Martin Garfield took note of the black eye. "I noticed that he had an awful black eye, an awful crack under the left eye that extended to the cheek," Garfield said. He said to Rich, "Well, Mr. Rich, you got a mighty good crack in the eye some way."

"Well, I got it in a very simple way," Rich replied, but he did not elaborate.

A few hours later, by the cistern, Rich told Ralph Baldwin that his horse had kicked a basket of pea pods he was carrying, and the basket hit him in the eye.

At other times, as Rich told the story, it was his pipe that hit his eye. According to his neighbor Mary Hutchinson, "he wasn't quite sure exactly how it did happen, but his impression was that when he went in his barn that the horse kicked and he had his pipe in his mouth and he thought the blow of the pipe struck his cheek."[25]

Rich repeated some version of the pipe story to a number of people, including Lewis Davis, who testified that Rich told him the horse "didn't strike him with her foot but her rump did strike his pipe, which broke the stem and it hit him in the eye."

Federal agents also got conflicting reports about Rich's injury. Agent Valkenburgh reported, "According to report of Agent Leighton of the Concord Office of this Bureau, Rich stated to him that he was entering the stall of his horse, who became startled and kicked at him, hitting a broom which he had in his hand and in such a manner that the handle bruised his face," On another occasion, Rich told agents he was carrying a box of pea pods and "the hurt came from having the box hit my face."

Regardless of exactly how it happened, a number of townspeople doubted that Rich's injury came being kicked by a horse. "I looked at his face and there was a doubt in my mind whether a horse did it," Iveretta Bingham said, and her mother, Katherine Kidder, added, "I suppose if a horse kicked him he would know."

Louis Cournoyer said, "I tried to find out how this thing had happened and I received from different people who questioned Mr. Rich different answers as to the manner in which he got his black eye. At last it seems that he could not tell how it happened and we thought that this was rather peculiar."

In all, federal agents counted six different stories that Rich gave regarding his black eye. "The mere fact that a man has an injured face on the day after a murder would not, of itself, be of much significance," Norman L. Gifford noted. "But when the man finds it necessary to lie about that injury, both as to how it happened and when it happened, grave suspicion justly attaches to him."

One other witness to Rich's black eye is worth noting. On the Friday after the murder, Ed Baldwin—who took care of Rich's horse for him—attended a meeting of the Odd Fellows lodge where he and Rich were members. Some men were talking about Rich being kicked by his horse and Baldwin was overheard to say, "Oh, hell, that horse never kicked anybody. Perhaps Mr. Rich can tell you how he got that black eye, but I cannot."

Baldwin would later deny ever making such a statement, though it is possible he had a good reason to do so.

59

THE HORSE AND THE BARN

According to Charles Rich, his horse kicked him shortly before Mr. Dean arrived at his home on August 13, around 9 p.m. or a little after.

At just about that time the night watchman at the Bean & Symonds factory, named Albany Pelletier, was beginning his hourly rounds. There were seven stations on his route, each with a distinct key attached to a post. The keys fit into the timekeeping device that Pelletier carried, recording precisely when and where he was at any given time.

At 9 p.m., Pelletier saw Ed Baldwin drive up with a horse and buggy to get some sawdust, which he had done many times before. The Bean & Symonds company gave away the sawdust, a byproduct of manufacturing matches and boxes, and Baldwin used it as bedding for the horse.

Pelletier knew Baldwin, who worked at Bean & Symonds during the day. He also knew that the horse and buggy belonged to Charles Rich.

"Hello, Pelkey," Baldwin said, referring to Pelletier by his nickname.

"Hello, Ed Baldwin," Pelletier replied. "Why don't you get the sawdust before six o'clock?"—kidding him because the factory was officially closed after 6.

Baldwin laughed and said he thought he could come any time and get sawdust. He filled five or six bags and loaded them on the wagon while Pelletier continued his rounds, a process that usually took 10 or 15 minutes. "I did not hurry that night because it was very hot," Pelletier recalled. By the time he finished, at about 9:15, Baldwin was driving out of the yard. Given the usual speed of a horse and buggy, Baldwin would

247

have arrived at Charles Rich's home no earlier than 9:25 to 9:30 p.m. that evening.

Ed Baldwin told a different story about the sawdust errand. According to Baldwin, he had left Rich's barn with the horse at about 6:30 that evening. He drove to Bean & Symonds, picked up one bag of sawdust, and dropped it off at Rich's barn. He then drove to Peter Hogan's house to pick up a woman who was visiting there and rode with her to see the garden of D.D. Bean, about halfway to Jaffrey Center. He returned to Hogan's house, dropped the woman off, and arrived back at Rich's barn between 7:30 and 8 o'clock.

At the grand jury, Baldwin was asked what he would say if someone reported that he had actually been at the factory an hour later than that. "I wouldn't care to say very plainly just what I think of it," Baldwin replied, and denied being there at the time Pelletier said he was.

Albany Pelletier also appeared at the grand jury, and County Solicitor Pickard questioned him at length about his account of Baldwin's trip to pick up sawdust.

PICKARD: How did you happen to notice it was nine o'clock?
PELLETIER: Because I had to know to start such a time, I had to get to my post. I carry my clock with me all the time, and I had to go every hour, and I always had the time from the clock I was carrying, you see.
PICKARD: How do you know it wasn't eight o'clock or ten o'clock?
PELLETIER: Well, I suppose I could tell. Don't you suppose a man could tell?

Pelletier tried to explain to Pickard why he could be so certain about the time. The entire system was designed to prove that he made his rounds on a regular schedule, stopping at each station, once every hour through the night. The average person, when asked when something had happened, might guess at the time, but Pelletier knew exactly. It was part of his job.[26]

The only other person who could confirm the time would have been Charles Rich. Rich did not remember whether Baldwin had taken his horse out that evening, though he acknowledged that it might have been possible, given that Baldwin often took the horse out after supper. Had he seen Baldwin at all that evening? "I can't be positive about that," he testified.

Baldwin, on the other hand, stated that he saw Rich when he picked up the horse and buggy at about 6:30. "I'm positive that I saw Mr. Rich on the doorstep that night," he said. He remembered telling Rich he was going to get sawdust and Rich asking if he needed any help.

According to Baldwin, after returning the horse and buggy he went home and was in bed at the time Pelletier claimed to have seen him at the match factory. Baldwin admitted that it was an early bedtime, but explained, "I am out early in the morning." According to Baldwin, he did not leave his house again that night.

The woman that Baldwin took for a buggy ride that evening was Elsie Crabe. Crabe had been visiting her mother—a tenant at Peter Hogan's house—when Baldwin stopped by and offered to take her and her little girl for a ride. The time was about 7:10, Crabe said, and when Baldwin dropped them off at the end of the ride, "It was close to eight o'clock."

But Crabe's mother, Marie Long, had a conversation with a neighbor the day after night watchman Pelletier's testimony appeared in the newspaper. "Oh dear, they have found that out," Mrs. Long said. She told the neighbor that Rich's horse was not in the barn all that evening. In fact, the horse and buggy had been standing outside her home at the time Mr. Dean drove home at 9:30.

The neighbor asked why she had not reported such an important piece of evidence and Long replied that "she did not want to get her family mixed into the affair," according to the neighbor. "She said she had been shaking in her shoes for fear they would find out the rest of it, that someone was riding in that team all that evening."

It seems clear now that Charles Rich's horse was not in the barn at the time he said it kicked him. It was at the Bean & Symonds factory, and then it was in front of Peter Hogan's house, a short distance from Rich's barn—which means he must have gotten his black eye some other way.

60

THE ACCUSATIONS

IN THE DAYS FOLLOWING THE MURDER, IT SEEMED CLEAR TO MOST PEO-
ple that Mrs. Dean was simply not capable of committing the murder,
let alone disposing of the body in the cistern. Nevertheless, rumors circulated that Mrs. Dean was the murderer, all of which seemed to originate
from one source.

On the very first day after the murder, according to Elizabeth Bryant,
Lana Rich said, "Mrs. Dean must have done it."

Later that day, Mary Lee Ware came to the farm and spoke with
Lana Rich and her sister, Georgiana Hodgkins. As they discussed the
events of the day, Mrs. Rich said, "Has it occurred to you, Miss Ware,
Mrs. Dean might have actually committed this act herself in a fit of
insanity?"

"No, not for an instant, Mrs. Rich, it doesn't occur to me for a
moment," Ware replied, shocked that she should even suggest such a
thing. "I was quite struck with the fact that Mrs. Rich showed very little
sympathy, she was as hard as she could be about it," Ware said, "and I
felt afterwards that she hadn't shown the tenderness and gentleness you
would to a woman under such circumstances, and she and Mr. Rich had
been the oldest friends and I would have said the best friends of Mrs.
Dean."

The following day, Margaret Robinson had a similar encounter with
Charles Rich at the Monadnock National Bank. Knowing that Mr. Rich
and Mr. Dean had been good friends, she stopped by and asked if he

could tell her anything about the murder. Rich made some comment that indicated his suspicions were of Mrs. Dean.

"Why, Mr. Rich," she told him, "do you mean to say you think she could have done it?"

"Well, I wouldn't like to be in her place," he replied in, what seemed to Robinson "a very pitiless way."[27] She did not, at the time, think that Rich had any connection to the case. "But what I remember very definitely is that the first suggestion I had of Mrs. Dean having done it was from Mr. Rich."

Imogene Mead, a neighbor and friend to Mrs. Rich, was interviewed by federal agents and told them, "You know after the murder there were rumors current and some of those were spread by the Riches that Mrs. Dean perhaps was the one who had done it. Not for a minute did I believe it and I don't want anyone to think so, but she—Mrs. Rich and her sister—made quite a sad story about it."

Jaffrey shopkeeper Charles Deschenes told federal agents that "certain women in East Jaffrey, would like to have it known and are continually spreading rumor, that Mrs. Dean committed the murder under a fit of insanity." Deschenes did not identify the women, though he most likely meant Lana Rich and Georgiana Hodgkins, who lived nearby.

According to William de Kerlor, Rich himself told Frederick Dean once or twice that he thought Mrs. Dean did it. And Daniel C. Mulloney, a bank examiner called in to go over the bank's books, said Rich told him Mrs. Dean didn't seem sorry to think that her husband was dead. "On the contrary, she seemed to be kind of satisfied that her husband was gone," Rich had said, and insinuated that Mrs. Dean wanted to get the estate for herself.

Even Rich's business associates linked the rumors of Mrs. Dean's guilt to Rich and his family. Federal agents asked Merrill Symonds where the rumors of Mrs. Dean's guilt originated and Symonds said, "I think some of it came from the Riches. They were very strongly inclined to think that she might have done it."

Rumors of Mrs. Dean's guilt also appear to have been spread by those connected to the Riches. On his very first day of investigation in East Jaffrey, Agent Robert Valkenburgh went to Hamill's garage, a place near the depot where locals were known to gather. He did not tell anyone who he was nor what he was up to, hoping to eavesdrop on their conversation about the murder.

The strategy paid off. Almost immediately, Valkenburgh overheard a conversation about Mrs. Dean and the murder. "Wasn't it a damn shame that she would do a thing like that?" one man said.

"Who?" someone else asked.

"Why, Mrs. Dean. Would you think she would commit a murder of that kind?"

The man made several such comments, and Valkenburgh approached Robert Hamill, the garage owner. "Who is this man always bringing out this murder story and always saying it's a damn shame Mrs. Dean did it?" he asked.

"That's Henchman, superintendent of the Water Works," Hamill replied—Russel Henchman, friend of Charles Rich. Russel Henchman, brother to Susan, who owned the car kept in Rich's garage. Russel Henchman, who had swept the barn floor the day after William Dean's body was found. Later, when interrogated at length by Agent Valkenburgh, Henchman would deny ever making any statement implicating Mrs. Dean in the murder, but Valkenburgh was positive in his identification.

Lawrence Colfelt also suggested that Mrs. Dean might have been capable of committing the crime, asserting that she was "far from feeble" and suggesting that "her strength had been greatly under-estimated by many people." At the Atlantic Shipyard where he had gone to work, Colfelt admitted to his supervisor that he was a suspect in the Dean murder case but claimed that "Dean was a feeble old man who had been shoved into a cistern by his wife who was much younger and stronger."

From the Rich family and their associates, the drumbeat of suspicion against Mrs. Dean was picked up early on by local and county officials, like Sheriff Walter Emerson. According to Martin Garfield, "Emerson came to me and asked me if Mrs. Dean had said anything to me about her husband being in deep water and I said she did not. He kept bringing that up, trying to put the words in my mouth."

Later, Garfield was questioned by George Wellington, who asked about Mrs. Dean's statements before her husband's body was found. "Didn't she say that Billy was dead?"

"She never did," Garfield insisted. Wellington returned later with reinforcements and told Garfield that if he knew anything, he had to share it with them because they were county officials. Garfield bristled. "We might as well talk turkey right here," he said. "You are hurting Mr. Rich much more by trying to say Mrs. Dean did it than by keeping your mouths shut." According to Garfield, "They looked pretty darn sober when they left here I can tell you."

Another time, George Wellington queried Arthur Smith about Mrs. Dean. "Don't you think it was her?" he asked.

"No," Smith replied. "She was too weak and feeble to drag him up from the barn to the well. That is quite a distance."

County Solicitor Pickard expressed his suspicions of Mrs. Dean in letters to the Deans' nephew, William Dean Goddard: "Mrs. Dean told Mr. Rich and others at eight or nine o'clock on the morning of Wednesday that Mr. Dean was dead and in deep water; that he was down deep where people could not see him and that he had fallen in because of a pain in his head," Pickard wrote. "As a matter of fact, Mr. Dean's body was not found until about noon on Wednesday and how she should be able to give information which later proved to be so extremely accurate is beyond my comprehension." Unfortunately, that "extremely accurate" information was stitched together from Mrs. Dean's muddled statements and later shown to be entirely false.

Pickard also told William Dean's brother, Frederick, that "probably Mrs. Dean in her deranged mind murdered her husband."

Finally, Pickard questioned Arthur Smith, the first person to arrive at the Dean farm on the day the body was found. During the conversation, according to Smith, "He said he was pretty sure Mrs. Dean did it and asked me if I didn't think so and I told him that she did not, that she couldn't do it. When I told him I thought it was Mr. Rich he said that there wasn't enough money in Cheshire County to bring Mr. Rich into it. His exact words were: 'that all the money in Cheshire County couldn't get Rich into it.'"

61

THE SANITARIUM

IT IS HARD TO RESIST THE CONCLUSION THAT RUMORS OF MRS. DEAN's guilt were spread to deflect suspicion from more obvious suspects. In many ways, Mary Dean was the perfect scapegoat for her husband's murder. She was the last person known to have seen him alive. She was among the people who knew his habits and knew the layout of the farm, including the location of the inconspicuous cistern.

Most importantly, there was a history of mental illness in her family, or so she believed. Mrs. Dean's mother and grandmother had both suffered from dementia, and Mary worried that she too would eventually lose her mind. (At the time, the difference between mental illness and dementia was not understood and often conflated in common usage.) According to her friend Miss Ware, "she had always told me she supposed she would end her life in that way."

Ironically, Mrs. Dean's illness could have eased the conscience of anyone accusing her of the murder of her husband, knowing that she would probably never be prosecuted for the crime because of her infirmity. County Solicitor Pickard confirmed as much during the argument about conducting an autopsy on Dean's body. According to Pickard, there was no use in having an autopsy, "as Mrs. Dean was the one that murdered Dean and she was crazy and could not be prosecuted."

She could, however, be put away. A week after her husband's death, Mrs. Dean was taken to a sanitarium in Worcester, a decision that may have originated with—or at the very least, met with the approval of— her brother-in-law, Frederick Dean. According to William de Kerlor, at

Frederick's first meeting with Charles Rich, he asked if the bonds from his brother's estate "would be sufficient to pay for the expenses of Mrs. Dean's transfer to Worcester in the sanitarium."

The relationship between Mary and Frederick Dean had not been good for some time according to Dr. Charles Thompson, who examined Mrs. Dean before her removal to the sanitarium. "She had not seen her husband's brother for a number of years and I was told that when he visited them she immediately left the house and remained away throughout the time that he was there visiting," Thompson said. "For some reason she heartily disliked him and would have nothing whatever, at that time, to do with him."

Mrs. Dean was taken to the sanitarium under the guise that she was just going for a ride. Elizabeth Bryant, who helped with the transfer, felt guilty about it afterward, telling federal agents, "that poor woman is not crazy, and has so much confidence in me and Miss Hiller, and it seems an awful dirty trick we played on that woman." There had been other options, according to Bryant. "They could have had two rooms here in East Jaffrey, here in the village," she said. "Mrs. Dillon offered to take her if she could get enough board out of her to get the help. Even I would have been glad to take her."

For Mary Dean, losing her husband and her home in short order was a hard blow. "Why am I here?" she asked Agent Valkenburgh when he interviewed her at the sanitarium. "Why don't they let me go home?" According to Valkenburgh, Mrs. Dean said that she "was feeling very well but sad, and that she could not sleep and was crying all night, for she loved Billy very much, and that they had been married 40 years, and above all she wanted to go home."

Sadly, the injustice heaped upon Mrs. Dean did not end, even when she was released from the sanitarium into the care of Rev. and Mrs. Enslin of East Jaffrey on October 26. A year after Mr. Dean's murder, another episode indicated that some were still trying to pin the blame on his wife.

Young Dick Eaves was working behind the counter in Duncan's drugstore when Mrs. Dean came in. "I knew Mrs. Dean well," Eaves said, noting that she seemed feeble. "She asked for poison that would kill a dog or man and she said she wanted a piece about so long, holding her hands about eight inches apart."

The request seemed suspicious to Eaves. "I asked her what she wanted the poison for and she said that a man had asked her to buy it. I asked her who the man was, and she said she didn't know, but that he would be waiting outside for her to give it to him."

Eaves rushed to the door hoping to catch a glimpse of the man, but whoever it was had disappeared.

The incident also seemed suspicious to the town's selectmen. "We concluded that it was nothing but another bit of theatrical stuff on the part of the local clique to shield the real suspects," Edward Boynton said. "We concluded that the opposition were still eager to saddle guilt on Mrs. Dean and that they figured if Mrs. Dean succeeded in getting the poison and turned it over to the stool who put her up to it, they would have something to crow over."

To demonstrate Mrs. Dean's innocence in the matter, the selectmen staged their own bit of theater. "We selected Frank Humiston to ask Mrs. Dean to buy poison for him and some of us watched the outcome," Boynton said. "She went in, and under a pre-arranged plan, the druggist sold her magnesia. We wanted to see what she would do with it. Sure enough, just as we expected, she came out and handed the little package of harmless powder to Frank Humiston and went on her way innocent of it all."

"The poison episode was very unjust," said Winifred Enslin, with whom Mrs. Dean spent the last year of her life. "Somebody tried to have her buy poison in order to renew the old suspicion and to keep alive the theory that she had homicidal tendencies, but her whole life with us was a contradiction of anything of the sort." Moreover, Mrs. Enslin said, "It was cruel to suspect her of the murder of her husband. It was worse than cruel, given that evidence pointed in another direction. The only charitable feature of it was that while they were putting her through the tests and while suspicion hung heavily over her in the minds of certain officials, but not to the majority of the townspeople, Mrs. Dean was entirely ignorant of it."

Mary Dean remained blessedly ignorant, and otherwise content in her new life, for just about one more month. She died on September 15, 1919, finally free from the lies and slander of those who saw her as a convenient solution to the Dean murder.

62

THE BUNDLES

Along with the real but mishandled evidence that might have helped solve the Dean murder mystery—the bloody doorknob, Rich's lantern, the missing cigarette case—other evidence appeared that may or may not have had anything to do with the case.

The day after William Dean's body was found, Oscar Howard was cutting brush near Contoocook Lake in Jaffrey and came upon a bundle of bloody towels wrapped in newspaper. The blood on the towels was fresh, indicating that the bundle had been placed there after the thunderstorm of the day before; if they were there before the storm, the rain would have washed out any blood.

Howard kept the package but said nothing to authorities for several weeks. "He was afraid of being ridiculed, or being implicated in this matter," according to William de Kerlor, who received the bundle from Howard in early October. De Kerlor showed the bloody towel to federal agents and brought it to the grand jury when he testified. It was, he suggested, the towel used to wipe the handle of the instrument with which Mr. Dean had been struck down.

Then, a month after Howard's discovery, there was another incident involving bloody cloths. Brothers Wesley and Malcolm Proctor were hunting in their woodlot two miles from the Dean farm when they stumbled upon some suspicious bundles. One bundle contained a blood-stained strip from a woman's dress, which had been creased as though it had been used as a head bandage. Other bundles held towels and strips of a curtain. The cloths were wrapped in newspapers dated September 13 and 14.

The Proctor boys took the bundles to their father, who alerted the selectmen. Edward Boynton went with William de Kerlor to the spot where the cloths had been found, a woodlot only one or two hundred yards from Russel Henchman's home. There they came upon another bundle, containing a bloodstained cloth with a salve of some kind on it. To de Kerlor, the conclusion was obvious, as he told Attorney General Young at the grand jury.

YOUNG: Do you connect this up in any way with the killing of Mr. Dean?

DE KERLOR: I think perhaps more with the nursing of somebody's face.

YOUNG: That is, your suggestion is that perhaps these are the bandages that Mr. Rich wore on his face after he got hit?

DE KERLOR: Yes.

Young had a different suggestion, one that perhaps made more sense, given the dates of the newspapers: the cloths were "sanitary towels such as a woman would use."

Neither federal agents nor state and county officials followed up on the bundles found by Howard or the Proctors, as there was no way to connect them to the Dean murder other than William de Kerlor's suspicions.

Some other bundles, however, were harder to dismiss.

Elizabeth Richardson lived off Main Street in East Jaffrey, on a road then called West Street (now Charlonne), perhaps a quarter mile from the Riches' home. At the time, there was a small dump right next to the Richardson home, on the same side of the street.

In the days after Mr. Dean's murder, Mrs. Richardson, like many people, was anxious about the possibility that the murderer was still at large, especially since she was alone at night with her three young daughters while her husband Frank worked a night shift. According to Richardson, "About two or three nights after the murder of Mr. Dean, I heard an auto stop in front of the house and as my husband works at the tack shop, I thought there had been an accident and that somebody was bringing him home in an automobile. I went to the front window and looked out; at the front of my house stood an automobile and I noticed Mr. Rich, whom I know very well, step out of the machine, then a woman stepped out, whom I recognized as Mrs. Rich. They went to the back of the machine, took out some bundles and threw them on the dump outside of my house. It was a very clear moonlight night and I recognized both of them."

The car, according to Mrs. Richardson, "was a little old car and looked like a Ford." Although Charles Rich did not own a car, he allowed his neighbor Alfred Hutchinson to store a Ford in his stable and which was available for his use. "He always told me to take the car if I wanted to," Rich said.

The car drove away, and fifteen minutes later Mrs. Richardson heard the town clock strike two. At the time, she didn't think much of the incident because she had no idea Charles Rich might be connected to the murder. Nevertheless, it unsettled her enough that she couldn't sleep the rest of the night, and she told her husband about the incident when he returned from work in the morning.

She told other people as well, and repeated her story at the *Rich v. Boynton* slander trial. But after she testified, Emily Webster took the stand. Emily Webster was the wife of Wilbur Webster, owner of the tack factory, Frank Richardson's boss and a close associate of Charles Rich. Mrs. Webster testified that Mrs. Richardson told her she was "only fooling" when she recounted the story of the Riches and the bundles. Mrs. Webster recalled Elizabeth Richardson saying, "I have been ill ever since and have not been able to eat, because so many people have called to ask me about it."

But the next day, Richardson was recalled to the stand and denied she had ever told Mrs. Webster or anyone else that she was joking about seeing the Riches toss bundles. "The statement is true," she testified, and went on to say that those who claimed she had said it was a joke were wrong. Perhaps when her story became known around town she worried about the repercussions for her husband's job and downplayed the story when speaking to Mrs. Webster. But by the time of the slander trial she was adamant about what she had seen.

The biggest flaw in Mrs. Richardson's story was her statement that it was a moonlit night when she saw the Riches toss the bundles at the dump. She had given the time as about 1:45 a.m., but Rich's lawyer rightly noted that the moon could not have been shining at that hour, having set at 11:45 p.m. on August 16. It is possible, however, that Richardson mistook a streetlight, which stood just past her house on the other side of the street, for moonlight.

There was more to the story. According to Richardson, "After the incident, Mrs. Rich and Miss Hodgkins, her sister, would come by the house nearly every night and look at the dump, turn around and go back." Then, a few days after the late-night dump run, Russel Henchman— who was superintendent of the water department—began to dig a trench through the dump to bring town water to a new house being built. "Henchman dug the trench but didn't start to lay pipe until nearly a year after," Richardson said. "The dirt was thrown up on the dump covering whatever had been thrown there."

It is perhaps entirely coincidental that Lana Rich and her sister walked past the dump during evening walks, and that Russel Henchman threw dirt where Elizabeth Richardson saw someone toss bundles. But it is hard to believe she would make up a story so incriminating to a well-known public figure, a story that would likely upset his associates and cause problems with her husband's employer. For his part, Charles Rich denied that he had thrown anything onto the West Street dump. And as with the other stories concerning mysterious bundles, no further action was ever taken in the matter.

63

THE GRAND JURY

IT IS CLEAR NOW THAT STATE AND COUNTY OFFICIALS HAD NO INTEREST in conducting a grand jury hearing into the murder of William Dean until Charles Rich's business associates pressured them into it. When the grand jury was held in April of 1920, the Soft Pedal Squad looked on it as a way to clear Rich's name, put rumors to rest, and get back to business.

Department of Justice officials and agents were unhappy at being excluded from the conduct of the grand jury and doubtful of state officials' impartiality in the matter. Jaffrey's selectmen and their supporters hoped for the best. The selectmen's attorney, Reginald Smith, prepared an extensive abstract of the case, which outlined in meticulous detail the events surrounding the murder, potential suspects, witnesses, and evidence. County Solicitor Pickard appears to have made no use of it, which did not necessarily surprise Smith. "Either he is playing the game fairly or he is trying to give Rich a whitewash," Smith said. "I am trying to face either eventuality."

Henry M. Dean, nephew to Mr. Dean and himself a lawyer, criticized the conduct of the grand jury in a letter to his cousin, William Dean Goddard. "Of course in the hearings before the Grand Jury the public is not admitted, simply one witness is before them at a time, and a great deal depends on the attitude of the prosecuting attorney. If he accepts the testimony of each and every witness with no attempt on his part to check up or cross-examine his statements and no one of the jurymen are enough interested to question the witness a lying witness might be able to produce a very good impression on the jurymen."

In retrospect, Pickard and Attorney General Young's conduct of the grand jury hearing seems to have been haphazard at best. Witnesses and evidence were presented to the jury in no particular order, and important points were sometimes glossed over while inconsequential matters were discussed at length.

A large number of witnesses were summoned, but many of those— some with crucial evidence to present—were never called to testify, including: night watchman Jean Bibeau, who saw the auto by the mill at midnight; a neighbor who saw signal lights flashing from the Colfelt place on the Dean farm; policeman Walter Lindsay, whom Mr. Dean asked about protection; Henry Ash, caretaker for the Colfelts in Temple; Camille Bruneau, who saw Charles Rich in downtown Jaffrey the night of the murder; Lester Ellsworth, who saw mysterious boxes in Colfelt's cellar; and Ed Baldwin and Frank Patterson, who recovered the cigarette case from the bottom of the cistern.

On the other hand, the psychologist William de Kerlor was called to testify, and Attorney General Young interviewed him for over three hours—far longer than any other witness. De Kerlor brought to the hearing a 30,000-word report of his investigation into the Dean murder, but neither Pickard nor Young appear to have paid any attention to it. Instead, Young focused on de Kerlor's astounding claim about seeing human faces in the photographs of blood spots he had taken at the murder scene.

Young began by reading an excerpt from the *Boston Post* article about the faces de Kerlor claimed to see, then spent several minutes asking him to explain the exact mechanism by which the images appeared, an arguably pointless exercise. As Young pressed the issue, even de Kerlor appears to have backed off on the value of the psychic pictures. "They are of psychological value and of scientific value, but I don't think they are of criminal value," he said. "They are interesting, but I don't think they would be used in any way."

It seems likely that Young's reason for spending so much time with de Kerlor was to establish that he was a crackpot and that nothing he said could be trusted. Federal agent Norman Gifford suspected that the intent went even further. He reported, "It is Agent's opinion that County

Solicitor Pickard's aversion to Kent [de Kerlor] is such, and his desire to discredit him so strong that he may so conduct the Grand Jury proceedings as to some extent be-cloud the main issue of the murder."

64

THE EXPERT WITNESS

In contrast to the appearance of the eccentric de Kerlor was the testimony of Dr. George Magrath, the Harvard-trained physician and medical examiner, who spoke confidently and with clinical precision. Magrath explained to the jurors that Mr. Dean had been choked to death, the pressure applied so forcefully that his neck had been broken between the third and fourth vertebrae. He also testified that, although Dean had been struck on the head hard enough to crack his skull, that blow had not killed him, though it might have rendered him unconscious.

On the second day Magrath was called to testify, he brought along the five-pronged hand weeder that Charlie Bean had found and turned over to him. Magrath had identified blood and hair on the weeder, though he could not confirm whether these were animal or human. Attorney General Young questioned Magrath at length about the weeder, asking whether it might have been the weapon that caused the wounds on Dean's skull and his skull fracture. "My best judgment at the present moment is, not having seen those wounds themselves, and having seen and made some broad studies of this implement, is that it is unlikely that it was the cause of the fracture," Magrath said.

Magrath also brought with him a piece of board taken from the porch of the barn at the Dean farm. The board had scratches and two holes in it, which William de Kerlor suggested had been made by the weeder. Magrath lined up the prongs of the weeder with the holes and confirmed that they could have been made by the weeder, though he could not say for certain that they were. De Kerlor had also theorized that scratches on the stone by the cistern, the cuts on Mr. Dean's head, and those on Charles Rich's face had all been made by the weeder. De Kerlor's report contains a blow-by-blow description of how this might have happened. According to de Kerlor, the tracing he had made of Dean's wounds at the exhumation matched those on Rich's face and lined up with the spacing of the prongs on the weeder.

Dr. Magrath allowed that the weeder might have caused the marks on the cistern stone, but he dismissed the idea that it had caused the wounds on Dean's head. These were not cuts, he explained, but contusion wounds, breaks in the skin caused by a blunt instrument. "I wouldn't say it's impossible but I would say it's unlikely this is the instrument that caused the marks on Mr. Dean's forehead and the one that made the fracture," Magrath said.

Attorney General Young, having dismissed the weeder as a murder weapon, showed little interest in pursuing it further, including whether it might have inflicted the cuts on Charles Rich's face, either from Mr. Dean defending himself, or accidentally in the hands of another attacker.

In a hearing beset by disorganization, hearsay, and palpably false claims, Dr. Magrath demonstrated a clarity and common sense—undoubtedly acquired during the many murder cases he had investigated—that appears to have gained him the respect of those in charge of the hearing. He spoke at length and the attorney general treated him with professional courtesy. But a number of other witnesses felt they were given short shrift and were not permitted to tell their stories fully. Daniel LaRose, who saw Charles Rich driving a car the night of the murder, said, "When I went before the Grand Jury I was examined by Mr. Young who did not let me tell my story but just let me answer his questions. He asked me questions in such a way as to make me feel he was trying to make me contradict myself."

Martin Garfield was among the first persons to arrive at the Dean farm, but among the last to be questioned at the grand jury. "Those county fellows have no use for me and if it hadn't been for the Federal men, I wouldn't have testified before the Grand Jury," Garfield recalled. "Sheriff Emerson said it was not necessary for me to testify."

Similarly, Arthur Smith told federal agents, "When I went before the Grand Jury hardly any questions were asked me, except by a Grand Juror who asked about the lights and the milk pail. To this day I still feel that Pickard wanted me to think as he did and answer questions the way he wanted, so that my impressions would be the same as his. This made me sick. I thought that remark about all the money in Cheshire County not getting a certain man into it looked funny to me."

Nor did Charlie Bean believe he had been treated fairly. Prior to the hearing, Sheriff Emerson and detective Harry Scott had taken a statement from Bean. "When the statement was finished, they asked me to sign it," Bean said. "I did not have my glasses and I asked them to read it. I then signed the statement."

Later, Bean was called to the grand jury. "When I went up to Keene to testify, they handed me a statement which they said I was to testify from, instead of letting me tell my story my own way under oath. When I read the statement in the Grand Jury room I was surprised to find that it was far different from the statement that I made."

A few witnesses were called to the grand jury who had never been questioned by county or state officials before, including Dean's neighbor, Charles Deschenes; Margaret and Annie Costello; and Charles Rich's neighbors, Alfred and Mary Hutchinson. Even Mrs. Hutchinson found this odd. Agent Weiss asked her, "Don't you think it out of the ordinary that the Sheriff in the county where a murder had been committed not too far from you, and he would not ask you some questions?"

"I think so, I should think he would try to find out, and I think it was kind of strange," Mary Hutchinson replied. "I was a newspaperwoman once, and would have asked everybody in the neighborhood if I had been on a murder case."

65

THE FINAL WITNESS

THE VERY LAST WITNESS TO BE CALLED TO THE GRAND JURY, ON THE final day of the hearing, was federal agent Robert Valkenburgh. Attorney General Young had returned to Concord the day before, leaving the conclusion of the hearing in County Solicitor Pickard's hands. Valkenburgh's appearance was the one concession the county and state officials were willing to make to the federal government's desire to be involved in the hearing.

Pickard began by questioning Valkenburgh about the Bureau of Investigation's involvement with the case and Valkenburgh's own investigation. Valkenburgh went on to speak about the suspects and various witnesses in the case, Dean's movements on the night of August 13, the signal lights, the available evidence, and several other topics. He challenged Charles Rich's statements about the events surrounding the murder, dismissed the idea of Mrs. Dean's guilt, and highlighted the importance of the missing cigarette case. He testified for over an hour, and the transcript of his testimony reads like a man trying to convey as much information as possible in the short time allotted to him.

Given the importance of Valkenburgh's testimony and his position with the government, it is hard to believe there was not some ulterior motive for bringing him in at the last minute and giving him short shrift. Even members of the jury wondered why such an important witness was not brought in until the last moment:

JURYMAN: Let me ask this other final question. The last witness has sort of thrown a key wrench into the case, to my reasoning. May I ask if there is any purpose in bringing him in last?

PICKARD: No. Simply because he happened to be here.

JURYMAN: I was thinking that had this evidence been introduced first, in the light of the other things that have come along, it would possibly look somewhat different to us.

PICKARD: Well, there was no purpose in it except simply that he happened to be here at this time. He has been here on previous days, but also other witnesses from farther away were here, and he said he would be available at any time, and so he happened to be brought forward at this time.

At the very end, at least one juryman seemed anxious to be done with the hearing. Valkenburgh was about to make a point when the unnamed juryman—perhaps the foreman—interrupted:

JURYMAN: What is the sentiment of the jury? Shall we sit right here and finish this up? It's now half past five.

JURYMAN: I move that we sit.

JURYMAN: How long will it take? (This to the witness.)

VALKENBURGH: I will have you out of here before six o'clock.

Apparently, getting home in time for supper was more important than achieving justice for Mr. Dean.

The witness most significantly absent from the grand jury was Mary Dean. Although Roy Pickard said this was "by agreement of everybody," it seems likely to have been largely his decision. Granted, testifying about her husband's death might have been traumatic for Mary Dean. But by all accounts, at the time of the grand jury she was stable and sufficiently lucid to have answered questions put to her. But rather than have her appear in person, Pickard presented a lengthy statement prepared by detective Harry Scott based upon the answers to questions he and Pickard had put to her.

The statement began, "On Tuesday, August 13, my husband went down to Jaffrey to Mr. Rich's place at 7:30 p.m." Given that he had a number of tasks that evening—grocery shopping, checking his mail, dropping off laundry—it seems odd that she would begin by highlighting a visit to the Riches. She describes her husband's purchases at Goodnow's store, then reiterates, "He told me when he got home that he had seen the Riches at their house."

The statement rambles in one or two spots, noting that "My husband loves ladies," and that "Mr. Colfelt didn't pay him for the last month." But otherwise, it is a fairly detailed account—the only account we have—of Mr. Dean's actions upon returning home that night.

It is also the only confirmation—apart from that of the Rich family— that William Dean had visited them that evening. And the experience of witnesses like Charlie Bean, Martin Garfield, and others suggests that Mary Dean's statement might not accurately convey her words, and that Pickard and Scott may have purposely or inadvertently guided her testimony in the questions they asked.

In fact, at several points in the grand jury hearing Pickard and Young seem to have led witnesses. William Coolidge testified he had heard a team go by his house on the night of the murder and Attorney General Young asked him, "Any possibility it might have been Dean on his way home after he left Rich's house at 10:40?" Granted, examiners are allowed more leeway at a hearing than at an actual trial, but this certainly sounds like a leading question.

At another point, County Solicitor Pickard asked Edward Boynton about Charles Rich's reputation and then proceeded to put words in his mouth: "A leading citizen and well respected?" Pickard suggested. At other times, Pickard asked witnesses who Dean's best friends were, with the apparent expectation that the answer would be the Riches.

Sometimes, the questions Pickard and Young *didn't* ask are more interesting than those they did. During his questioning of Dr. Dinsmore—the first person to examine Mr. Dean's body—Pickard did not ask if anything was found on the body; that question was left to a juryman, who was perhaps looking to corroborate Arthur Smith's testimony about the cigarette case found in Dean's pocket.

When Daniel LaRose testified about the car he saw in downtown Jaffrey on the night of the murder, he mentioned that he recognized the driver. Attorney General Young then proceeded to ask him about the speed of the car, whether the moon was shining, and whether LaRose had been able to buy any tobacco that evening. It was not until several minutes later that he got around to asking who the driver of the car was. "Mr. Rich," LaRose replied, which may explain why Young had been in no hurry to ask the question.

Finally, Charles Rich and Lawrence Colfelt—both of whom were arguably suspects in the case and whom some suggested shouldn't even have been there—appear to have been treated somewhat differently than other witnesses.

66

THE SUSPECTS

SHORTLY AFTER MR. DEAN'S MURDER, ROY PICKARD INTERVIEWED LAWrence and Margaret Colfelt at his Keene office. Later, he wrote to Attorney General Young, "Mr. and Mrs. ____ were very free in talking with me here on Sunday and it seems to me that they ought to be eliminated entirely as suspected witnesses." (The letter, as quoted by the *Boston American* newspaper, omitted the Colfelts' name so as not to be accused of libel.)

Young responded, "Replying to your letter of August 28, will say that in view of the circumstances, you and I agreeing that there is absolutely nothing to connect the ___s with the Dean case in any way and that the talk among the neighbors in Jaffrey is so far as we are able to discover entirely unfounded . . ."

Similarly, Pickard and Young appear to have ruled out Charles Rich as a suspect early on. On September 13, Young wrote to Pickard, "While I appreciate that it would be a misfortune to overlook any facts or circumstances of the crime, irrespective of whom they might implicate, the suggestion that Mr. [Rich] is in any way connected with the death of Mr. Dean strikes me as ridiculous."

Pickard responded, complaining about the actions of William de Kerlor, aka Kent. "It is Kent who is now endeavoring to fasten this crime upon Mr. [Rich]," Pickard wrote. "The story is too long for one letter which Kent told me last night, but he certainly feels, or says he feels, that [Rich] is the guilty man and he has promised to give me chapter and verse in due time."

That same day, Young wrote to Pickard about a request from Chief of Police Nute for information related to Mr. Rich. "I have since been told by some of the men connected with the Department of Justice that the detective [is] working upon the theory that Mr. [Rich] is implicated in the matter," Young told Pickard. "I cannot imagine the possibility of there being any foundation for such a suggestion."

Given the attitude of Pickard and Young, it is not surprising that Charles Rich appears to have been handled with kid gloves at the grand jury. When Rich was first called to testify, Attorney General Young questioned him at length about the Deans, their finances, their home, and Rich's friendship with them. Then Rich was dismissed. It was not until after lunch and the calling of other witnesses that Rich was recalled and Young asked him about the night of Dean's murder. And while other witnesses felt they had not been able to tell their own stories, Young encouraged Rich to relate events "in your own way"—a phrase he repeated three times and a courtesy he extended to no other witness.

Even more telling is the report of Agent Feri Weiss, who was camped out in the antechamber to the judge's office throughout the grand jury. Margaret and Natalye Colfelt were also present in the room, but they did not know Weiss. According to Weiss, "While Attorney General Young, County Solicitor Picard, and Sherrif [sic] Emerson, came into the room, they did not notice Agent, who was hiding behind a newspaper, and it was certainly an education to see what a hearty welcome these gentlemen of the prosecution gave to the two ladies, who we appointed as suspects, and how they felt guilty the minute Agent dropped the paper, and thus gave them to understand he saw them."

One other criticism may be leveled against the conduct of the grand jury hearing. Early in the proceedings, Attorney General Young gave these instructions to the jury. "I presume that you gentlemen may not have a very clear idea about the strict realities of the evidence, but I assume everybody knows you can't convict a person of a crime by testimony that comes through three or four different persons before it comes to the person who finally tells it on the witness stand, and I think you ought to know there is about ninety percent of that kind in here, as with Mrs. Morison and Miss Ware." With that, he effectively discounted most of what the jurors had just heard.

67

THE DISSATISFACTION

THE DECISION OF THE GRAND JURY, THAT DEAN WAS MURDERED BY "person or persons unknown to them," satisfied no one. It did not, as Charles Rich's associates hoped, put an end to the affair. Nor did it satisfy the demands of justice for William Dean and his ill-used wife, Mary.

William Dean Goddard slammed the handling of the grand jury in a lengthy letter to the *Keene Sentinel* that he never sent, or if he did, it was never published. Regarding Pickard's attitude to the grand jury, Goddard wrote, "He called it, he told me last August when I saw him the second time, 'against his better judgment,' which being translated means 'without any intention to prosecute.' He conducted it, he says, liberally that 'the testimony of each witness was received with a fulness of detail not restrained to the rules of evidence,' a plausible phrase which when critically examined amounts to a confession that he did not 'conduct' the hearing at all . . ."

Goddard went on to criticize the manner in which Pickard handled witnesses and concluded, "in short his only contribution was to befuddle the minds of the jurors if possible by calling the witnesses in as helter-skelter an order as possible."

Even members of the grand jury were unhappy with the handling of the case. "I was a member of the Cheshire County Grand Jury in April 1919, and throughout the entire session," said Franklin L. Lang of Troy, New Hampshire. "I was not satisfied with the hearing, and I know some other members of the Grand Jury were dissatisfied. I don't think they

277

used all the evidence they could get. I don't think they got from the witnesses all they could have gotten."

According to the *Boston American*, "Members of the grand jury admitted later that evidence related to signal lights was offered in such a vague and jumbled manner as to mean nothing to them."

Rollin Angier, a farmer from Fitzwilliam, said, "I was a member of the Cheshire County grand jury in April, 1919 and sat through the hearing on the Dean murder case. There was testimony about lights but at that time it didn't impress me very much. Since then, from what I have heard and read, I am convinced that there is more to it than I thought at the time."

For his part, Charles Rich believed that the grand jury exonerated him, but even County Solicitor Pickard, in his summation to the jury, denied that. "There is nothing final about the action of any grand jury," he told them. "It is simply an investigation that takes place upon the state of facts at that time. Every effort will be made by the Federal authorities, and by the County authorities, and by every law-abiding citizen, to trace down this thing."

The words echo Pickard's refrain throughout the Dean case. As the *New Hampshire Sentinel* reported, "he is now and always has been urgently desirous to receive all possible information that anyone has or believes can throw light upon the murder of Dr. Dean of aid to fix the responsibility for that crime."

Others found those assurances to be hollow, if not outright lies.

68

THE MISHANDLED CASE

The murder of William K. Dean will go down in New Hampshire history as one of the most brutal of crimes. The blundering stupidity of the officials whose duty it was to investigate will always be regarded by the citizens of East Jaffrey as equally criminal.
—*BOSTON AMERICAN*, APRIL 19, 1920

IT IS EASY, WITH THE 20/20 VISION OF HINDSIGHT, TO CRITICIZE THE actions of the officials charged with investigating the Dean murder. But a review of all the information now available suggests that those officials were at the very least inept, and possibly corrupt.

First, there was the handling of the investigation. Andrew J. Sweeney, a former police officer in Keene, New Hampshire, described County Solicitor Pickard as an aggressive prosecutor, except when it came to the Dean murder. "When the Dean case was reported to Pickard on the 14th of August, he did not seem to be in any hurry whatsoever to investigate it," Sweeney told federal agents. "As a matter of fact, he was sitting around for more than an hour before he took an auto from Keene for Jaffrey and he has ever since tried to delay rather than to speed up the investigation."

The initial search of the murder scene was disorganized, to say the least. *Boston American* reporter A.J. Daniels, who was on the scene the day after Dean's body was found, described Pickard's investigating technique. "While his enthusiastic helpers ran willy nilly around the place destroying evidence of the first importance with their blundering, the district attorney organized his forces for a hunt for a milk pail which Mr. Dean was supposed to have used on the night of the murder. The hunt for a murderer became a hunt for a milk pail."

Nothing was done to protect the scene of the crime. Selectman William Coolidge testified that 150 people were at the Dean farm when the news came out, perhaps more, walking around the barn and through the yard. According to A.J. Daniels, "I saw a white porcelain door knob with blood stains on it and everybody was permitted to handle this door knob, thus destroying fingerprints which might have furnished a valuable clue."

Martin Garfield's son, Roger, who was with his father the first day, told him he had seen blood on the ground. "I noticed more on the inside of the doorknob on the inside of the barn and I noticed good, big fingerprints on it," he said. But by the time the doorknob was sent to a fingerprint lab in Boston, any fingerprints had been smudged.

The barn had been left unguarded, allowing Russel Henchman to sweep up the floor. Whether this action was intentionally criminal or not, it nevertheless made any subsequent investigation impossible and may have destroyed evidence. At the grand jury, William de Kerlor criticized the local and county authorities for not preventing Henchman's actions, at which point Attorney General Young quickly changed the subject.

When Dean's body was found, the medical examiner performed only a partial autopsy. It was not until January, five months later, that Dr. George Magrath was called in by the selectman to perform a complete autopsy. Later, Magrath met a Pinkerton agent who told him that he had tried hard to call on Magrath for the Dean murder, but that County Solicitor Pickard had balked and told him that "the County could not see their way clear to have Dr. McGrath [sic] to [per]form the autopsy as it was a loss of money and of no use."

69

THE TAMPERED WITNESSES

QUESTIONS WERE ALSO RAISED AS TO THE RELIABILITY OF WITNESS statements obtained as part of Pickard's investigation. Most of these statements were taken by Deputy Sheriff Walter Emerson, a part-time officer who had never been trained for such work. Emerson wrote the statements down in longhand and had witnesses sign them, but they were not sworn statements.

When Emerson and detective Harry Scott interviewed Charlie Bean, they asked him about the buggy that left Charles Rich's home on the night of Dean's murder. According to Agent Feri Weiss, Bean's statement said, "I did not hear or see a wagon leave the barn."

"If they have that they have cooked it," Bean told Weiss. "I told Scott in Boston and Emerson that he and Emerson were damned crooks and that fellow up in Keene [meaning Pickard], God help him if I meet him—if I land in jail I don't care."

Early on, Sheriff Emerson told Father Hennon that he had come from Keene with the authority to arrest Charles Rich. "I would have done so if three of my witnesses had not gone back on me," he said. At that point, Emerson appears to have accepted the possibility that Charles Rich might be involved in the murder. He soon changed his mind, however, and engaged in actions that amount to witness tampering.

Case in point: Emerson confronted Oscar Dillon, who had challenged the identification of the cigarette case found in the cistern. According to Dillon, "Sheriff Emerson told me in Keene, recently, that if I and some other people in Jaffrey didn't keep our mouths shut, we'd get in serious trouble. I told him I was going to talk as much as I wanted to, as long as I told the truth."

Similarly, Mary Lee Ware told federal agents that within a couple of weeks after the murder, Emerson had told her to "lay low" and not be so active in regard to the Dean murder. "Mr. Emerson, County Sheriff, told me not to talk so free or talk so much as I was a very wealthy woman, and someone might sue me for liable [sic]."

It appears that Emerson was sent to Ware by Roy Pickard, who had also warned William de Kerlor and Frederick Dean that Colfelt "wouldn't hesitate to bring a libel action against anyone, including Miss Ware," as de Kerlor recalled. According to de Kerlor, the visit from Emerson "so unsettled Miss Ware's nerves at the time that Miss Ware asked me if I thought it advisable for her to leave her home in Rindge to go to Boston for some time."

Emerson also attempted to influence Frank Humiston, who had worked for the Colfelts before entering the service. When Humiston returned from overseas in the summer of 1919, he was driving with a friend through Fitzwilliam, New Hampshire, when he passed the home of Emerson, who called to him. "He asked me what I knew about the Dean case and what I had told about Colfelt," Humiston said. "He asked me if the Federal authorities or anybody had talked with me about it." Humiston replied that they had not.

"That's good," the sheriff said, and invited Humiston into his house.

Humiston declined, but asked Emerson, "Have you fellows got a motive?"

"We didn't until we got ahold of that letter which gave us [the] perfect motive for Mrs. Dean killing Mr. Dean," Emerson replied.

Humiston, perhaps doubtful that such a letter existed, asked to see it.

"Well, I tell you Frank," Emerson said, "you come in the house or I'll come over and see you and I'll have a little paper all fixed up and you sign it and I'll take you up to Keene and you'll see Pickard and the letter and everything will be fine."

Humiston had no intention of signing anything Emerson put before him, but told Emerson that he would talk with him any time he came to his house.

"You don't seem to want to talk to me," Emerson said, "but when certain ones get ahold of you, you'll have to talk."

Later Humiston told federal agents, "I was afraid that there was some funny business there; that he might try to mix me up and get me to sign [something] that was against the case in general. Mr. Dean was one of the best friends I had, and I wouldn't sign anything that would go against Mrs. Dean or Mr. Dean either, because I don't believe Mrs. Dean did it, or could have done it."

County Solicitor Pickard was also suspected of having influenced witnesses unduly. Frederick Dean, who came to Jaffrey determined to investigate his brother's murder, abruptly abandoned the effort after meeting with Pickard at his office in Keene, and it is unclear what happened to make him give up the case. Frederick's cousin, Henry Dean, spoke about the matter with federal agents Weiss and Valkenburgh after the grand jury.

"It continues to puzzle Mr. W. and Mr. V. as also myself why Fred Dean dropped the case in the way and at the time he did," Henry Dean said. "No definite light has yet been shed on the cause. Apparently after a conversation with Pickard at Keene he had an entire change of heart."

According to Agent Weiss, "Mr. Dean said that he was so disgusted with de Kerlor that he decided to go back to New York and not have anything more to do with the case, particularly as Pickard impressed him with the fact that probably Mrs. Dean in her deranged mind murdered her husband." But it seems equally likely that Frederick Dean was scared off by Pickard's warning that Lawrence Colfelt would sue anyone who connected him to the crime and that, unlike Mary Lee Ware, Dean had neither the resolve nor the deep pockets to stand up to such pressure.

Daniel LaRose also believed that Pickard tried to railroad him just prior to the grand jury. LaRose had borrowed money from a woman and paid her back more than the original amount, but she claimed he still owed her and took him to court. In the end, LaRose owed the state $17, and for this amount Pickard threatened to arrest him and send him to jail for a year. LaRose hired a lawyer, put up a fight, and the case was dropped.

LaRose had felt pressured by others as well. "The night before I went to Keene to testify in the Dean murder case, Mr. D.D. Bean had sent for me to come to Stratton's livery stable," LaRose told federal agents. "As I reached there, he said to me, 'Are you going to Keene tomorrow to make a damn fool of yourself?'"

LaRose, who worked for Bean, said, "I felt my job was gone to Hell right there. They made it so disagreeable for me at the mill that I was forced to quit two weeks after I appeared at the hearing in Keene."

Charlie Bean believed that someone was worried enough about his testimony to want him out of the picture entirely. "In fact, I saw so much in this case, that I found a note tacked on my barn door one morning," Bean said. "It was typewritten and said that if I would leave town, there would be $100 pinned up on the same door to pay my expenses." According to Bean, he had already purchased a rail ticket for a trip to Detroit, but returned it after finding the note. "Somebody knew I was going West on a trip and thought that offer might be an incentive to insure [sic] my absence, but smelling a rat and fearing they might try to lay blame on me as they tried on Mrs. Dean, I decided to stay and help clear up the case." There is no independent corroboration of the attempted bribery, and it is impossible to know whether Bean, who was clearly a gifted storyteller, was making it up.

70

THE EVIDENCE

THROUGHOUT THE INVESTIGATION OF THE DEAN MURDER, KEY EVIdence was mishandled. The murder scene itself, the bloody doorknob, the hairpin found by the cistern, and the lantern belonging to Charles Rich were not safeguarded as they should have been.

Other evidence was simply ignored if it did not support the investigators' working hypotheses. County Solicitor Pickard and Attorney General Young discounted the hand weeder as a murder weapon, but refused to consider that it might have caused the cuts on Charles Rich's face, whether in the hands of Mr. Dean defending himself, or accidentally from another attacker.

After the grand jury, the evidence from the Dean case was entrusted to Sheriff Edward Lord. Two years later at the *Rich v. Boynton* slander trial, Lord was deposed and asked about the evidence, but he had not brought it to court with him. The judge told him he would be summoned again and instructed him to produce the evidence when he came.

Later, Lord told County Solicitor Pickard he was to return to court with the evidence. In short order, Pickard and Attorney General Young requested a superior court judge to impound the evidence and he did. It took another order of the court to have the evidence presented at the slander trial. Pickard never gave a reason for the impounding other than the "safety" of the evidence.

The most egregious mishandling of evidence however, involved the cigarette case found at the bottom of the cistern. This was a vital piece of evidence, the only thing that might have been linked to the murderers.

It seems likely, as federal agents believed, that the case had fallen from the pocket of one of the murderers as they dumped Dean's body into the cistern. It is also possible that the owner did not realize the case was missing until later, and even that he returned to the scene to look for it that night or the next day.

According to witnesses, Sheriff Walter Emerson took charge of the cigarette case found in the cistern. Later, Emerson also came into possession of William Dean's initialed snuff box. He carelessly left it on a shelf at his boarding house and then allowed his landlady to hold on to it for several days. Emerson also had access to the candy cigarette case, making him perhaps the only person to have handled all three of the cases.

By the time of the grand jury, Emerson had given Dean's snuff box and the candy case to Sheriff Edward Lord. Emerson claimed that Dean's initialed snuff box was the case found in the cistern, a claim that other witnesses flatly contradicted. When asked how Dean's case got into the cistern, Emerson replied, "It could have slipped out of his pocket very easily."

It could have, except that witnesses saw the initialed snuff box being taken from Dean's pocket, not from the bottom of the cistern. And other witnesses testified that the cigarette case recovered from the cistern was quite different from the box that Dean carried his cigarette makings in. The case from the cistern, a thin, silver cigarette case marked "Made in Germany," had vanished. After coming into Sheriff Emerson's possession, it disappeared from the official records and has never been seen since.

71

THE WHITEWASH

THE INVESTIGATION INTO WILLIAM DEAN'S DEATH WAS ALSO HAM-pered by county and state officials' stubborn persistence in accusing Mrs. Dean of the crime. Was this their honest belief or an intentional effort to shield other, more likely suspects? That suggestion is hard to ignore, given that most people—including the doctors who examined Mrs. Dean, the people who knew her best, and federal agents who investigated the case—said it was a physical impossibility for her to have committed the murder.

In retrospect, the letter that Roy Pickard sent to William Dean God-dard on September 11, 1918, is shocking in its willful ignorance: "We are still seeking for some ray of light which will cause us to look elsewhere than to her but at the present time there is nothing which would arouse any suspicions at all in any other direction." In fact, there was a great deal that should have aroused suspicion in one or two specific directions.

For most of the investigation, Pickard was of the opinion—as he wrote to Goddard—"that the act was done by somebody upon the premises and somebody who remained there." This essentially eliminated everyone but Mrs. Dean. Goddard had seen Pickard's file and said, "I spent the whole night studying his documents till 5 a.m. I was puzzled to explain why he had not followed up the evidence of his own inves-tigations as to the presence of outsiders on the Dean farm the night of the murder."

When it became clear that Mrs. Dean could not have committed the murder, perhaps Pickard was simply unable to admit that he had been wrong. According to D.D. Bean, "My idea of Pickard is this. He got discouraged on his first judgement and ought to be a big enough man to come out now, and say what he found out . . ."

When William Dean Goddard wrote to Pickard to question the notion of Mrs. Dean killing her husband, Pickard's response was dismissive. According to Goddard, "His answer, brushing aside all that I had to offer, convinced me that he was not seeking the truth, that he had got his mind on investigating the fabrications only, and that he had no plan for investigating the murder except to wait until someone else should do all the work and make everything so clear that he would have to follow."

Federal agents initially attempted to work alongside County Solicitor Pickard, Attorney General Young and their deputies. But the agents quickly became doubtful of the state and county officials' ability, if not their integrity. Just one month after the murder, Agent Valkenburgh reported, "The officials working on the case seemed to change their stories daily. It seems to agent as if they are trying to cover someone."

Agent Feri Weiss was even more blunt, saying, "It is clear that the Attorney General, as well as County Solicitor, and perhaps even Judge Kivel, are in a conspiracy to whitewash the suspects, namely, Rich and Colfelt."

72

THE SUPPORTERS

WHY WOULD LOCAL, COUNTY, AND STATE OFFICIALS HAVE COVERED FOR Charles Rich and Lawrence Colfelt, or at the very least soft-pedaled any investigation into their actions, as some charged?

To begin with, Charles Rich was an influential person, closely tied to local business interests as well as social and political circles. People who lived in East Jaffrey understood this all too well. Ethel Fish, who had lived in town for years, said, "I knew Mr. Rich and do not say that he had anything to do with the case, but I will say this, that if anyone who is living in Jaffrey who didn't have so much influence as he had and had been the last man known to have been with Mr. Dean and appeared the next day with a black eye and could not explain satisfactorily how he got it, [he] would [have] been arrested and put in jail at once."

Even Herbert C. Sawtelle, a friend and business associate of Rich, acknowledged the influence that Charles Rich wielded. "The whole thing in the Cheshire County is this: Rich is a political power there and he domineers Pickard and Young and that is the reason the case has fallen flat," Sweeney said. "This case should be opened and tried before a County Solicitor who is unbiased and not controlled by the ring in Cheshire County."

Sawtelle was not alone in claiming that Pickard was unduly influenced by political considerations. Former Keene policeman Andrew J. Sweeney described Pickard as "a regular tool of the political ring of Keene, which is in close touch with Concord."

The *Keene Sentinel* newspaper was unflagging in its support of Roy Pickard, and some of its articles read as if Pickard had dictated them himself. In December of 1919, following the publication of Bert Ford's articles in the *Boston American*, the *Sentinel* published an apologia for Pickard's handling of the investigation and the conduct of the grand jury. "Everything possible was done by the state to aid the United States secret service men, and their cooperation with the state was always sought," the paper noted. The article rehashed the case against Mrs. Dean, dismissed any other explanation for the crime, and argued that to criticize state or county officials bordered on treason. "Certainly, to cause or stimulate a frame of mind that would hold up to undue ridicule or censure officials of the law who are an essential part of the government of the state would be almost tantamount to spreading 'Red' propaganda in the community."

William Dean Goddard, incensed by the article, wrote a letter of protest to the newspaper, which it declined to publish. The editor responded to Goddard privately, "This paper has opened its columns to no communications about the Dean murder, which manifestly would be endless in number if once the columns were opened, and for the present at least declines to do so."

Bert Ford wrote to Goddard the same day, explaining the decision of the *Sentinel*'s editor not to print his letter. "The selectmen tell me he is a tool of the county ring and that everything he has published about the case has been distorted or biased."

Perhaps even more important than Charles Rich's political connections was his fraternal affiliation. Like many of Jaffrey's leading businessmen and several of the officials connected with the investigation into the Dean murder, Charles Rich was a Mason.

73

THE MASONS

"Further, that I will keep a worthy brother Master Mason's secrets inviolable, when communicated to and received by me as such, murder and treason excepted."

—Masonic oath

Charles Rich was Worshipful Master of the Charity Lodge of Masons in East Jaffrey, the presiding officer of the lodge. The lodge met on the second floor of the bank building where Rich worked, and all the leading businessmen in town were members: D.D. Bean, Merrill Symonds, Homer White, Wilbur Webster, and Louis Meyers. Other members of the Charity Lodge included Russel Henchman, who swept the Dean barn shortly after the murder; Lewis Davis, who was appointed executor of the Dean estate and Mrs. Dean's guardian; Rich's doctor, Frederick Sweeney; Rich's minister, Rev. Myron Cutler; banker Herbert Sawtelle; liveryman Fred Stratton, who said he'd never seen Dean in better spirits the night of his death; liveryman Robert Hamill; and a number of other townspeople.[28]

Others involved in the case were members of lodges in other towns, including Dr. Frank Dinsmore, who testified that there was nothing in William Dean's pockets when he was pulled from the cistern; Rich's lawyer, Major Orville Cain; Attorney General Oscar Young; and even Governor John Bartlett.

For the most part, Rich's fellow Masons believed him to be innocent of any connection to the Dean murder. There is no evidence that they knew him to be guilty and were involved in a conspiracy to cover it up. However, they were undoubtedly inclined to give Rich the benefit of the doubt, unable to believe that a person with his background and reputation could be implicated in such a crime. "I cannot conceive of any man of Rich's standing or character having anything to do with an affair of that sort," said Dublin postmaster Henry Allison, another Mason.

Given their bias in Rich's favor, his fraternal brothers were unlikely to press for a full and complete investigation of the murder. In fact, they rejected any investigations beyond what had already been done unless, as County Solicitor Pickard said, new evidence were to be found.

That was an untenable position, as Bert Ford pointed out. "The County and State authorities say that the Dean case is open and that they will welcome any new evidence," he wrote. "But they are not now spending a single dollar or making the slightest effort to track the assassins or to unearth new evidence themselves." And new evidence was not likely to be found if no one was looking for it.

The residents of East Jaffrey took the Masons' support of Charles Rich for granted and gossiped about it endlessly, to the chagrin of businessmen and Masons like D.D. Bean, who said they would welcome a resolution to the case regardless of whom it might indict. "But you can go around town and what do you hear?" he demanded. "That Bean and Symonds and Webster, and the leading men in the Knight Templars and the Masons are stalling this case."

While most of the Masons defended Rich, a few—like Herbert C. Sawtelle—saw limits to their support. "I will state again that Rich is a good friend of mine, a brother Mason," Sawtelle said, "but if he had anything to do with the Dean murder he ought to be arrested and punished."

A few lodge members went further. Selectmen Edward Boynton—a past master of the lodge—and William Coolidge led the charge for a fair and complete investigation. Following the slander trial in 1921, Charles G. Whitney—another past master—was outspoken in his criticism of Charles Rich, raising the ire of other members. According to George Duncan, D.D. Bean called Whitney to a meeting at his office to discuss "matters of Masonic propriety." When Whitney realized that half a dozen other Masons were waiting at the office, he became alarmed that "plans of physical violence might be in the making," according to Duncan. Whitney asked Duncan to accompany him, and they took William Coolidge to even the numbers.

The conference began peacefully enough, but then tempers rose and a Mason named Charles Davis approached Whitney with fists raised. The others separated them and Duncan and Whitney decided it was best to leave. "As we stepped off the steps some of the other group started to follow when Mr. Coolidge drew a revolver, which I didn't know he had, and ordered them not to come near," Duncan said. "We departed without further incident."

It also appears that the Big Five were not above wielding political influence through their workplaces. Jaffrey's chief of police George Nute died in June of 1919 of heart and liver disease. William W. Preston was appointed to replace him and became allied with the friends and associates of Charles Rich. The selectmen, who continued to investigate the Dean murder, accused Preston and postmaster Russel Henchman of spying on them as they were questioning witnesses. They fired Preston, who told D.D. Bean of his dismissal.

"Get back on your job," Bean demanded. "Don't pay any attention to that order of the selectmen. They have no right to dismiss you. I'll call a special town meeting and found out who's running this town."

When Preston declined to fight the dismissal, Bean gave him a job. "Go down there and I'll give you thirty dollars a week if you don't have to do anything but sit and watch the smoke go up the chimney," Bean told him.[29]

Just before the 1920 town elections, according to Robert Charlonne, William Preston came around asking his fellow workers if they would support him for election as police chief. "He also asked us if we wanted a new board of Selectmen or if we were satisfied with the present board," Charlonne said. "I told him I was satisfied with the present board."

On voting day, Charlonne and another worker left the shop to vote. "When I returned at 11 o'clock, the boss told me that there wasn't any work for me," Charlonne said. He asked if he was being fired because he had voted but was told it was simply because of a reorganization.

Despite opposition from the town's business leaders, the selectmen were all reelected in a landslide. The businessmen tried again in 1921, nominating a full slate of candidates for town positions. This time, Webster, White, Bean, and Symonds distributed flyers which contained, in George Duncan's words, "a veiled threat" to their employees: "Are you even sure that, if the present antagonistic attitude is continued, you can retain the industries you now have? Larger plants than any in Jaffrey have been discarded overnight."

Average workers may have faced pressure if they didn't toe the company line regarding the Dean case. But businessman George Duncan took the strongest stand and paid the greatest price for it.

74

THE OUTCAST

GEORGE DUNCAN WAS A MASON, BUT UNLIKE MANY OF HIS MASONIC brothers he was a lifelong Democrat. Duncan had advocated an active approach to the Dean murder investigation, in contrast to the hands-off attitude of his fellow businessmen. Over the course of the investigation he corresponded with County Solicitor Roy Pickard who was, coincidentally, his first cousin.

In one letter, Duncan tried to explain why locals at the town meetings suspected the Masons of involvement in the case: "I think I voiced the sentiments of most of us when I said at the meeting, 'The county solicitor is a Republican; the leading Republicans of Keene are Knight Templars; the latter naturally believe what they learn from the solicitor; when we hear from Keene Knight Templars that Mrs. Dean is thought to have committed the murder, a thing which to us who know her is ridiculous, it is the most natural thing in the world for someone to think, and say, that these men are working together to throw suspicion from some Knight Templar; especially when the 'some Knight Templar,' whom those of us who know him best know is absolutely incapable of committing such a crime, has been by an unfortunate coincidence placed in a suspicious position." The Knight Templar in question, of course, was Charles Rich.

Duncan had been present at the first meeting of the group that came to be known as the Big Five and argued that a grand jury should be held to clear Rich's name. "That was the last time up to the present day that any of this group ever discussed the matter with me," he noted.

In the aftermath of the grand jury, the rift between Duncan and his fellow Masons widened. The final break came in December of 1920, at the annual meeting of the Charity Lodge. Duncan had served as lodge secretary for 13 years, but that December he was opposed by Rev. Myron Cutler and lost by a vote of 17 to 4. "That being the last officer to be chosen by ballot, I realized that I was persona non grata and left the lodge room," Duncan said. From then on, he attended no meetings and received no communications from the lodge other than bills for his annual dues, which he paid promptly.

Finally, four years later, Duncan requested and received a dimit (honorable discharge) from the lodge. But the fallout from his parting with the Masons was not over. "Having previously been rather closely associated with most of those herein called the 'soft-pedal squad,' and enjoyed their business, I must say that in the intervening years, until the death of some of those and even up to now with those still living, they have not recognized me in a business or social way except in dire necessity," he said.

In 1920, Duncan took on a partner at his drugstore. Shortly thereafter, members of the Soft Pedal Squad approached his partner about opening a competing drugstore. The partner declined and Duncan's adversaries then backed another man who opened a rival store.

Duncan served as a lecturer for the Exchange Club, a nationwide service organization that opened a chapter in Jaffrey in 1925. As reported in the *Peterborough Transcript*, "The new organization starts with a charter membership of twenty-five leading business and professional men of the town." George Duncan was not among them. James H. Fitzgerald and Merrill Symonds, both Masons, were elected president and vice president of the club, but Duncan was never invited to join or even attend as a guest at a meeting. Later, the club became the Jaffrey Service Club and Duncan applied to join but was turned down. "On one occasion I was a guest speaker," he wrote, "but before I spoke about one-half the members present pointedly left."

In 1933, Duncan went to Washington, DC, to serve as secretary to U.S. Senator Fred Brown. He hired a manager to run his store while he was away; within six months, the manager was invited to join the Service Club.

Duncan lived on Main Street in East Jaffrey, a four-minute walk to his pharmacy that took him past the homes of Merrill Symonds and Wilbur Webster. But in the aftermath of the Dean murder, he would walk around the block to get to work rather than pass their homes. "So you can see the hostility there was in town," Archie Letourneau said. "It was terrible."

George Duncan died in 1958, having served "in practically every capacity on committees and town offices in Jaffrey," according to the *Peterborough Transcript*. Over 300 people attended his funeral, and among the 14 honorary bearers was D.D. Bean, the last surviving member of the Big Five. Bygones—at least to that extent and on that occasion—were at last bygones.

75

THE MEANS AND THE OPPORTUNITY

IN CRIMINAL INVESTIGATIONS, STANDARD PROCEDURE HOLDS THAT A suspect must have the means to commit the crime, a motive for committing the crime, and the opportunity to commit the crime.

In the case of William Dean's murder, the means—the items used to strangle, bind, and conceal him—were all present at the farm and available to anyone who might have been there. Given that the murderers did not bring weapons with them—a gun or a knife, for example—it's possible they did not come intending to kill Mr. Dean. His death may have come about when the situation got out of hand, the result of too forcefully attempting to convince him to keep his mouth shut. On the other hand, the murderers could have purposely used items from the farm in order to cast suspicion on the only other person living there at the time, Mrs. Dean. If so, they failed, because Mrs. Dean was physically incapable of committing the crime; practically speaking, she did not have the means.

In terms of opportunity, anyone who was in the town of Jaffrey that evening could have been at the Dean farm at the time of the murder, unless witnesses positively placed them elsewhere. Charles Rich said he was in bed at the time, but the only ones who could confirm that were his wife and sister-in-law. As Ralph Davis noted, "As for Rich going out at night, any man could go out after a certain hour and even his wife would not know about it." At any rate, witnesses testified they saw Rich downtown at a time when he claimed he was in bed.

Another person implicated in the crime, Ed Baldwin, said, "I went to bed early that night," but he offered no proof to substantiate his claim.

Others, like Russel Henchman, were never asked where they were at the time of Dean's murder. Even Lawrence Colfelt, who argued that he had an alibi because he was working in Portsmouth at the time, is not completely clear in terms of opportunity. "While it is true that Colfelt was in Portsmouth at 7 p.m., it is also true that a fast car can cover the distance from Portsmouth to Jaffrey in 3 hours," said federal agent Norman Gifford. "A man could leave Portsmouth at 8; be in Jaffrey at 11; leave Jaffrey at 2 and be in Portsmouth at 5 a.m. and go to work at 7 a.m."

Bureau of Investigation agents tried to establish whether Colfelt was actually in his Portsmouth hotel room on the night of August 13. Unfortunately, the chambermaids and other staff working there that night had quit by the time agents arrived, so there was no one to confirm or deny Colfelt's story. "The manager further stated that it would be very easy for anyone to leave the hotel in the evening after he had stirred up the bed so as to make the people believe that he spent the night at the hotel," said Agent Weiss. "It is not certain by any means that Colfelt was at the hotel during the night of August 13th even if the books show he lived there according to the manager."

Clearly, a number of people had both the means and the opportunity to murder William Dean. The question of motive is far more complicated.

76

THE MOTIVE

WHY WOULD ANYONE WANT TO KILL WILLIAM DEAN, A MAN WHO seemed to be universally liked? What motive could there be?

Regardless of the allegations made against Mrs. Dean, she had no motive to kill her husband. The suggestions of jealousy or desire to inherit the estate simply do not wash with her history and personality. However, other suspects may have had motives related to espionage, financial issues, or some interplay between the two.

At first, the suggestion that German spies were traipsing around southwestern New Hampshire, flashing signals to each other and to collaborators on the seacoast, might seem absurd. It is true that many of the reports of signal lights can probably be chalked up to mistakes, imagination, or hearsay.

Many, but not all. We now know that Germany had developed a spy network in the United States even before America entered World War I. Count Johann von Bernstorff, the German ambassador to the United States, was given a slush fund of $150 million dollars to set up a spy network that would conduct sabotage operations in the United States. Germany's agents, operating at arm's length from the ambassador, targeted chemical plants, munitions dumps, and Allied shipping.

In September of 1916, von Bernstorff visited friends in Dublin, New Hampshire, not far from Jaffrey. His host, Mrs. Wesley J. Merritt, was the young widow of a Civil War hero who had died in 1911. The visit, which von Bernstorff acknowledged in his book *My Three Years in America*, was not public knowledge. "His presence here was kept fairly quiet," said

Charles Thomas, telephone operator in Dublin at the time. "Ordinarily it is hard for a person of prominence to visit this town without it being known by everybody, but only a comparative few knew that von Bernstorff was in the town at that time."

Von Bernstorff probably came to know Mrs. Merritt via the social world of Washington, DC, her year-round residence. "Mrs. Merritt is the wife of the late General Merritt and her knowledge of American Military affairs is quite great and her knowledge of German ways and her decided progerman [sic] feelings are well known," said Dublin resident Almeim McGowing.

Merritt was also a riding enthusiast. "Mrs. Merritt is very fond of horseback riding and twice while going up what is known as the Pumpelly trail on Monadnock I saw Mrs. Merritt and the Count riding along the trail on the mountain side," McGowing said.

Von Bernstorff's visit may have been simply a social call to a friend. But he returned later with a much more malign purpose, if we are to believe a story told by Charlie Bean.

According to Bean, he received a visit from two men in the fall of 1919. "They were staying at Shattuck's Inn," Bean said. "They told me that they had heard I was a photographer and asked if I would do some work for them."

The next day, the men came for Bean in an automobile. "The first thing which they asked me was whether I understood German and when I told them I didn't they talked German entirely among themselves."

The three men drove to Mount Monadnock and took the car as far as it would go, then parked and proceeded to hike to the summit. One of the visitors was older, perhaps 50, and seemed out of shape. The other was younger, athletic, and carried himself like a military man.

When they arrived at the summit, Bean said, "They asked me to take photographs of the mountain ranges." In fact, they only seemed interested in the outlines and the tops of the hills, including Mount Wachusett, which lay southeast over the state line in Massachusetts.

As the men hiked down the mountain, Bean took them to a shelf of rock that provided a sweeping view of the countryside. "The older one of the two was delighted with the place. He said he liked the view better than at the summit, because it was less windy and exposed."

The visitors proceeded to tear their handkerchiefs into strips and used the strips to mark bushes as they continued down the hill, "leaving a trail just like boys play hare and hounds," Bean said. (Hare and Hounds, also known as "paper chase," involves one player leaving bits of paper as a trail that other players must follow.) "At the time I thought that they were simply marking the trail, so that they could find the place alone to take friends there," Bean said.

The men asked Bean if he had any maps of the region. "I told them I had some small charts of folders which sold at a local store for 10 cents, showing the outline of the mountains and hills and giving the altitude," Bean said. They asked him for six of the maps. "They paid me a quarter apiece for them," said Bean, who netted a tidy profit on the deal.

The next day the men called for Bean again, and once again they asked him to take photographs of the surrounding hills, this time from the northern side of the summit, facing Dublin. They were met on the summit by a third man, who had apparently climbed up from Dublin. Once, and only once, Bean heard one of the other men call the third man "Bernstorff."

It was not until later that Charlie Bean realized for whom he had acted as trail guide. "Later I saw Bernstorff's picture in the paper and recognized it as the man I had out that day and I felt quite proud to have been in such distinguished company," he said.

His pride was short-lived. "After we got into the war, I kicked myself when I put two and two together and awoke to the fact that I had helped Germans with photographs and maps of the region," Bean said. "I would have shot them before I would have lifted a finger to help them if I had known."

Within two weeks, according to Bean, signal lights began to appear from the secluded shelf to which he had guided the Germans. "Dr. Dean was murdered as a result of those German lights, and everybody in town knows it," Bean said.

It is a remarkable tale, too remarkable for some people, who simply chalked the story up to Crazy Bean and his overactive imagination. But the level of detail and conformity to the timeline of von Bernstorff's visits to New Hampshire makes it hard to ignore.

Then, as now, there were those who scoffed at the idea of German espionage in rural New Hampshire. "They couldn't for the life of them understand why the enemy should want to blink and flash signals from the mountains," Bert Ford said. "They couldn't grasp the purpose of such operations so close to home."

If German agents were involved in espionage on American soil during World War I, to what end? What information might they hope to pass on that would aid Germany?[30]

77

THE SIGNALS

Even before the United States entered the war, Germany was preparing for that possibility. Sabotage operations had been ongoing since 1914. In 1915, the sinking of the *Lusitania* caused an outcry and Germany suspended unrestricted submarine warfare, but resumed the practice on February 1, 1917, knowing full well this would draw the United States into the war. The aim of unrestricted submarine warfare was to break the British blockade of Germany and disrupt the shipment of Allied supplies to England. But to be successful, Germany needed information about the movement of troops and supplies from the United States.

According to Bert Ford, Germany's agents could pick up such information at Camp Devens in Massachusetts, where the 12th, 26th, and 76th army divisions were trained and shipped out. "Much information could be gathered in and around Camp Devens, carried by automobile to the mountain retreats and relayed to points nearer the coast where it could be picked up and decoded by German submarines which were discovered lurking along the New England shore," Ford said.

The trick, of course, would be relaying the information. One possibility would be to signal the information by way of flashing lights. Along with all the dubious reports of signal lights in Jaffrey and the surrounding area, a few accounts stand out as more plausible. One of those came from Herbert L. Baldwin, reporter for the *Boston Post* newspaper, who had been among the first to report on the Dean murder. "Right away I heard stories of German spies working in the vicinity and of mysterious lights flashing from the mountains at night," Baldwin said. "Naturally, I was skeptical of these stores at first. I thought they might be the products of rural imagination or war hysteria, but I hadn't been working on the case more than a few days when I was convinced that they were true."

Baldwin's change of mind came one evening as he was filing a story on the murder from the Western Union office in Keene. The telegraph operator remarked, "You fellows are missing the real motive back of this killing."

"What's your dope on it?" Baldwin asked.

"Why, it's mixed up with the signal lights in some way and I'm willing to bet on it."

Baldwin dismissed the notion, hoping to draw the operator out more. "I heard some talk of lights over at the Dean place today," he said, "but didn't pay much attention to it because I hadn't been on the trail long enough to see how the lights could figure in the murder. I thought the lights a lot of rural chatter."

"Chatter nothing," the operator snapped. "They're real. When we finish here, if you're not in a hurry, I'll take you to my room and show you."

Baldwin agreed and went to the man's home. They sat on a balcony that looked out toward Mount Monadnock, smoking and waiting. At first they saw nothing, and Baldwin wondered if it was a wild goose chase. Then glimmers of light began to appear. "There they are now," the operator said.

"Those are nothing but Northern Lights," Baldwin said.

"The Northern Lights don't speak in code," the operator insisted. "I can read the letters, but can't make out the code. I have watched a great many nights."

Baldwin's curiosity was piqued. "That night, after I filed my copy, I ran my car right into the heart of the hills to get a closeup," he said. "I had hardly reached a place of vantage before there was a play of flashes which almost blinded me. They were weird, so weird in fact, that I felt I had been rather reckless in going there alone. After that I was satisfied that signals were being operated in the mountains and that there was something queer back of the murder of Dr. Dean."

78

THE NEIGHBOR

ANOTHER SIGNIFICANT REPORT OF FLASHING LIGHTS CAME FROM LEON Turner, who lived on his father's hilltop farm very near the Dean place, with a clear line of sight between the two farms. (It was Turner's windmill that William de Kerlor had erroneously identified as a wireless tower.) Turner had known the Deans since he was a boy and had fond memories of them. In an affidavit provided to the Jaffrey selectmen, Turner testified, "My father's farm is located on a hill east of the Dean farm, scarcely a quarter of a mile away. I saw signal lights from a point about 25 feet from the house on the Dean estate hired by Colfelt, on the southerly side of the house, facing the village and away from the Dean bungalow.

"The first time I saw the signals was a hot night in the summer of 1918, and I first thought it was heat lightning. About a week later, between 9 and 10 o'clock at night, when I went up on my windmill to shut it off, I saw the light again and it was then I discovered what it was. It looked to me like a searchlight sending signals over the mountains in code. It was either a searchlight or acetylene light. It was not in the Colfelt house but on the hill outside. It was not an automobile light, it was too powerful. It seemed to be set off the ground about four or five feet, just about the height of a searchlight on an automobile windshield, but I am satisfied that it wasn't an automobile light. It shot the rays at an angle of about 45 degrees so that the rays could be seen from the mountain.

"I have studied the Morse code but could not understand this code. It would shoot long flashes and two or three short ones and I thought it was a private code; answering flashes shot up from the other side of

Monadnock mountain. These lights appeared a little fainter but plain enough to be read. The lights on the Colfelt place would shoot for four or five minutes and then there'd be a wait of about two minutes and then the lights over beyond Monadnock would answer.

"After I found out what they were I used to go up there purposely to watch them. After Colfelt moved over to Temple I saw the lights coming from the direction of Temple mountain."

Another person who saw signal lights coming from Temple was William Cleves. According to Bureau of Investigation records, "About a week after Colfelt arrived in Temple, William S. Cleves, an employee of Miss Ware, while returning at 10:30 in the evening from Rindge to West Rindge, saw a revolving searchlight coming from the direction of Temple Mountain or Peterboro Hill, he could not tell which, but he thought Temple Mt. The light was thrown first to the southwest then circled through all the points of the compass to the southwest again. This occurrence took place for 10 or 15 minutes on July fifth or sixth."

To determine whether such reports were plausible, the Bureau's Norman L. Gifford held a conference with Dr. Louis Bell, the head of General Electric's electrical transmission department and an "expert on light signals," according to Gifford. The meeting convinced Gifford that, at the very least, some system of communications with lights was being experimented upon in southern New Hampshire. Of course, if it was an experiment, it may have been a failure—the distances too long, the operators too inexperienced, or watchful eyes too many to allow for success. Nevertheless, it seems plausible that some of the reports of signal lights may have had a basis in reality.

Frank Humiston, at least, was adamant that the lights were real and were related to Mr. Dean's murder. "Too many intelligent persons in this district saw the lights and hunted them down to be bothered by the skepticism of people who live in other New England states," Humiston said. "Those lights were real, and it's a pity that those who operated them weren't rounded up and shot in their tracks. That would have been a good way to deal with them. Dr. Dean was killed because he knew too much about the work of German agents in these parts."

If German spies were transmitting information to fellow agents—by signal light or some other method—they would undoubtedly try to protect the privacy of their messages. But how? Perhaps by using a code.

79

THE CODES

A NUMBER OF PEOPLE SUSPECTED THAT THE COLFELTS USED CODED language to communicate over the telephone or by telegram. Their suspicion even extended to Colfelt's wealthy mother, Rebecca Colfelt.

In the aftermath of the murder, Mrs. Colfelt was living at the Hotel Touraine in Boston, whose telephone operator—a Mrs. Polley—was interviewed by Agent Weiss. According to Weiss, "The Colfelt messages appeared to Mrs. Polley as being in code because they were to her mind, a lot of foolish talk about packages, etc., with neither head nor tail to it, unless the other party at the telephone understood what was meant." Needless to say, this is inconclusive evidence of espionage, at best.

On the other hand, there is the testimony of the Greenville telephone operator who told Agent Weiss that "she transmitted some messages over the telephone to Fitchburg which were absolutely code words," as Weiss reported. Federal agents were unable to find copies of any of these messages, but Weiss noted, "we did learn that the manager of that office was intimately acquainted with Colfelt, which may account for our not finding said messages."

Then there were the postcards. In July of 1918, after the Colfelts moved to Greenville, Natalye Colfelt brought three rolls of film to photographer C.T. Johnson in East Jaffrey to be developed and printed. "These negatives showed two teddy bears and a dog," Johnson said. "One teddy bear was black and the other white." The arrangement of the animals varied from print to print, he said. "On one negative the dog would be at one side of the grouping, and on another it would be in the centre [sic] and the different colored teddy bears were changed in location."

There were 49 images in all, and Johnson printed them on postcard stock. "At the time I thought it very queer to think that a household where they were all adults should have teddy bears and be interested in teddy bear photographs," he said.

Johnson kept one of the postcards, and during the investigation of the murder he turned it over to Selectman Boynton. Boynton passed the postcard on to federal agents, who took little notice of it. To William de Kerlor, however, the significance of the teddy-bear postcards was obvious: they were coded messages. The teddy bears, he argued, represented Ursa Major (the Big Bear) and Ursa Minor (the Little Bear), also known as the Big Dipper and Little Dipper. The stuffed dog was the Dog Star, Sirius. The arrangement of the elements indicated which direction the recipient was to look for signal lights.

The postcard also had what appeared to be the double-exposed image of a clock on it. This, de Kerlor stated confidently, indicated the time at which a signal would be sent.

Initially skeptical, Agent Valkenburgh came to accept de Kerlor's explanation of the teddy bear postcards by the time of the grand jury. "The government has found out it is a code, an astronomy code of the stars in the heaven," he testified.

But according to Natalye Colfelt, the photos were simply a silly pastime that she and her friends had undertaken. "At Radcliffe there was a girl who had a little toy dog, and another who had a doll, and I had a teddy bear, and it seems a crazy thing for a college girl to do, but they do a lot of crazy things," she said. She explained that the girls would take the toys around campus, arrange them in different positions, and photograph them.

"Was there any sinister motive or design in taking those pictures by you?" County Solicitor Pickard asked.

"You must excuse me, but that's a rather amusing question," Natalye responded. "Absolutely none."

Margaret Colfelt also scoffed at the suggestion that her daughter's photos represented some kind of secret code. "I didn't think there was a human being on earth as stupid as that, who would suggest a thing like that," she said.

The question remains, if the images were simply playful photographs, why have them printed as postcards? "I don't think those teddy bears were ever sent through the mail," Margaret Colfelt said. But Natalye testified that she had sent some of the photos to college friends and perhaps to Mr. Dean and Mrs. Robinson, though she was not sure.

One could excuse the teddy bear postcards, the puzzling telegrams about tainted candy, and even the Colfelts' cryptic telephone messages as innocent activities that were misconstrued in the heightened atmosphere of war hysteria and a brutal murder. But there is another suggestion that is harder to dismiss, and far more damning.

80

THE DEVICE

PUBLIC TELEPHONE AND TELEGRAPH SYSTEMS MAY HAVE BEEN TOO insecure for a spy to use, but there was always the option of setting up one's own, private, telegraph system.

At the time of World War I, the term "wireless" referred to telegraph signals sent via radio waves; broadcasting audio signals such as voice and music was only just being explored. Wireless telegraphy, originally developed for use by oceangoing vessels, would have been the best method for a spy to transmit information about troop or ship movements.

The first telegraph transmitters were large, heavy devices, often mounted in boxes resembling a large suitcase. Much of the device's weight was due to the power source, typically one or more large batteries akin to today's automobile batteries. The batteries accounted for another characteristic of a wireless apparatus: it was important not to tip or overturn it, as the acid in the batteries could leak out and destroy the wiring.

The batteries in a portable device would need to be recharged periodically using a generator, perhaps powered by a bicycle or an automobile. Just such a recharging operation may have been taking place at the Dean farm according to Leon Turner, who had seen lights flashing from the farm. "Several time[s] I approached the Dean farm to try to find out what these lights were and heard Colfelt's motor working," Turner said. "It seemed to me as if he were charging some battery with it; it lasted about an hour or so. It does not seem possible that he would let his motor run in the barn for over an hour and waste gas, unless he had some object in view."

Selectman Boynton, recalling how protective Colfelt was of his auto, suggested that it "might contain a wireless apparatus which they could go out and operate and would want to protect."

A wireless unit also requires an antenna. Today, antennae are omnipresent and everyone knows what they look like. In 1918, however, they were relatively new and perhaps easier to disguise.

In the aftermath of William Dean's murder, rumors spread that he had discovered a wireless apparatus in Colfelt's house. According to Father Hennon, Frank Humiston told him, "that there was a wireless outfit or part of one in the house."

George Mayhaver, the police chief in Peterborough, reported that a woman had done washing for the Colfelts and Lawrence Colfelt had told her he wanted to put up a wireless antenna but Dean objected to it.

According to William Leighton, "Mr. Dean made a remark sometime that if people would get into the Colfelt cellar they would see something surprising."

Finally, a Mrs. Griffith, friend of the Deans, said, "I have heard various persons say that Mr. Dean discovered that Colfelt had a wireless apparatus in the house and that he, therefore, ordered him away."

Unfortunately, all of these statements are secondhand or thirdhand at best, and there is no hard evidence that Colfelt installed a radio antenna at the summer house. If he had, the chimney would have been a good place to hide it; during World War II, spies and freedom fighters often hid radio antennae in chimneys, and it is possible that Colfelt anticipated that method 30 years earlier. Agent Robert Valkenburgh, at least, believed this was the case. Valkenburgh spoke to the Humiston family, who told him that Frank Humiston had seen a wireless apparatus being pulled out of the chimney of the summer house.

"Now, did he inform Mr. Dean of that fact?" County Solicitor Pickard asked Valkenburgh at the grand jury.

"No, I don't think so," Valkenburgh replied, "but I think Mr. Dean fell upon it himself, the way the Humiston family related it to me." Valkenburgh admitted that he had no evidence of this and did not know if Mr. Dean had spoken to anyone about finding such a wireless installation.

At the grand jury, Roy Pickard asked Lawrence Colfelt directly if he'd had a wireless apparatus on the Dean property.

"No," Colfelt replied, though he acknowledged that Mr. Dean suspected him of having one. According to Colfelt, the rumors started because he had an unusual trunk. "It's the sort of style trunk that you hang your clothes in and it stands up endwise," Colfelt said. He had showed the trunk to Dean because, he said, "I came to the conclusion they must have thought I had something to do with a wireless apparatus or something."

The "unusual trunk" to which Colfelt referred was undoubtedly the heavy case that Robert Hamill moved to Greenville. But Colfelt's explanation notwithstanding, his description does not match that of the heavy case, which Hamill would undoubtedly have recognized if it were a wardrobe trunk, a relatively common item at the time.

Nor does Colfelt's description match the box that Charlie Bean testified he saw in Colfelt's living room, which Attorney General Young asked him about. (In the following, bear in mind that "keyboard" likely meant a single key attached to a board, unlike today's computer keyboards.)

> YOUNG: Can you give us any better description of it?
>
> BEAN: Well, that keyboard, do you mean?
>
> YOUNG: Yes, the thing you saw in the box that you are talking about.
>
> BEAN: This thing in the box had a little round thing, like that, and something like this, and about two cylinders here, and this little knob up here to press down, and then there were wires connected, as if there was a battery in here somewhere.
>
> YOUNG: Do you know what kind of batteries they were?
>
> BEAN: Well, the batteries were concealed so I couldn't see what they were.
>
> YOUNG: It was something—you don't know exactly what it was?
>
> BEAN: I never saw anything like it before. Never saw anything like it before.
>
> YOUNG: Did you ever see the sending part of a wireless machine?

BEAN: No, not that I know of. Not unless that was one.

YOUNG: Was that on a board, or how was it?

BEAN: It was fixed onto this valise so you could turn this valise and it looked as though you could connect wires and use it right off.

All of this sounds very much like a telegraph apparatus, with a key, a battery, an induction coil, and a tuning coil.

Charlie Bean's story was at least partly confirmed by Frank Humiston, who was working at the Colfelt place the day Bean saw the device in the living room. Agent Weiss asked Humiston, "Do you remember when Charlie Bean went there to cut the puppies [sic] tail, what was he looking at?"

"I remember he looked into a box," Humiston replied.

"Did he make any remarks that it was either a wireless or a flashlight outfit?"

"Not that I remember, and I didn't look deep into it enough to make out what it was, but [we] were pretty sure that it was some kind of an outfit."

81

THE MONEY MOTIVE

IT WAS EASY FOR PEOPLE TO BELIEVE THAT A FLASHY STRANGER LIKE Lawrence Colfelt was a spy. It was harder to suspect a well-known, long-time resident like Charles Rich. But some did. Following the death of Mr. Dean, witnesses reported signal lights flashing from Charles Rich's home, which sat on a hill behind the town library.

At the time, Rich's house could be seen as far away as the Dean farm two miles away. It could certainly be seen from the Humiston home, a mere quarter mile east on Main Street. From there, Ruth Humiston kept a record of lights she saw over a period of about two weeks in October of 1918. She did this, according to her nephew David Humiston Kelley, at the suggestion of William de Kerlor. "There seem to have been about five principal locations from which the lights came, one of which was the tower room in Rich's house," Kelley said.

Ruth Humiston also saw lights from surrounding hills that looked like the dots and dashes of Morse code, although she admitted, "At Mr. Rich's house the lights very selom [sic] gave dots and dashes, although on one or two occasions they did."

When interviewed by federal agents, Ruth Humiston said, "We could see lights coming from Rich's house as if he was pulling down his shade and then letting it up again at intervals of about 3 minutes. Rich's stable light in front of the big stable door was also used."

Not surprisingly, Charles Rich denied flashing signal lights from his home. And it seems highly unlikely, even if he had been engaged in such activities prior to Dean's murder, that he would have continued in

October of 1918, given the level of suspicion and scrutiny to which he was being subjected.

Apart from the Humistons' suspicions, there appears to be nothing of substance to allegations that Charles Rich was involved in espionage. As a motive for being involved in the death of William Dean, the allegation lacks credibility. But there is another area worth examining as a possible motive: Rich's finances.

When it came to money, Charles Rich had his fingers in a lot of pies. In addition to his role at the Monadnock National Bank, he was a trustee of the Monadnock Savings Bank and ran his own insurance company. He served on the finance committee for the Masonic lodge, as treasurer for the Odd Fellows Lodge and for the local school district, and he managed a fund to help the poor in town.

Rich was also a key player in bringing new business to town. In 1912, he joined with other businessmen in a syndicate to finance D.D. Bean's and Merrill Symonds's purchase of land in East Jaffrey where they planned to construct a new manufacturing facility. Rich invested $7,500 in the enterprise, and other backers invested similar amounts, although one unnamed investor put in $50,000, according to bank examiner Daniel Mulloney.[31]

To fund his investment in the syndicate, Charles Rich appears to have borrowed the $7,500 from his own bank without any collateral. According to Mulloney, "I told Rich that it was a very poor move, because the bank has nothing on Bean & Simons [sic]." The move was not illegal, but perhaps unwise, and it supports the contention that Rich was, at the very least, loose and disorganized in his financial dealings.

D.P. Emory, president of the bank and fellow investor in the syndicate, found Rich's administrative abilities to be lacking, according to Herbert Sawtelle. "Mr. Emery [sic], who was formerly president of the Monadnock National Bank, told me before he left the presidency that the bank was run in a very loose way and that as soon as he could see his way clear he would get out from under," Sawtelle said. [32]

Even Rich's supporters disparaged Rich's business abilities on occasion. D.D. Bean noted that "he is a stubby short-fingered man, which proves to me that he hasn't got any executive ability, but he is a worker himself, and I could always notice that there is no system to his bank."

Judge Robert A. Ray complained about Rich's handling of estates for which he had been appointed executor. Regarding the settlement of one estate, Ray said, "It went on for years and I could not get any settlement from him. I had to order him into court and tell him just what is what before I could get the accounting that he ought to have rendered two years before." In the end, Ray did not accuse Rich of any wrongdoing in the matter. But Rich's handling of a few other transactions are more problematic.

In January of 1917, Dr. Lawrence B. Hatch of Jaffrey was called up to serve in the army. He made arrangements with Rich to have his government paycheck sent to the bank and then to his wife.

Hatch shipped off to France on July 4, 1918. In late July, his wife, Marian Hatch—who had moved to Fitchburg while her husband was at camp—visited Jaffrey and stopped at the bank to ask if her husband's allotment check had arrived.

"No. Not yet," Lana Rich told her.

Two months passed with still no checks. Mrs. Hatch wrote to the paymaster general and was told that three checks had been sent to the Monadnock National Bank. Upon receiving the letter, she promptly drove to Jaffrey and went to Charles Rich's house, arriving that evening.

"Mr. Rich was sitting in the parlor and I noticed that he had a black eye," Mrs. Hatch said. She asked Rich if he knew why she had come.

"Yes, I received a check for you," he replied.

"You should have three checks," she said and showed him the paymaster's letter.

According to Mrs. Hatch, "After Mr. Rich read the letter, he got very nervous and pale, and I thought he was going to faint."

Rich tried to excuse the mishandling by saying that he had not known who the checks were for. Mrs. Hatch reminded him that her husband had made the arrangements before he left for France. "As soon as I said that, Mr. Rich jumped up, put on his hat and left the house."

Mrs. Hatch talked to Lana Rich for a time, then asked if Mr. Rich was going to give her the money.

"Just wait here, Mrs. Hatch, I will go out and try to find Mr. Rich and bring him back."

Rich returned eventually and said, "I will go to the bank and give you my personal check for the amount due you." He did so, minus $75 that he said her husband owed the bank—an amount she knew nothing about but didn't want to argue over.

At the grand jury, Rich was at pains to dismiss the matter as simply a mix-up. Federal agents suspected it was fraud. At the very least, it was further indication that Rich's recordkeeping and handling of money left something to be desired.

As to his personal finances, Rich told bank examiner Mulloney enough to indicate that "he was not good for a very large sum of money," according to Mulloney. Rich told Mulloney that he had a mortgage of $3,500 on his house. Mulloney asked who held the mortgage, but the conversation was interrupted, and Rich did not answer.

In fact, the mortgage was held by Rich's own bank. In 1913, Rich mortgaged the house for $4,500, according to bank president D.P. Emory. Rich later repaid $1,000 of the principal, but he stopped making the interest payments in May of 1917, according to William de Kerlor. "This, much to the disgust of his mortgagee, Mr. Derastus E. [sic] Emory, who is also President and Director of the bank," de Kerlor noted.

The most potentially damning of Rich's financial affairs involved his dealings with the stock market and the sale of Liberty Bonds. It was widely rumored that Rich had lost money in the stock market. According to Norman Gifford of the Bureau of Investigation, "general gossip as well as some definite information of a more confidential nature indicates that Rich speculated and inside of two years sustained a loss of eight thousand dollars, which in some manner he tided over, although obtaining a salary as bank cashier of only two thousand dollars per year." The president of the Monadnock Savings Bank, Alfred Sawyer, countered the rumors, stating, "I have never seen any indications at any time of Mr. Rich speculating in stocks." This does not, of course, prove that Rich did not.

At the grand jury, Rich tried to downplay his involvement with the stock market. Attorney General Young asked him, "Have you bought any stocks, speculated at all in the last, well, I won't limit—ever speculated on stocks?"

"Well, I suppose you would say speculated," Rich replied. "I never bought over $5,000 worth at any time, I think." (In 1918, $5,000 would be the equivalent of $80,000 or more today, a tidy sum.)

"Did you sell it at a loss?" Young asked.

"No, I didn't lose anything," Rich said. "Didn't make enough so that I'd write it down anywhere."

Rich conducted his investments through Pearman and Brooks, a Boston stock brokerage firm that William de Kerlor believed was somehow connected to the Dean murder. De Kerlor visited the firm's office demanding to see their books but was denied access. According to Bert Ford, "de Kerlor's visit caused a flurry which was intensified when agents of the Department of Justice a few days later called on the firm to produce the books." A short time later, the company went into receivership and then declared bankruptcy. The ostensible cause of the company's failure was an employee's embezzlement of funds, though Bert Ford suggested that it might have been related to a different activity: mishandling of Liberty Bonds.

82

THE LIBERTY BONDS

IN THE SPRING OF 1917, THE UNITED STATES TREASURY BEGAN SELLING Liberty Bonds to finance the war effort. The bonds were sold through banks, stock brokerages, insurance companies, and even retail stores. Each bond came with coupons attached, which purchasers could redeem periodically for the interest accrued, or retain and collect the full interest upon maturity.

Charles Rich handled the sale of Liberty Bonds at the Monadnock National Bank, though his participation was perhaps less than enthusiastic. Jaffrey resident Alfred Burgoyne recalled approaching Rich during one of the Liberty Loan drives and telling him he had money to invest.

"Put it in the bank," Rich told him, according to selectman Edward Boynton. "You didn't want this war and I didn't want this war. Let them settle for it."

Rich's attitude toward the bonds may have been due to the amount of work they entailed. One aim of the Liberty Loan program to was to encourage those with low to moderate incomes to invest in the war effort. The large number of people who invested and the small amounts of money involved necessitated a great deal of bookkeeping, which may have grated on Rich. One prominent loan official complained that "Rich did not cooperate, that his bank was the last to send in its returns, that it took a sharp letter to get them in at all."

Even Rich's supporters acknowledged the stories of his mishandling Liberty Bonds. "Rich has been accused of holding up the Liberty Bonds," D.D. Bean said. "Everybody in this town knows that is a fact. Tobey who is at the head of the Liberty Bond Bureau in this state said that Rich must be pro-German because he would not deliver the Bonds."

A few witnesses testified that Rich's handling of Liberty Bonds went beyond mere dislike or disorganization. Selectman Peter Hogan reported that he had purchased three $50 Liberty Bonds from Rich, one each for himself, his wife, and his mother-in-law. According to Agent Valkenburgh, "His wife's mother received her check for the interest from Washington, but Mrs. Hogan didn't receive any. When the fourth loan was on, Mr. Hogan called at the bank and asked for his bonds. Mr. Rich handed Mr. Hogan two registered $50 Bonds and two envelopes, in which Mr. Hogan found cash for the interest due on said bonds." This was not the way it was supposed to work, as Valkenburgh correctly noted. "A person buying a registered bond receives a check for interest from Washington direct and not cash."

Alice Humiston also bought a $50 bond from Rich and received a receipt, but not a bank receipt. "This receipt is a personal receipt of C.L. Rich and on the right hand upper corner rubber stamped, 'Monadnock National Bank,'" Humiston said. Five months later, when she was interviewed by Valkenburgh, Humiston had still not received her bond, nor had she received any word from Washington or the Monadnock Bank about it.

Edward Boynton spelled out his suspicions about Rich's handling of Liberty Bonds to Agent Norman Gifford, telling him that "some deliveries on the same order had been several months late and the dividends had been paid in cash instead of government check." Boynton and others suspected that Rich was buying second-hand bonds at a discount and selling them to people who had intended to purchase new bonds directly from the government.

Bert Ford spelled out the scheme. "It is known that a local suspect bought many Liberty bonds through Pearmain & Brooks, and that one of the firm had a summer place in this vicinity. It was also discovered that Liberty bonds subscribed to by many of the people of Jaffrey were bought at low figures, unregistered, the coupons detached and the bonds then sent to Washington to be registered. In this way a margin was cleared by local persons and the defunct firm. It is alleged that this method was operated on a most profitable scale and that subsequently subscribers hereabout received their Liberty Bonds in envelopes which contained cash as interest instead of coupons. This irregularity was called to the attention of the authorities in Washington, but no action was taken."

Ford also alleged that federal agents had observed an unnamed suspect working at night, transferring Liberty Bonds to new envelopes and destroying the envelopes in which they had come. He was undoubtedly referring to Charles Rich, who was known for working into the evening at the bank, a two- or three-minute walk from his home.

At the grand jury, Attorney General Young questioned Rich about his handling of Liberty Bonds. "Did you personally have any trouble with anyone about any bonds or about the delivery of any bonds subscribed for at your bank?" Young asked.

"Not a bit," Rich replied.

That seemed to satisfy Young, who did not follow up, either unaware or unconcerned with the allegations people had made about Rich's handling of the bonds.

If the aim of the Liberty Bond program was to get people of modest means involved, William Dean certainly qualified. At the time of his death, Dean's financial situation was dire. Although the Deans had come to East Jaffrey with $50,000, they appear to have used that up over the course of their 30 years in Jaffrey "Where the money has gone no one seems to know," Dean's cousin Henry Dean wrote to William Dean Goddard.

The Deans had moved to the small bungalow so they could rent out the big summer house to make ends meet. Their precarious financial situation could explain why Dean had hesitated to ask the Colfelts to leave despite the issues he'd had with them, dependent as he was on rental income from the big house. The Deans' money problems may also explain the dunning telegram Dean sent Colfelt requesting payment for hay he had used, a message that struck Colfelt as very unlike Dean.

Dean's only other income appeared to be the occasional interest or dividend payments from bonds issued by the Rochester Telephone Company and the American Clay Company. Dean kept whatever cash he had at a bank in Rochester, New York, and maintained a very small balance—occasionally overdrawn—at Monadnock National Bank.

Despite his straitened circumstances, Dean managed to purchase Liberty Bonds to support the war effort, a total of $1,800 in value. He paid for them with money from his Rochester bank account, essentially emptying it. He bought a few large bonds and a number of smaller $100 bonds. Charles Rich supposed he bought the smaller bonds so that he could sell them later, should he need the money.

The severity of Dean's financial situation was highlighted by an incident that occurred in July of 1917. During a severe thunderstorm, lightning struck the Dean bungalow, tearing up flooring, damaging the fireplace, and knocking dishes off the mantle. Dean filed a claim with Rich's insurance agency, but Rich felt that Dean set too a high value on his losses. According to Rich, he hesitated to settle for fear the insurance carrier would think he was showing favoritism to a friend. A year later, the case had still not been settled and Dean, apparently needing the money, decided to sell one of his $100 Liberty Bonds.

"You don't have to do it," Rich told him, offering to give Dean a personal loan of $60 against the money expected from the insurance company.

Perhaps this was an act of friendship, or perhaps Rich did not want Dean to sell the bond and discover that it was one Rich had purchased and resold rather than an original government issue. To some, this might simply have seemed like a shady business practice. But William Dean, a man of high principles and intense patriotic fervor, would have viewed it as treachery.

Dean's finances continued to decline right up to the end. The last check he wrote was for $5, made out to Goodnow's store during his final trip to town. At that point, his bank account was overdrawn by $21.96.

83

THE SECRET

Why was William Dean murdered? The most likely answer is that he knew something that someone didn't want him to tell. Of course, it is possible that the timing of Dean's murder, just before he intended to give information to the government, was coincidental, though this seems unlikely.

If Dean was murdered to keep him from telling what he knew, what was it? The leading theories are that it was information related to espionage or to financial misdeeds. Other motives have been suggested, such as Dean becoming aware of an affair between Charles Rich and Susan Henchman. But Dean would have had no reason to report that to the government, nor would it explain his sense of urgency.

In regard to espionage, Charles Rich seems unlikely to have been involved, or only peripherally involved at most. Edward Boynton suggested that Rich's pro-German sympathies might have drawn him into activities that did not seem disloyal at the start. "At one time before this country went to war, it was possible that a man, a loyal citizen, might have been mixed up in German intrigue, and that after war was declared he might have been in so deep that he couldn't get out," Boynton said. At any rate, regardless of Rich's alleged pro-German sympathies, there is no firm evidence he was involved in espionage.

What of Lawrence Colfelt? Was he a spy, or the victim of prejudice and war hysteria? Admittedly, much of the evidence pointing to Colfelt is circumstantial, like his frequent travels around the region, trips that he took on foot, horseback, or by automobile, day and night, at all times of the year. Was Colfelt gathering information, or was he simply a wealthy man with little to occupy his time?

Could Colfelt have been connected to Count von Bernstorff? He could easily have met von Bernstorff during one of his visits to the Monadnock region. But this is speculation, with no evidence to back it up.

Financially, Colfelt was well off, but he lived well and was not frugal, so he may not have been immune to financial inducements from foreign agents. According to Colfelt's doctor, Robert J. Carlisle, "Colfelt is one who might easily be induced to do most anything in case he found himself in a tight place for financial consideration."

More incriminating, there is Colfelt's stunned reaction to Frank Humiston saying he had come to the Dean farm to catch Colfelt as a spy, and Colfelt's query as to how Humiston did it.

Then there are the reports from Leon Turner and Eva Sweeney of the lights seen from Colfelt's house on the Dean farm, and Turner's suggestion that Colfelt was charging a battery with his automobile. The mysterious teddy bear postcards could have been innocent keepsakes, or may have been part of some coded messaging system.

Countering the idea of Colfelt being involved in espionage is William Dean's belief that Colfelt was simply not smart enough to be a spy. A former business associate of Colfelt's, Beakman O. Meyers, agreed. Meyers told federal agents he thought Colfelt was "incapable, for want of intelligence, to engage in any spy activities or anything of that character."

Another intriguing possibility is that Margaret Colfelt was actually the spy in the family and that Lawrence was merely an accomplice. Frank Romano, who worked for Lawrence Colfelt and may have known them better than anyone, said that Margaret "was directing all his strange activities and causing the trouble." It seems certain that Margaret Colfelt harbored pro-German sentiments, but her comments to Romano on the matter were inconsistent. "Mrs. Colfelt told me one day that she knows the Kaiser very well and when she was in Berlin last, she went to the Theatre and sat two seats from the Kaiser, and then again she would say he was no good and she would like to kick him," Romano said.

According to Bert Ford, "Mrs. Colfelt went frequently to Ayer, Mass., to see a relative who was in the army at Camp Devens. She was seen there on various occasions talking with an officer in an American uniform." An American soldier was also reported visiting them at their Greenville home and holding conversations behind locked doors.

However, as with Charles Rich, all this is circumstantial and speculative. The only really incriminating evidence that the Colfelts were engaged in espionage is the mysterious device Charlie Bean saw in their house and the heavy box that was moved to Greenville.

Did William Dean know or suspect that Colfelt might be involved in undercover activities? Frank Humiston said he asked Dean on several occasions if that might be the case. The first time Dean replied, "You don't think for a minute that I would have a spy living in my house."

Later, however, Dean appeared to take the question more seriously, and by the time Humiston left for overseas, Dean seemed fearful. "I think he got pretty wise to Colfelt then and got to be afraid of him," Humiston said. "In fact, of both of them."

Even Colfelt acknowledged that Dean suspected him of being a spy. At the grand jury, Colfelt explained how he and Dean had fallen out over the use of the barn. "And then he got in his head this German spy situation and worried about the war," Colfelt said. "The man was beginning to worry himself to death about it."

At one point, Colfelt overheard Dean suggest that he was a spy, which he dismissed as a joke. "I heard he said over the phone to someone, someone was asking who we were and what we were doing up there, and I heard he said perhaps that we were spies, in a jocular way," Colfelt said. "He was always that way, had to be sarcastic or jocular."

When Dean met with Agent Bradley just weeks before his death, he said he had seen nothing that he would consider pro-German, apparently unwilling to accuse anyone without firm evidence. According to Bradley, "I came to the conclusion that he was an exceedingly cautious man. I was convinced that he would not be apt to discuss a subject unless he was sure of his ground."

A month later, however, Dean *had* uncovered something and it was so disturbing that he would not share it with Mrs. Morison for fear of putting her in danger. By then, the Colfelts had moved. The summer house was empty, and Dean would have had plenty of time to look for anything suspicious there. Dean's comments to Mrs. Morison about signal lights and the Colfelts just before his murder suggest that something of the sort was on his mind.

84

THE THEORY

THE PROBLEM WITH WRITING A BOOK ABOUT AN UNSOLVED MURDER IS exactly that: the murder has not been solved. The author can't gather the suspects like the detective in a TV show or movie, eliminating them one by one until only the murderer remains, revealed at the end with a flourish.

In writing this book I have read thousands of pages of documents, scanned hundreds of newspaper articles, and filed dozens of Freedom of Information requests. I have retraced the steps William Dean took on the last night of his life. I have driven the winding country road to his home, walked the path he took to the barn, followed the footsteps of his murderers as they carried his body to the cistern. I have spoken to the children and grandchildren of eyewitnesses. In the course of my research, I have been asked dozens upon dozens of times, usually in a whisper, "Who did it?"

Here is my confession. I cannot tell you who killed William K. Dean. Now, a hundred years after the fact, the precise truth is almost certainly unknowable. However, I can present a scenario that fits the reams of evidence we have.

Here then is my suggestion of what might have happened on the night that William Dean was murdered. Let me be clear, I am not saying that this is definitely what happened. I am saying that this is what could have happened, a scenario that fits the facts as we know them.

Lawrence Colfelt may have been a spy, or he may simply have been a dilettante who imagined himself as a spy and toyed with activities he thought would be useful to Germany: gathering information, wireless telegraphy, hobnobbing with German sympathizers. On the other hand, the Colfelts may simply have been the innocent victims of gossip and war hysteria.

In any event, William Dean became convinced that Lawrence Colfelt was engaged in subversive activities. Whether true or not, Dean's suspicions were enough to cause him to contact federal authorities. The Colfelts had already fallen out with Dean over financial matters, and the dunning telegram from Dean about the hay put them over the edge. Margaret Colfelt was furious and penned an anonymous letter telling him to keep his mouth shut.

As far as we know, Dean spoke to no one about what he planned to tell federal authorities—not his wife, his friends, nor anyone in town. This was more than just Dean's usual circumspection. His actions were those of a man who suspected his every move was being observed. Nevertheless, Colfelt somehow became aware that Dean was about to report him to the government. Arria Morison came to believe that when she visited Dean the day before his death, someone was hiding behind a nearby hedge, overheard their conversation and passed it on. William de Kerlor accepted this suggestion, as did federal agents.

It is also possible that Dean told one person of his concerns, someone who had once been a close friend: Charles Rich. "It would have been a natural thing for Dean to give his evidence to Rich, as his friend and as the local magistrate," lawyer Reginald Smith said. "There is evidence that he did so but that Rich, for reasons best known to himself, refused to act."

According to Frank Humiston, Rich's refusal to act brought on a quarrel with Dean, as Humiston told Robert Hamill. "The story about Rich was that Dean as a friend came to him and told him as a police justice some things of importance about certain people and Rich would not act on it so Rich got into a fight with Dean," Hamill said.

When Charles Rich became aware of Dean's intentions he alerted Lawrence Colfelt, with whom he had become quite friendly. Colfelt and Rich shared a sympathy for the German cause and had interacted in social and business settings, although both tried to play down their relationship later. Colfelt admitted that he and Rich were friendly and had dined together one or two times, but claimed their connections were mostly business oriented, related to the bank, the insurance company, and the purchase of Liberty Bonds. Rich claimed that he mostly knew Colfelt as a customer of the bank. "I never knew him except as I would any depositor," he said, though he admitted that they had played billiards at Mr. Dean's house now and then.

But other witnesses indicated there was more to it than that. "I heard Colfelt speak a lot about Mr. Rich what good friends he and Rich were," Frank Humiston said. "He said Rich was the best fellow in town and he used to talk with him a lot."

Similarly, Mary Lee Ware noted, "Colfelt is continually going to East Jaffrey to see the Riches."

Alice Humiston—who seemed to have a particular dislike for Charles Rich and may be an unreliable witness—said, "Colfelt and Rich were so thick for quite a spell that they used to send their shirts to the laundry together."[33]

If Rich became aware that Dean was about to report Colfelt to the federal government, he undoubtedly told Colfelt. At this point, Lawrence Colfelt had had enough. He told Rich to make his friend shut up. "I don't think he actually would do the deed, but might have hired somebody else to do it," Merrill Symonds said, speaking of Colfelt. "He was too smart to do it himself."

Why would Rich listen to Colfelt? Because Colfelt, with his background in stock trading, knew that Rich had been mishandling Liberty Bonds; his own purchase of bonds from Rich would have tipped him off to that. Or perhaps Colfelt knew that Rich was having an affair with a young woman at the bank. At any rate, Rich knew that Colfelt could make life miserable for him and agreed to cooperate in the effort to stifle Dean.

Charles Rich was undoubtedly present at the murder of William Dean. He was seen heading in that direction just prior to the murder, in the company of at least two other people. According to Jaffrey resident John Tonry, Rich would have needed help if he was going to strong-arm

Dean. "Now, Eddie Baldwin would be the man," Tonry said. "Henchman is a meek and humble fellow, while Baldwin is a bull-dog." There was another factor, Tonry explained: "Henchman, Rich, and Baldwin know every inch of land around the Dean farm, and they certainly know Dean's habits as nobody else in the town."[34]

Recalling the murder decades later, Archie Letourneau argued against the idea that Dean had been killed by outsiders brought in for the job. As far as he was concerned, it was an inside job, committed by local residents. "Henchman, Baldwin, and Rich," Letourneau said, ticking the names off on his fingers. "There's three of 'em, right there. Inside job."

Ed Baldwin may have driven Rich's buggy, as he was the most familiar with it. Rich and Henchman rode in Susan Henchman's auto. Daniel LaRose saw three people in the car but said the two people in the back seat hid their faces as it passed. Perhaps there was a reason for that. "There was a lady in there too, in that car," Homer Belletete said years later. "Miss Henchman."

At the Dean farm, Rich and the others met Lawrence Colfelt, who had come from Portsmouth in a rented car. Or perhaps they met Margaret Colfelt, though this seems less likely. The hairpin found at the cistern places her in the vicinity of the crime, although this could have been dropped there earlier, when she was living in the summer house.

The group of three or four people confronted Dean, first trying to reason with him, then threatening him. William Dean was older than his attackers and outnumbered by them, but he was not a man to cower. He refused to keep his mouth shut. A fight ensued and Dean, an amateur boxer, managed to get in a few good blows, including at least one at Charles Rich. This was the cause of the black eye that Rich sported the next day, not a kick from his horse.

Things got out of hand as the more aggressive members of the party tried to subdue Dean, tying a rope halter around his neck. Dean continued to struggle, and then the unthinkable happened: his neck was broken, killing him. After the murder, Natalye Colfelt visited Margaret Robinson and asked if anything had been found out. Robinson, suspicious and hoping to draw Natalye out, said, "You probably know that there are people in East Jaffrey who suspect Mr. Rich."

"Is that so?" Natalye replied. "Well, if he did it I don't suppose he went up intending to do it, but they probably quarreled."

Having accidentally killed Dean, the gang panicked. They knew they had to dispose of his body, somewhere it would take searchers a while to find it. They settled on the cistern by the summer house, a location that anyone who did not know the property would have had trouble finding in the daylight, let alone on a moonless night.

The men hog-tied the body so that it would be easier to carry and grabbed a rock from the stone wall near the barn to help sink the body in the cistern. A dead body is not easy to carry and it took all three men to lug it up the slope to the cistern. As they deposited the body into the murky water, Charles Rich did not notice that the cigarette case Dean had given him years ago slipped from his shirt pocket. Rich would not realize the cigarette case was missing until he returned to Jaffrey. There, he consulted with the others outside the mill building—where they were seen by the night watchman—then Rich raced back to the Dean farm, taking the roundabout route by Mrs. Morison's house so as to avoid going through town again.

Lawrence Colfelt, if he was present, sped back to Portsmouth in time to show up for work the next morning. Even if not present, he would have been afraid that his part in the affair might come out; when questioned by federal agents, Colfelt seemed nervous, as did most of the parties mentioned here. Charles Rich was particularly fearful. He was a man of business, not action, and those who had taken the more active role in the murder undoubtedly threatened him and his family with grievous harm if he talked, the same kind of harm that had befallen William Dean. According to the Riches' neighbor, Imogene Mead, "I am just as positive that Mr. Rich did not do it as I am Mrs. Dean did not do it, but I am awfully afraid that he knows something about it."

"If he would only tell us about it?" Agent Weiss asked Mrs. Mead.

"He would not be alive twenty-four hours if he told, I think," she replied.

By 1:00 a.m. on the morning of August 14, 1918, the deed had been done. William Dean was dead, his body hidden in a cistern on his own property.

The farm was quiet now, apart from the rustling of leaves in the wind. On a high branch of a maple tree by the barn, an owl scanned the grassy slope that led up to the summer house, wondering what the whispering figures had been up to earlier.

The murderers had gone, and now the only human within a mile was Mary Dean, who paced her small kitchen, wondering what was keeping Billie. She lay down, then rose, expecting him to come at any moment. She went on pacing. The soup she had prepared grew cold. The clock in the kitchen ticked off the minutes, then the hours. She kept her vigil through the night, with a growing certainty that something had happened to her husband. He would not have otherwise left her alone for so long.

Finally, the morning came. Steeling herself, Mary Dean headed for the barn.

EPILOGUE

THE COLFELTS

A MONTH AFTER WILLIAM DEAN'S MURDER, MARGARET COLFELT LEFT Temple, New Hampshire, and moved to an apartment in New York City. The next month, Lawrence Colfelt left his job at the Atlantic Shipbuilding Company and joined Margaret in New York.

Federal agents tracked Colfelt to Portsmouth and followed his trail to New York where they tried to interview him but were never able to gain access to his apartment building.

In December of that year, the flu epidemic was still raging, and Lawrence apparently worried that he was infected. Federal agent William Poling interviewed Colfelt's doctor, Robert Carlisle: "He states that he had been called to see Lawrence Colfelt quite frequently in the past three months, the last time he had seen him was on December 6, when he was called up at 3 o'clock in the morning by subject's wife and was requested to come to the house at once, that Lawrence was dying. When he arrived, he found that Lawrence Colfelt's temperature was normal and apparently there was nothing the matter with him. He states that he had been annoyed by these frivolous calls a great deal of late and that he had tried to rid himself of these people."

By the spring of 1919, the Colfelts appear to have moved back to their home in Harrison, New York. That September, Lawrence's mother died and he and Margaret relocated to her house—his family home—in West Whiteland, Pennsylvania. There, he continued his high-society lifestyle, which included serving as an officer of the Whitelands Hunt club and Master of the Hunt, and Margaret was recalled as "a well-known local equestrienne." They had two servants, according to census records, although by 1940, there were no servants.

In 1942, Lawrence registered for the World War II draft at age 63, listing his employer as the Fox Munitions Corporation in Philadelphia. One could ask why a man of his age and income bracket would need to work at a munitions factory. Apparently, the question also concerned Daniel LaRose, who had moved to Troy, New York, shortly after the Dean murder, perhaps feeling he had worn out his welcome in Jaffrey with his appearance at the grand jury.

On May 24, 1943, LaRose wrote to J. Edgar Hoover about his concerns. "Dear Chief, I have had a feeling of late that a person named by Lawrence Maens [sic] Colfelt Jr. is sure on the spot in doing in [sic] American Activities," LaRose wrote. He explained that he had been a witness in the Dean murder case and that Colfelt was suspected of having German ancestry and pro-German sympathies. He offered his help to the Bureau and said, "I honestly think this Colfelt is playing an important part in World War #2 and has furnished information from here."

Hoover responded a few weeks later, thanking LaRose for his interest and instructing him to contact the FBI office in Albany if he had information to share. If LaRose did so, I could find no record of the communication.

Margaret Colfelt died of a cerebral hemorrhage in 1946, brought on by hypertension and "previous apoplexy." Lawrence died from cancer in 1954 at the age of 76. A brief mention in the *Philadelphia Inquirer* noted that he would be buried in his wealthy grandfather's mausoleum at the North Laurel Hill Cemetery in Philadelphia.

CHARLES RICH

The shadow of the Dean murder followed Charles Rich for the rest of his life. At Rich's slander trial against Edward Boynton, he tearfully recounted that children would cross the street to avoid him because of the rumors spread about him. Rich's efforts to restore his reputation were met with skepticism by some of his fellow townspeople. "He had always been hateful and surly to people in the bank, but lately he has tried hard to be pleasant," Alice Humiston wrote. "He has even offered to do unheard of kindnesses for people with whom he has never been particularly friendly." Fred Croteau told his wife, "How does it happen that Mr. Rich never spoke to anyone before and now he bows? He is getting pretty good natured all at once."

Although Rich lost the slander case against Edward Boynton, he successfully sued the *Boston American* for libel and the newspaper settled for $5,500 rather than bearing the expense of a trial. Rich believed that this was a complete exoneration, though it was not. He continued working at the Monadnock National Bank and was active in social and civic affairs, including the Jaffrey Republican Club, Universalist Church, Jaffrey Service Club, and New Hampshire National Guard, among others. In 1930, he suffered a stroke that forced him to resign from most of his positions. A second stroke felled him in January of 1933, and he died on January 11 from "apoplexy," as his death record reads.

Rich's obituary appeared in the *Monadnock Breeze* and *Peterborough Transcript* and read, "He was a man of absolute incorruptibility, of fearless independence, and sympathetic generosity. The interest of his neighbor was always first with him. His hand was open and his decisions just. If he ever erred in judging men, it was through over-generosity and belief in the purity of their motives. For years he served as moderator of the town meetings and as a judge in the local police court. His standards of character and ideals were high and exacting as they applied to himself; but he was tolerant of those less well-equipped to meet the demands of life. Today he rests from his labors, and his works do follow him." No mention was made of the affair that had dogged him for 15 years.

Rich's funeral was held on January 13. Among the bearers were Wilbur Webster, Homer White, Merrill Symonds, John Townsend, and Dr. Frederick Sweeney.

Lana Rich died on January 18, 1938, following surgery for a twisted intestine and peritonitis. The honorary bearers at her funeral included the same five men who had borne her husband's casket: Webster, White, Symonds, Townsend, and Sweeney.

RUSSEL AND SUSAN HENCHMAN

Russel Henchman was appointed postmaster in Jaffrey on September 19, 1918, roughly a month after the murder of William Dean.[35] William de Kerlor believed that Henchman was given the job thanks to the influence of Charles Rich. So did Rich's friend Herbert Sawtelle. "Henchman has got to thank Rich for every job that he ever had and I have it from good authorities that Rich made him postmaster in East Jaffrey," Sawtelle said.

Prior to the Dean murder, Russel Henchman had lived a mile and a half from East Jaffrey with his daughter, son, and sister, Susan. (His wife had died in 1915.) After the murder, the family moved to a house on Main Street near the center of town. In 1928, Russel and Susan Henchman built a home near the end of Bradley Court, a short, dead-end street off Main Street next to the library. Their neighbors, at the very end of Bradley Court, were Charles and Lana Rich.

Over time, in addition to being superintendent of the town water works, Russel Henchman served as selectman, supervisor of the check list, and town auditor, among other positions. He was Jaffrey's postmaster until shortly before his death in August of 1931. According to the obituary in the *Peterborough Transcript*, "His work in reorganizing the local Post Office, at a time when complaints were frequent in regard to poor service, was appreciated by the business men of the town in particular ..."

After the deaths of Russel Henchman and Charles Rich, Susan Henchman appears to have resigned from the Monadnock National Bank and moved to Massachusetts for a time. Then, on April 23, 1936, a brief item in the *Peterborough Transcript* noted that she had returned to East Jaffrey, "and is staying with Mrs. Lana M. Rich at present." By 1939, Susan Henchman appears to have lived in Athol, Massachusetts. Upon her death in 1951, her body was returned to Jaffrey and is buried with those of her parents and brother in the town cemetery.

Before coming to work at the bank, Susan Henchman had been a teacher at the high school and a favorite of Alice Humiston, who nevertheless suspected Henchman of involvement with Mr. Dean's death. "This part of the story hurts me a good deal, because Susie was one of my teachers in high school and the one I liked best of all the women teachers I had," Humiston wrote in 1919. "From hints that have been given me at different times at home, I am very much afraid Mr. Rich met her some-where that night because they say a woman was mixed up in the affair, as well as two or three other men."

FRANK ROMANO

The mysterious Frank Romano stopped working for the Colfelts shortly before the murder of William Dean. He went to Port Chester, New York, where he found work at a bolt and nut foundry. In the aftermath of the murder, people remembered the comment Romano had allegedly made about Dean being found hanging up in his barn. Among those who cast suspicion on Romano was Charles Rich, according to Edward Boynton. "One day he came to me on the street and he said, 'Have you examined Romano? Have you found him?'" Boynton recalled.

The suspicion led Pinkerton agent Harry Scott and federal agents to interview Romano, who could not at first account for his whereabouts on the night of William Dean's murder. He told investigators he had taken time off work and gone to Silver Lake near White Plains, New York. "I picked up a girl at the lake one night and slept there," Romano said. "You know, a man has to have a woman that way once in a while and I'm no different from other men. I don't know the name of the girl or where she lives or anything about her."

Romano told the investigators he had tried to find the woman to corroborate his story but could not. Nevertheless, both Scott and federal agents cleared Romano of any involvement in Dean's murder. According to Harry Scott, "while we were unable to find the woman with who [sic] he spent the night, the Federal officers have gone into it very fully and so far as we can find, we cannot place him within two hundred miles of Jaffrey on any of these days. No person answering his description was seen around East Jaffrey where he is known fairly well. That result has been concurred with by the Federal officers, but I also investigated it."

Agent Valkenburgh had interrogated Romano aggressively. "I even tried to get his goat, as the saying goes, and see if I could get anything out of him," Valkenburgh said. Finally, Valkenburgh asked Romano point blank why he had made the comment about Dean being found hanging in his barn some morning.

"Damn him," Romano said, meaning Lawrence Colfelt. "That's what he told me."

"Are you willing to get on the stand and swear to this?" Valkenburgh asked.

"Yes. Whenever you are ready, send for me and I will make that statement under oath that Colfelt made that remark to me."

WILLIAM DE KERLOR

It is difficult to assess William de Kerlor's contribution to the Dean murder case. There are undoubtedly things we would not know if not for his rambunctious persistence. But his unorthodox methods, lack of real experience, and tendency to jump to conclusions may, in the end, have hindered the investigation more than helping.

Although de Kerlor had agreed to work on the case for expenses only—and was reimbursed for those expenses—he later submitted a bill to the town of Jaffrey for his services as well. When the selectmen refused to pay, de Kerlor sued the town for $4,000, but his own attorney eventually decided the suit was meritless and withdrew it.

While the Dean investigation was ongoing, de Kerlor and his wife, Elsa Schiaparelli, relocated from New York to Boston, where they continued the self-aggrandizing promotional schemes that had gotten them in hot water elsewhere. In 1920, their one daughter was born, but de Kerlor almost immediately deserted Elsa and the child. Thereafter, Schiaparelli would tell her daughter that her father was dead. De Kerlor and Schiaparelli both took other lovers and only officially divorced in 1924.

After leaving Schiaparelli, de Kerlor appears to have traveled widely and ended up in Tampico, a wild west oil boomtown on the Gulf of Mexico. There, he engaged in oil prospecting, palm-reading, and heavy drinking. On April 29, 1928, at a bar called the Yaqui Club, an inebriated de Kerlor got into an argument with the bartender, who shot him in the stomach. The circumstances of the altercation are unclear, but de Kerlor did not seek medical attention until two days later. He was operated on and died later that day. He was 39 years old.

De Kerlor, for all his eccentricities and bull-in-a-china-shop approach to the Dean murder investigation, was perceptive in some areas. In regard to Germany, he noted that "our government was not acquainted with European trickery and diplomacy and therefore was an easy prey to the villainy of the so-called diplomats"—a statement proven true when it was revealed that Count von Bernstorff had been behind a massive espionage scheme while serving as the German ambassador to the United States.

De Kerlor also displayed a surprising prescience even as he attempted to explain the "science" behind the faces he saw in the blood spots on the barn door. "Psychology, as a means of detecting crime, will be the most potent agency of the trained police of the future," he said, a statement with which today's experts in criminal profiling would probably agree.

ADDENDUM I

THE HOODLUM THEORY

IN THE DECADES SINCE WILLIAM DEAN'S MURDER, A FEW ALTERNATIVE theories have been floated to explain the crime. One theory, especially favored by those who supported Charles Rich, was the "hoodlum theory." This narrative suggested that Mr. Dean stumbled upon a group of young people who were using his barn or the summer house as a meeting place for drinking and sex. A fight ensued, Dean was accidentally killed, and the culprits disposed of his body so as to hide the evidence. This theory collapses upon even the most cursory examination. To begin with, no evidence was ever found to support the idea, and the earliest primary sources contain no suggestion of it.

The hoodlum theory does, however, play a prominent role in a fictionalized account of the Dean murder that Georgiana Hodgkins wrote after Charles Rich's death. *Prominent Citizen: Prime Suspect* is a *roman à clef*, a retelling of the Dean murder using invented names for the real-life characters involved. The manuscript of Hodgkins's book remained unpublished until it came into the hands of the Jaffrey Historical Society. In 1996, with the permission of the Hodgkins family, the society published the book, replacing the fictional names with the actual names of the people involved, most of whom were easily recognizable. As Margaret Bean wrote in a foreword to the book, "It must be understood that Georgiana Hodgkins was inescapably subjective in the telling of the story." Nevertheless, the book does provide insights into Georgiana Hodgkins's feelings about the Dean murder.

The storyline of *Prominent Citizen: Prime Suspect* hews closely to the Riches' account of the murder, including Mrs. Dean's jealousy, the friendship between Charles Rich and Mr. Dean, the horse kick that resulted in Rich's black eye, Dean's visit to the Riches' home on the evening of the murder, the suggestion that Dean committed suicide, Mrs. Dean's deep water comment, and the implication of Mrs. Dean's guilt, among other details.

The hero of Hodgkins's book is Charles Rich, "the soul of truth and honor" as she describes him, and the unjustly accused victim of a conspiracy to blacken his name and convict him of Dean's murder in the court of public opinion.

The chief criminal is William de Kerlor, a charlatan masquerading as a detective and playing upon the prejudices of townspeople to indict an innocent man. But the story suggests that de Kerlor was acting at the direction of the mastermind behind the conspiracy to implicate Charles Rich: the Catholic priest, Father Hennon. The priest's motive, according to Hodgkins's tale, was to conceal the identity of the real murderer, Harold Griffin, the son of Father Hennon's housekeeper and—Hodgkins strongly implied—Father Hennon.

The novel suggests that Griffin and Oscar Dillon were with some girls at the Dean farm on the night of August 13, and Dean's death played out along the lines of the hoodlum theory. Hodgkins buttressed this conjecture with reference to a real-life attack on a young woman in Boston that Griffin was accused of participating in and which bore all the marks of the attack on William Dean.

The facts, however, do not support Hodgkins's story. The attack Griffin was accused of took place on October 19, 1920, two years after the murder of William Dean. The manner of the attack was not similar to that of Mr. Dean, and more importantly, Griffin was released and never charged with participating in the attack. No investigators at the time found any connection with the Dean murder.

Nor do the facts support the suggestion that Father Hennon was protecting his illegitimate son. According to public records, Griffin's father was Michael J. Griffin, who died in 1905. In the 1910 census, Michael's widow, Elizabeth, was listed as the housekeeper for Father Hennon in Plaistow, New Hampshire, and her son, Harold, was living with her. It appears that when Father Hennon came to Jaffrey, his house-keeper and her son came with him.

In short, the hoodlum theory and the implication of Harold Griffin have nothing beyond mere conjecture to support them. However, Hodgkins's book does contain an interesting suggestion: that before his death William Dean told the Riches he was contacting the government with important information. At the grand jury, Charles Rich denied that Dean had told him anything about information he had for the government. "No, not a word," Rich said, "and that's the strange part of it to me, for we talked together often about everything in that way."

In Hodgkins's book, Dean tells the Riches he does did not believe the reports of signal lights. "However," he says, "I've notified the Boston Federal authorities of the situation and the suspicion, and asked their assistance in running the rumors down."

It seems just possible that Georgiana Hodgkins based the scene on an actual conversation with Mr. Dean. If so, the information could have been passed to Lawrence Colfelt, or to another party that wished Dean to keep mum.

Addendum 2

Spy Caves

In the Monadnock region, rumors of spy caves from which German agents might have operated have circulated since the time of World War I. One such cave, located on the eastern side of Mount Monadnock near the summit, provides a clear view to the east, including Temple Mountain and the seacoast in the distance. Just after the war, according to the rumors, the cave was found to contain food, beds, and electronic equipment. There are nearby ledges that could well be the spot to which Charlie Bean led his mysterious guests prior to the war.

Another rumored spy cave lies closer to town. In May of 1919, children picking flowers in the woods near the Bean & Symonds factory came upon a suitcase and a traveling bag that had been covered with leaves and branches. The children brought the bags to their father, Samuel Taylor, who looked inside and found a nearly new pup tent, canvas, candles, pencils, paper, an electric doorbell, riding spurs, and 17 test tubes.

Taylor was justifiably concerned, given all the talk in town about spies. He reported the find to a local official and was told that the matter would be looked into at once. It never was, nor was the incident ever reported to the selectmen. The person to whom Taylor reported the mysterious bags was Judge Charles Rich.

Almost a year later, the bags came to the attention of Agent Robert Valkenburgh, who interviewed Taylor and went to the woods to investigate further. Not far from where the bags had been found, Valkenburgh came upon a cave entrance covered with planks. He cautiously removed the planks and entered. "The cave is twelve feet in length, eight feet in width and six feet in height," Valkenburgh wrote in his report. "The walls are reinforced by wooden planks. There are ledges out in the side of the walls and reinforced by wooden boards and can be used to store food; four boxes on ground possible [sic] used as seats; an old hanging lamp suspended from ceiling of cave. The cave is large enough to hold from eight to ten persons."

The cave was a quarter mile away from Sawyer's Hill, which provided excellent views of Monadnock to the northwest, Temple to the East, and Rindge to the south. At the time, before trees grew up, it also provided a clear line of sight to the Dean farm.

Whether the caves in Sawyer's woods or on Monadnock were ever used by spies has never been proven; it is possible that they were outfitted and used by locals. On the other hand, the possibility that they were part of a spy network has never been conclusively ruled out.

ACKNOWLEDGMENTS

THIS BOOK WAS MADE POSSIBLE BY A GRANT FROM THE BEAN FAMILY Foundation administered by the Jaffrey Historical Society. The Jaffrey Historical Society provided access to their archives, including the largest collection of material related to the Dean murder in existence. Bruce Hill, Rob Stephenson, Richard Boutwell, and Bill Driscoll—members of the Society's Dean Murder Group—were tireless in their support and willingness to share their knowledge of local lore and research arcane details about people and places mentioned in the story. Endless thanks.

I also indebted to a number of individuals and institutions for assistance with the writing of this book. It could not have been written without Margaret Bean's transcription of the grand jury hearing into William Dean's murder. Margaret's son, Mark Bean, was generous with his time and insights into the case.

Many thanks to my early readers for their time and thoughtful feedback: Lenora Arntson, Ann Harvey, Deborah Huegel, Susan Allen Jacobs, Donna Kuethe, Susan Lamb, Gloria Lodge, Karen Nixon, Eric Poor, Gary Sheldon, and Jane Stein. Thanks also to my dear wife, Christine Halvorson Sheldon, who had to listen to more discussion of the Dean murder than any person should have to.

The Peterborough Town Library, the oldest tax-supported library in the nation, maintains a digital archive of local newspapers going back to the 1800s including the *Peterborough Transcript*. This archive proved to be an invaluable resource for researching individuals and details of their lives and I am forever grateful. Also, I will return that overdue book any day now.

The historical societies of the Monadnock region are treasures and were immensely helpful. Thanks especially to Michelle Stahl at the Monadnock Center for History and Culture for assistance with details related to the town of Peterborough and to the Historical Society of Cheshire County for permission to use photographs taken at the exhumation of Dean's body.

I'm grateful to Stillman Rogers, former clerk of the Cheshire County Courthouse, for details about the discovery of the Dean murder grand jury transcript.

Dr. Tom Perera provided invaluable insights into World War I–era radio telegraphy. Dr. Perera is a noted expert on cryptographic systems and provided the Enigma machines used in the feature film *The Imitation Game*.

Dr. Mark Stout of Johns Hopkins has served with the CIA and other intelligence services and as the historian at the International Spy Museum in Washington, DC. He was more than generous in responding to my questions about espionage during World War I and I am grateful.

For assistance in my attempt to track down missing documents related to the Dean murder, I am grateful to: Milli Knudsen, a member of New Hampshire's Cold Case Unit and early member of the Dean Murder Group; Brian Burford, director and state archivist at the New Hampshire State Archives; and Cheshire County officials and staff members Kathy Ruffle, Jenn Tomer, and Christopher Coates.

Thanks to Rob Deschenes, descendant of original witnesses in the Dean murder case, for walking me around the Dean farm and sharing his family's story.

Karen Clement and Richard Jordan cleared up a mystery about the automobile wiper factory in Peterborough founded by Karen's grandfather George, a neighbor to Arria Morison.

Louis Jeffries, head of archives at The Hill private school in Potsdam, Pennsylvania, provided information regarding the Cadet Corps that existed there in the late 19th century and to which Lawrence Colfelt belonged.

Thanks to Andrew Begley, archives specialist at the Boston office of the National Archives for insights into records of the Office of Naval Intelligence.

NOTES

1. Frederick Dean did not live in the area and probably would not have known who to choose for the role of guardian and administrator of the estate. According to some reports, he relied on the advice of those who had known his brother best, specifically Charles Rich.

2. Later, de Kerlor would admit that at least a part of his expenses was for the studio apartment that he and his wife occupied in Manhattan.

3. Smith was kinder, but similarly critical of Jaffrey's selectmen, referring to them as "honest and mentally slow moving."

4. In fact, about nine months had passed since the murder; either McCabe—or Ford, quoting him years later—misremembered.

5. In a strange coincidence, Lawrence Colfelt's mother died the very same day.

6. A full-page advertisement in the November 29, 1919, issue of the *Monadnock Breeze* attempted to counter the negative press Jaffrey was thought to have received. "Why Come to East Jaffrey?" the ad ran, extolling the virtues of the town, and paid for by Bean & Symonds, White Brothers, the Monadnock National Bank, and the Granite State Tack Company.

7. A few newspapers incorrectly reported that the suit was for $100,000, an unheard-of sum at the time.

8. In fact, there were rumors at the time that saboteurs were putting ground glass in candy and other foodstuffs, later proven to be false, but the telegram may simply have referred to that.

9. Still later, Ware admitted that she wasn't positive about the "dropping in the well" comment. "The only thing I can say was that afterwards, and I think it might have been important, we thought that it said something about dropping in the well, or something of that sort, but I don't know that that was anything more than a thought that came afterwards."

10. In the agents' reports, as in some other sources, Colfelt is referred to as residing in Temple, New Hampshire; the rented house was located between Temple and Greenville, and the distinction was often lost.

11. According to Bert Ford, "Mrs. Colfelt went frequently to Ayer, Mass., to see a relative who was in the army at Camp Devens. She was seen there on various occasions talking with an officer in an American uniform." This person has never been identified. Margaret had three brothers, all of whom were in their 30s and registered for the draft

357

in September of 1918—after William Dean's death—so it could not have been one of them.

12. One could ask why Dean didn't contact the person that Agent Bradley mentioned to him a few weeks earlier—George E. Kelleher of the Bureau of Investigation—rather than ask Mrs. Morison to contact someone she knew? Apart from his concerns about using the phone or mail himself, Dean may have felt that Mrs. Morison would be more comfortable contacting someone she already knew.

13. A 13-year-old boy named William Bunce claimed he saw Mr. Dean standing on the steps of the town hall, but he did not see Mr. Rich, and no one who might have known Dean better reported seeing him at the concert.

14. Charles Rich told federal agents that Dean told him, "I'll stay here until the moon is gone down"—which seems odd, given Dean's general anxiety about leaving his wife alone. At the grand jury, a jury member asked Rich if he had ever known Dean to be away from home as late at night as he was that night, and Rich admitted, "Very rarely away from home at night."

15. In the aftermath of Dean's murder, the steel-tired buggy disappeared from his property, creating suspicion among some as to what happened to it and why it had been removed. This mystery was resolved at the grand jury when Fred Stratton explained to County Solicitor Pickard that Mrs. Robinson had asked him to recover it for her.

16. Many early car models had the steering wheel on the right side rather than the left.

17. Russel Henchman claimed he did not receive the message until that evening when he returned home from work, and he did not remember what time Mrs. Dean called his house.

18. Bert Ford came to believe that the hairpin was planted to implicate Mrs. Dean and that no woman was present at the crime.

19. According to Bert Ford, when Emerson knocked on the Colfelts' door Margaret answered it with a revolver in her hand. But both Emerson and Margaret Colfelt denied this and there is no other testimony to confirm it.

20. Later, there would be rumors that Charles Rich had told Henchman to clean up the barn, but there are no witnesses to substantiate this.

21. Lemire may not have been the most conscientious of town employees. When called to give his deposition in the *Rich v. Boynton* slander trial, his first comment was, "I want my two dollars," apparently referring to the fee that witnesses were to be paid.

22. A month later, Agent Valkenburgh would find another tortoiseshell hairpin at the Colfelts' home in Greenville, which he believed also matched the hairpin found at the cistern. "It might be a little cleaner, but I think it matches up with the same one," he testified. Valkenburgh then visited Mrs. Dean at the sanitarium and surreptitiously took a hairpin from her hair. "And it doesn't match up with the other pin at all," he said.

23. Federal agents came to believe that Rich had said, "I have one similar to this," meaning the cigarette case found in the cistern, which would have been incriminating. But the belief was based on hearsay, probably related to Rich's statement about the candy case that Dean had given him.

24. Later, at the slander trial, Christian reiterated that Rich had said he had a board in his hand, not a box, nor basket.

25. Mrs. Hutchinson's husband, Alfred, who admitted to being hard of hearing, was also apparently nearsighted when it came to Rich's black eye. "If he hadn't spoken about it, I wouldn't have noticed that anything happened to him," Hutchinson said.

26. Albany Pelletier left Bean & Symonds a week after the murder. According to D.D. Bean, "We have a night watchman here in our factory, who gave up his job because he was scared on account of the murder." But Pelletier could not have been that scared because he remained in town and later worked as a night watchman at the tack factory.

27. At the grand jury, Charles Rich denied that he'd ever made such a remark. "I never would have thought of it," he said.

28. Ed Baldwin, who was seen with Rich's horse at the time it was supposed to have kicked Rich, was not a Mason. He was, however, the financial secretary of the local Odd Fellows Lodge, and Charles Rich was the treasurer.

29. Reporting on the incident, the *Boston American* noted however that the former chief was "doing an honest day's work" at the factory.

30. In the aftermath of the Dean murder, a rumor spread that Lawrence Colfelt was the illegitimate son of Count von Bernstorff, and even federal agents came to believe this, but it could not be true. Colfelt was born in 1879 at a time when von Bernstorff was only 17 and living in Germany. No evidence exists that he was in the United States at the time and he did not become Germany's ambassador to America until 1908.

31. It has been suggested that perhaps Lawrence Colfelt was the unnamed investor, which could have given the businessmen reason to shield him and Rich from suspicion. However, Colfelt did not arrive in Jaffrey until 1916, four years after Bean & Symonds moved to East Jaffrey, so he could not have been involved. "I think it is one of these Amorys [sic] if I am not mistaken," Daniel Mulloney told federal agents, probably referring to Warren W. Emory, a Rindge businessman, Mason, and brother to another investor, D.P. Emory.

32. Emory did not appear at the grand jury, but County Solicitor Pickard read a statement from him which appears to contradict Sawtelle's testimony: "Mr. Rich is a very hard working man and tends to business. My business transactions with Rich have always been entirely satisfactory. In fact, all his dealings with the bank have been satisfactory. If they hadn't been so, he would have been dismissed." On the other hand, Emory did admit that "Mr. Rich is a man who has received a very small salary up to the beginning of the war. He received only about a hundred a month, but since that time he has received up to $2,000 a year."

33. In her account of the Dean murder, Alice Humiston wrote of the relationship between Colfelt and Rich, "I don't know I'm sure which one the Kaiser would approve the most, but it wouldn't surprise me at all to find out that both of them have iron crosses. I've never heard anyone express such a suspicion, however."

34. At the slander trial, attorney Robert Murchie suggested a different reason for Rich to be present at the scene of the crime. "It is probably true that Rich never wished anything but good to Dean," Murchie said. "His black eye was received in defence [sic]

of his friend, who was killed by men who were desperate and undertook to hide all the evidence in the cistern."

35. At the *Rich v. Boynton* slander trial, Henchman stated that he had begun work as postmaster on November 16, 1918, but postal service records show that he was appointed on September 19 of that year. Henchman was not questioned on the discrepancy.

Bibliography

Bean, Margaret. *Hearing by the Grand Jury on the Death of William K. Dean*. Jaffrey, NH. 1989.

Bean, Mark. "The Death of William K. Dean: Murder by Person or Persons Unknown." Jaffrey, NH. Unpublished paper. 2013.

Bernstorff, Count. *My Three Years in America*. New York. Charles Scribner's Sons. 1920.

Brandon, Craig. *More Than a Mountain*. Keene, NH. Surry Cottage Books. 2007.

Bowers, Q. David. "A New Hampshire Murder Mystery." *The Numismatist*, September 2002. Colorado Springs, CO. 2002.

Blum, Howard. *Dark Invasion 1915: Germany's Secret War and the Hunt for the First Terrorist Cell in America*. New York. HarperCollins. 2014.

Clark, Betsy. "Jaffrey's Greatest Mystery" from *1773 Jaffrey Bicentennial 1973*. Jaffrey, NH. N.p. 1973.

Doerries, Reinhard R. *Imperial Challenge, Ambassador Count Bernstorff and German-American Relations, 1908–1917*. Chapel Hill, NC. University of North Carolina Press. 1989.

Dooley, John F. *Codes, Ciphers, and Spies: Tales of Military Intelligence in World War I*. New York, NY. Copernicus Books. 2016.

Ford, Bert. *The Dean Murder Mystery*. Pawtucket, RI. Privately printed. 1920.

Hodgkins, Georgiana. *Prominent Citizen: Prime Suspect*. Jaffrey, NH. Jaffrey Historical Society. 1996.

Kean, Sumner. "Who Murdered 'Dr.' Dean?" *Yankee Magazine*, February 1959: 32–79. Dublin, NH. 1959.

Kidd, Coburn. *Jaffrey Roads and Streets 1773-1980*. Jaffrey, NH. Jaffrey Historical Society. 1982.

Lehtinen, Alice. *History of Jaffrey New Hampshire, Volume III*. Peterborough, NH. The Transcript Printing Co. 1971.

Nicolai, Walter. *The German Secret Service, By W. Nicolai.* Translated with an Additional Chapter, by George Renwick. n.p. 1924.

Rogers, Stillman. "Murder and the Mountains" from *It Happened in New Hampshire.* Guilford, CT. Globe Pequot Press. 2004.

Secrest, Meryle. *Elsa Schiaparelli: A Biography.* New York. Alfred A. Knopf. 2014.

United States Department of Justice, Bureau of Investigation. *In re: Charles L. Rich,* case # 335271. Washington, DC. 1918.

United States Department of Justice, Bureau of Investigation. *In re: Lawrence M. Colfelt, Jr.,* case # 182615. Washington, DC. 1918.

United States Department of Justice, Bureau of Investigation. *In re: William K. Dean Murder,* case # 182613. Washington, DC. 1918.